Java™ Elements

Principles of Programming in Java™

Java™ Elements
Principles of Programming in Java™

Duane A. Bailey

Williams College

Duane W. Bailey

Amherst College

Boston   Burr Ridge, IL   Dubuque, IA   Madison, WI   New York   San Francisco
St. Louis   Bangkok   Bogotá   Caracas   Lisbon   London   Madrid
Mexico City   Milan   New Delhi   Seoul   Singapore   Sydney   Taipei   Toronto

McGraw-Hill Higher Education

A Division of The **McGraw-Hill** *Companies*

JAVA ELEMENTS: PRINCIPLES OF PROGRAMMING IN JAVA

This book is printed on acid-free paper.

1 2 3 4 5 6 7 8 9 0 FGR/FGR 9 0 9 8 7 6 5 4 3 2 1 0 9

ISBN 0-07-228357-2

Publisher: *Thomas Casson*
Executive editor: *Elizabeth A. Jones*
Senior developmental editor: *Kelley Butcher*
Developmental editor: *Emily J. Gray*
Senior marketing manager: *John T. Wannemacher*
Project manager: *Christine Parker*
Senior production supervisor: *Heather D. Burbridge*
Freelance design coordinator: *Gino Cieslik*
Cover design: *Michael Girard / Z Graphics*
New media: *Christopher Styles*
Printer: *Quebecor Printing Book Group/Fairfield*

Library of Congress Cataloging-in-Publication Data

Bailey, Duane A.
   Java elements : principles of programming in java /
Duane A. Bailey.
     p.   cm.
   ISBN 0-07-228357-2
   1. Java (Computer program language) I. Title.
QA76.73.J38B33 2000
005.13'3—c21   99-42391

http://www.mhhe.com

Contents

for our parents and spouses and children,
teachers one and all

the line between teaching and learning
lies before us like a log:
some never see it,
others leap across it,
and the truly fortunate bestride it with joy

Preface

"I shall be telling this with a sigh
Somewhere ages and ages hence:
Two roads diverged in a wood, and I—
I took the one less traveled by,
And that has made all the difference."

—Robert Frost

GENTLE READER, it gives us great pleasure to bring this book to you. This work is the product of two decades of discussions about the art of programming, as well as the art of *teaching* programming. We feel the result is a positive step toward introducing our craft to students with all levels of interest in computer science. Teaching, as we do, at liberal arts institutions, it is interesting that frequently the best students in introductory classes dabble in programming as passersby. Our special hope is that this book conveys to those individuals what makes us computer scientists.

Pedagogy. At the time of this writing, the academic community is considering many fundamental questions; their answers will dictate the immediate future of computer science education.

Is Java an appropriate teaching language? We believe it is. Historically, it has been unusual that a single language has determined the direction of both academics and industry. Today, Java[1] plays an important role in bringing relatively modern programming design concepts to both the classroom and the office. To the extent that this is true, it is easy to see that concepts learned in the classroom can become lifelong skills for young programmers. Most importantly, though, we see that Java is an effective pedagogical tool that should be used to teach students the successful programming strategies that have been developed over the past several decades.

Should object-oriented languages be taught early in the professional life of a programmer? We guardedly answer *yes*. Java is a powerful object-oriented language, and many of the features of Java are important to understanding how effective programming can be done in light of, say, portable computing and the Internet. Yet, when considering the limited time students have to learn basic material, it behooves the teacher to limit features to the most potent and palatable few. This book does just that.

Why not use graphics to motivate students? Indeed: why not! We have used graphical examples in our classes for many years and have been quite successful. Now that a rich graphical environment is widely available within

---

[1] Java is a trademark of Sun Microsystems Corporation.

a language suitable for teaching, we are all the more likely to be successful. We must not, however, be distracted from teaching students the fundamental principles of programming that are so often overlooked.

To help instructors develop a stable environment (in light of the sifting sands of Java), we developed the `element` package—a free, open, clean, well-defined environment that supports a simple toolbox for object-oriented graphics. It may be downloaded from `http://www.mhhe.com/javaelements`, the McGraw-Hill web site. Avoiding direct use of the AWT (Abstract Windowing Toolkit) has enabled us to insulate the sprouting programmer from a system whose motivation in design is not necessarily ease of use in the classroom. When the student is ready to make the transition to using the AWT, we have sought to maintain as consistent a viewpoint on graphics as possible. This package also provides textual input and output facilities that (we believe) are necessary in one's first programming environment.

Using the Text. The path through the text involves a number of important steps. First, we introduce the *use* of objects almost immediately. The *design* of objects occurs relatively late in the book. At that time, we believe the student will have the maturity necessary to construct larger projects.

Recursion is introduced relatively early and can be avoided, but our experience is that students enjoy the naïve novelty of the use of recursion to solve all sorts of problems. At one time, recursion was considered wasteful of machine resources, but now it is an important programming tool at nearly every level of programming.

We have had to select a particular order for Chapters 5 (strings) through 8 (classes), but there is nothing particularly important to approaching this material in this order. For example, we introduce strings before arrays, but nothing within the chapters obviates approaching the material in the reverse order. In particular, some instructors looking for an "objects-first" approach will find they can get a significant jump on the development of classes by addressing the material of Chapter 8 first.

The later chapters should be considered hooks into subsequent parts of the computer science curriculum—recursive data structures (here, lists) are, of course, a useful introduction to the subtleties of data structure design. They provide, in fact, an alternative implementation to the one discussed in the follow-on book, *Java Structures*. The chapter on threads is provided for those students interested in programming multiple-agent programs. Concurrency is an increasingly potent tool for solving problems, and Java makes that possible within the first semester. Finally, our chapter on machines is a light introduction to three architectures—the Java Virtual Machine, the Turing Machine, and the P-RAM. Each is a *virtual machine* that has had a significant effect on the course of computer science.

We have worked hard to build in a number of resources for students to test their progress.

- Within the running text of each chapter are a number of *exercises*. These are the type of problem often written in the corner of a board during lecture, and are meant to test progress as you read along. Some exercises are solved immediately, and some are left completely to the reader. Timing is, we believe, everything.

- Near the end of each chapter we include *problems*. Earlier problems are usually more easily solved than the later problems. The final problems in each chapter may be potentially very difficult to solve at this level. They are proposed to demonstrate that not everything interesting can be solved by a semester of programming. Most have been recently considered by one of the authors in a context other than this text. Answers (or distillations of answers (or hints)) to the starred ($\star$) problems are found in Appendix A (for *A*nswers).

- At the very end of each chapter are more formally presented *laboratory projects*. Many institutions teach this course with an attendant lab section; these labs are important forms of mental exercise and incorporate the material of the preceding chapter or chapters. Resources associated with these labs are also available on-line at the McGraw-Hill web site.

- Finally, we include, in Appendix C (for *C*ontest), some of our favorite programming problems. We believe that solutions to these problems can be developed by thoughtful, first-time programmers. With time, we expect that a student's solution to these problems will become more informed. These problems are the type often considered in programming contests, and we cast them in that light here.

Successful students of this text will have become *programmers*. The *practice* of programming is only a matter of development. As with players of games like chess or go, there should be some pride in simply having learned the rules in the process of having played a few experimental games. From then on, the process involves a considerable amount of continued experimentation. We hope we've provided the motivation to write lots of Java programs. The process, it seems, rarely ends. We write programs as frequently as possible and we hope we never drop the possibility of honing our skills.

Following Along. A number of features of this book make it unique. First, all the software in this book was extracted from on-line code. Thus, we can be reasonably sure that everything we say here is "as true as possible." We've placed two different icons in the margin (see right) to highlight the details of the text. The "meshing gears" icon is used to highlight working programs that can be found at our web site. The "compass" icon identifies important principles of program design we have sprinkled throughout the text. For example, we suggest that

example

Principle 1 *A useful principle is not fact, but a guide.*

The observant reader realizes that even *with* a compass, true north is slightly elusive. We hope our principles set you in the right direction.

Acknowledgments. The process of bringing a book to life is unlike any other. We found our best conversations on Java were held at the many informal restaurants in and about Amherst. The establishments mentioned in this text have literally given us the energy to attack a sticky problem, and we recommend them to you. Our collegial working environments—Department of Mathematics and Computer Science at Amherst and the Department of Computer Science at Williams—have provided a fruitful medium for discussing nearly every detail of this text. Paul Buhler (College of Charleston), Scot Drysdale (Dartmouth), David Jacobs (Clemson), John Rager (Amherst), Jim Roberts (CMU), Dale Skrien (Colby), Lou Steinberg (Rutgers University), Roman Swiniarski (San Diego State), and Deborah Trytten (University of Oklahoma) reviewed our text. Their comments have made this a more accurate and accessible book, and we thank them for sharing their time. Discussions with John Rager, Lyle McGeoch (Amherst), and Andrea Danyluk (Williams) have directly shaped our approach. Lyle, in fact, authored the original console windowing model; we thank him for his insights there. Jonathan Kallay (Williams '00) helped to bullet-proof the `element` package. Our editors, Betsy Jones, Kelley Butcher, and Christine Parker have been extraordinarily patient with this work. We are indebted to Betsy Blumenthal for her careful proofreading of these pages. Gino Cieslik designed our cover. Finally, we would thank our families—Leeta, Mary, Megan, Kate, Duane "Ryan"—for their love and enduring support.

Enjoy!

Duane A. Bailey, Williams
Duane W. Bailey, Amherst

Chapter 0

Welcome

"'Now we are all here!' said Gandalf, looking at the row of thirteen hoods—the best detachable party hoods—and his own hat hanging on the pegs. 'Quite a merry gathering!...'"
—J. R. R. Tolkien

DURING THESE TIMES IT IS DIFFICULT TO IMAGINE a student that would not be improved with a little knowledge of computers. The question is: How much and in what environment? This book is our answer to that question. We assume that the typical reader will have done no computer programming. It is not our objective to train professional programmers, much less to provide a treatise on the language of the day. We *do* hope to help beginning students to experience computer programming with all its ups and downs. We both remember fondly the thrill of seeing our first programs run, of seeing the machine follow our instructions. We have also experienced hours of discouragement looking for those last mistakes in our programs. Both of these emotions are probably necessary, but we aspire to give our readers principles and practice that will enable them to write bug-free programs consistently. We have chosen to do this using the relatively new language Java. We think that this language is particularly well suited for beginners. More than that, it provides the best and most secure language for programming on the Internet, though we can only touch on that aspect. One last point: Java is an *object-oriented* language. The meaning of this will unfold in the following chapters; suffice it now to say that object-orientation represents a modern view of computer programming that is quite different from traditional languages.

Mistakes in computer programs are called "bugs," and the process of detecting and removing them is called "debugging."

Computer programming is essentially a creative activity similar to creating a painting or other work of art. Both of the authors have found it a stimulating and rewarding experience. Nothing quite rivals the satisfaction of carefully designing a program and perhaps seeing it used by others. Computer programs can be beautiful, but the poorly considered are not. That is why most courses in computer science are as much about taste and æsthetics as they are about the details of a particular language. We hope to convey some sense of these æsthetics by the examples we provide.

0.1 Let the Show Begin

Now it is time to turn to the first example. One of the advantages of Java is that Java programs can be run on a wide variety of computers. An unfortunate consequence of this is that the readers of this book may be using different computers that handle some of the organizational details a bit differently. For example, all of the information in a computer is stored in the form of *files*. (There are two useful analogies: the computer as a filing cabinet, and a file as a stream of single characters like a single file of soldiers.) To write a computer program, we need to create a file of *characters*, and this may be done in different ways on different machines. Some implementations of Java have an environment that provides a built-in text editor, and on other machines you may have to use a separate editing program. This could be an ordinary word processing program, but you need to be sure the editor stores files without any formatting information (often called "text only"). Note that Java is *case-sensitive*, which means that it distinguishes between upper- and lowercase letters. Thus `main`, `Main`, and `MaIn` are all different. In any event, with a little local help it should be possible for you to create the following file:[1]

Greeting

```
public class Greeting
{
    public static void main(String[] args)
    {
        // welcome the user
        System.out.println("Welcome to Java.");
    }
}
```

Once this program has been stored in a file named `Greeting.java` there are two more steps (see Figure 1) you must take before you can enjoy the fruit of your labor. First the program must be *compiled*. This is accomplished by running the Java compiler for your system, naming your file. The compiler translates your program into a more compact form that can be understood by a large number of different computers. This enables you to exchange the program you've compiled on a Tangerine FruitStation 2000 with a friend who uses an Apiary Busy Bee Plus.[2] While performing this translation, the compiler keeps an eye out for mistakes in your program. These include typing errors (such as typing `publik` for `public`) and Java grammatical errors (such as leaving out the word `class`). The compiler can't find all errors, of course. It can't detect errors in a grammatically correct program that just doesn't do what you thought it would. It has no way to detect whether the words you so carefully typed between quotation marks are correctly spelled or whether they make sense. What you typed there is what you'll get. If the program compiles correctly, you will find a new *class file* that contains the translation of your program into a cryptic language that only the computer is meant to understand.

The fallibility of compilers relates to Gödel's first incompleteness theorem, proved in 1931.

---

[1] Recall that all of the examples used throughout this book are available on-line. The margin reference at this point indicates the name of the file where the example is located (`Greeting.java`). Still, we believe that you should get used to constructing files on your own: type in this one!

[2] All trademarks are acknowledged.

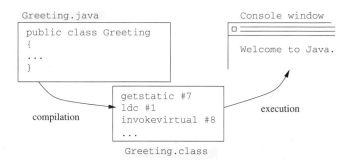

Figure 1 The process of running a program in Java: first it is compiled to more compact (but less readable) code; then the instructions are interpreted by the Java Virtual Machine.

The final step is to *run* the program, or cause the computer to perform (or *execute*) the instructions you have given it. Again, this depends upon the system you are using, but in all cases you should eventually see

```
Welcome to Java.
```

What can we say about this program? We are defining a new Java `class`. All procedures for doing things in Java are stored within classes, and programs are the simplest example. In later chapters we will encounter classes that can simulate, for example, physical objects that may be manipulated in many different ways. Our `Greeting` program is, essentially, an entity that does one main thing: it greets you. (In today's world, this is a significant step forward!) The class is declared `public` so that the Java environment can perform the instructions. Removing the word `public` makes the program inaccessible; in such cases the Java environment takes offense if you try to run the program, so we declare things as public as possible. Formally, the definition is called `Greeting` and includes everything between the matched pair of curly braces '{' and '}' that immediately follow. The word `main` identifies (we call it an *identifier*) the instructions contained within the following pair of curly braces as the main purpose of the program. The keyword `public` describes the accessibility of the `main` instructions. The keywords `static` and `void` are technical details we will get to later, but are important to include even in simple programs such as `Greeting`. The construct `String[] args` is, likewise, an incantation that describes `main`'s *parameters*—a feature we don't make use of here but is necessary in any case. The structure of a Java program definition—its *syntax*—must be followed without variation, or the Java environment will not understand what you are trying to say. The result is, usually, a *syntax error*.

The action takes place on the third line of `main`. The designers of Java have thoughtfully provided us with a collection of useful recipes for doing things (*methods*) called `System`. A component of this collection, named `out`, contains methods that enable the computer to communicate the results of its actions to the user. This communication is called *output*. One of these methods is `println` that writes a line of output (thus the cryptic suffix "ln") to the screen of your terminal. A sequence of letters appearing between quotation marks is called a *string*. When a string is placed inside the parentheses of a `println` statement, it will be displayed on your screen when the program is run. Two strings can be *concatenated*, or glued together as one, by placing a '+' between them. So the string in our example might have been written as `"Welcome"` + `" to " + "Java"`. Finally, a pair of slashes ('//') signals that the entire rest of the line is a *comment*. Comments are disregarded by the Java compiler, but are included to help a human reading the program to follow the reasoning of the programmer. That human may well be *you* at some later time, so you are encouraged to use comments in all of the programs you write. This point is so important, we highlight it as a principle of programming:

Principle 2   *Use comments to make your programs readable.*

We should take pride in the programs we write. Commenting our programs demonstrates we have an interest in sharing our work with others.

Exercise 0.1 *Type in the above program, compile it, and run it.*

Exercise 0.2 *Modify your program to print out a different greeting.*

Exercise 0.3 *What happens if you change a `public` keyword to `publick`?*

Since our first example dealt with words, we'll construct a second example that deals with numbers. Suppose we would like a table of squares of the first

Natural few natural numbers:
numbers:
$1, 2, \ldots$

```
public class Squares
{
    public static void main(String[] args)
    {
        int i = 1; // declare and initialize an integer variable

        while (i < 10) // "loop" as long as i is less than 10
        {
            System.out.println(i*i); // print the square of i
            i = i+1;                 // increment (add 1 to) i
        }
    }
}
```

Squares

This program produces the following output:

```
1
4
```

```
9
16
25
36
49
64
81
```

This program is more complicated. We see from the declaration in the third line that it uses a *variable*, i, which takes on integer values and is *initialized* to have a starting value of 1. As is true with most statements in Java, this declaration is terminated by a semicolon (';').

The next statement—a `while` loop—tells us that the statements enclosed in curly brackets

```
System.out.println(i*i); // print the square of i
i = i+1;                 // increment (add 1 to) i
```

are to be repeatedly executed in sequence as long as i is less than 10. This is an example of a *loop*. Of course, if i never exceeds 10, these statements will execute forever, forming an *infinite loop*. But, as we shall see, this is not the case. When the computer first encounters the `while` statement, i equals its initial value, 1. This being less than 10, the computer executes the two statements above, with i replaced by 1. The first statement results in a 1 appearing on our screen. (Note that i*i stands for the *product* of i with itself.) The next statement,

```
i = i+1;                 // increment (add 1 to) i
```

is an *assignment* statement. It says that the variable on the left side is to be assigned the value computed on the right side. Thus the new value of i is to be the old value of i, plus 1. Again, note that both of these statements are terminated by semicolons.

Having executed the two statements within the `while` statement, we loop back to check i (now 2) against 10. Since 2 is less than 10, we go through the loop again. What we see is that i increases by 1 at each repetition of the loop. The last time through the loop i is 9, which accounts for the last line of the output, 81. Now i is increased to 10 and no longer is it true that i<10, so the program moves to the statement that follows the `while`. There being none, the program halts. Since the `while` statement is delimited by its curly braces, it does not require a final semicolon (this is the only exception to the rule).

It should be clear that by changing the values of 1 in the fifth line (the `int` declaration) and 10 in the sixth line (the `while` loop), any range of consecutive squares could be printed. If the squares were very large and unfamiliar, we might not know the corresponding square root—the value of i. Suppose that the value of i is to be printed out on the same line as its square. We can either make changes to the original file, or we can go back to our editor and create a new program. We've chosen to create a new file, so you can download both versions from over the network.

Numbered-Squares

```
public class NumberedSquares
{
    public static void main(String[] args)
    {
        int i = 1; // declare and initialize an integer variable

        while (i < 10) // "loop" as long as i is less than 10
        {
            System.out.print(i+" "); // print i and a space
            System.out.println(i*i); // followed by the square
            i = i+1;                 // increment (add 1 to) i
        }
    }
}
```

The program generates the output

```
1 1
2 4
3 9
4 16
5 25
6 36
7 49
8 64
9 81
```

Readers familiar with old-fashioned typewriters will recognize newline as the full action of the "carriage return" arm.

Here you will notice a subtle distinction between `print` and `println` methods. The `println` method writes its characters *and then* sends a "newline" character, positioning any output that follows on the next line. The `print` statement writes its output characters to the screen without the terminating newline.

Exercise 0.4 *Modify the* `NumberedSquares` *program to print out the squares of the numbers* 10 *through* 19. *Widen the space between* i *and its square to five spaces. Insert an appropriate statement to print a nice title at the top of your table. You will probably want a line or two of blank space between the title and the columns of numbers.*

As our last example illustrates, `print` and `println` statements can print out more than one item; the `print` statement prints both i and the space following it by concatenating them together with a '+'. We could have accomplished both printing statements by the single statement `System.out.println(i+" "+i*i)`.

Exercise 0.5 *Why doesn't* `System.out.println(i+i*i)` *work? Or does it?*

We encourage you to experiment with these little programs, possibly causing them to break, or to compute different values.

Principle 3 *Experiment.*

While you may not have thought up this first program, the computer doesn't know. If things are working out well for you, print out a copy of your code and save it away for a rainy day. Looking back at this first creation, you'll be amazed at how much you've progressed!

0.2   Chapter Review

We've seen a little hint of programming. Since much of what programmers do is to communicate with the computer, it is not surprising that they have developed *languages*. Thus, the pitfall of expressing oneself in any language can occur with Java as well: errors in *syntax* or confusion of logic. Still the rewards are great—already we've seen programs capable of quickly computing things that would be difficult to do by hand.

- Programs are stored in files. We use editors to construct these files.

- Without much trouble, simple programs can be written and understood.

- Programs have a very particular form. Straying too far from the prescribed form makes the program difficult for a computer to understand.

- Adding comments to a program makes a program potentially easier for a human—perhaps yourself—to understand.

- There are some things computers will never be able to do.

Having made it this far, you might consider some challenging problems. We think you can guess how to do these things!

Problems

0.1⋆   Visit our web site:

http://www.mhhe.com/javaelements

0.2   Write a program to print out a poem. If you're so inclined—how about a poem about computer-written poems!

0.3⋆   Where is the answer to this problem?

0.4   Figure out how to send your poems to one of the authors at

bailey@cs.williams.edu

0.5⋆   Where in your local library can you find out about Java?

0.6   Sun Microsystems developed the Java standard. Where at Sun can you find out more about Java programming? Do you hear much about Java in the news?

0.7⋆   Suppose a "competing standard" for Java was developed. How might this be helpful (or harmful) to programmers and their programs?

Chapter 1

Values, Variables, and Expressions

"After demonstrating that there was nothing
up his sleeves, in his hat, or behind his back,
he wrote quickly:
$$4+9-2\times16+1\div3\times6-67+8\times2-3+26-1\div34+3\div7+2-5 =$$
Then he looked up expectantly.
'Seventeen!' shouted the bug,
who always managed to be first with the wrong answer."
—Norton Juster

WE DEPEND ON COMPUTERS TO PERFORM computations quickly and accurately. In most calculations, it is necessary to store intermediate results or *state*. In Java programs, most state information is stored within its *constants* and *variables*. As we plan or *design* our programs, it is important to determine *what must be remembered* as state information and *how it is to be represented*. We consider these issues in this chapter.

Most computers depend on *digital* storage techniques, where values are represented by numbers whose digits are explicitly stored within the machine. Most digital machines are particularly adept at remembering bits of information in one of two states: *on* and *off*, much like the state of a common light bulb. We might just as easily interpret these two states as representations of the binary digits or (*bits*) '1' and '0'. Long strings of bits can be grouped together to represent long binary numbers that, with some effort, we can interpret as decimal values. The particular form of the interpretation is not important here (we can leave that to Java), but it is useful to know that all "chunks" of memory in a computer are composed of a number of bits (say n) that can be used to represent as many as 2^n different states (see Figure 1.1). For example, a *byte* of memory is made up of 8 bits and is capable of storing any of $2^8 = 256$ different configurations or values. Because of its small range of values, the byte is useful for representing a single keyboard character. Larger ranges of values are needed for storing other primitive types including integers and numbers with decimal points (*floating point* values). Again, the precise details of the representation of the data are unimportant, but the fact that the machine uses a binary representation helps to explain some details we will see in this chapter.

Another subtlety of storing data within a computer is that while the physical structure of memory is little more than a few billion individual bits, the logical structure of the memory is usually *interpreted* to have a more abstract

The term "bit" was coined by John Tukey over lunch.

Binary	Decimal
000	0
001	1
010	2
011	3
100	4
101	5
110	6
111	7

Figure 1.1   There are 8 different states that 3 binary digits can encode. In general, n bits can encode 2^n different states.

structure. Box scores and medical records are typical types of things stored within a machine. Languages like Java are responsible for associating the type of interpretation, or, more technically, the *type* of the data, with each chunk of memory. Thus, an understanding of the types of data that can be stored within the machine allows programmers to be more effective in determining how to *represent* their data in Java.

1.1   Identifiers

Every program can be viewed as a long sequence of symbols. Some of these symbols are part of the syntax of the Java language itself, and we will be learning what they mean. These symbols include operators, such as, '+','−','*','/', and '='. Other symbols (for example, `class`) identify key parts of the Java grammar; they're called *keywords*. While we don't yet know the meaning of many of these keywords, it is important to quickly review them (see Figure 1.2) since these words are reserved. When we give a name to or identify the purpose of something with our own symbols, we're not allowed to use any of the keywords. Even so, it appears that many exciting and descriptive words are still available for our use!

Symbols that we make up for describing our own data and programs are called *identifiers*. An identifier must begin with a letter, or one of the characters '_' or '$'. The subsequent characters must be a sequence of letters ('a'–'z', 'A'–'Z'), digits ('0'–'9'), or the characters '_' and '$'.[1] Upper- and lowercase letters are considered different. Thus all of the following are distinct and valid identifiers:

```
max             MAX             Max
```

---

[1] Somewhat more than this is possible. To accommodate non-English-speaking programmers, the characters from several alphabets can be used. Usually, the character '$' is avoided.

abstract	boolean	break	byte	case	catch
char	class	const	continue	default	do
double	else	extends	final	finally	float
for	goto	if	implements	import	instanceof
int	interface	long	native	new	package
private	protected	public	return	short	static
super	switch	synchronized	this	throw	throws
transient	try	void	volatile	while	

Figure 1.2 The keywords of Java. These words may not be used as identifiers.

```
dayOfTheWeek    day_of_the_week    dayoftheweek
_token          sun$spot           long_sequence
main            Char               java
```

while the following are not

```
%right          #missing           30day_month
this            class              return
```

When labeling entities within a program, it's important to give them reasonable identifiers. Names serve to document the use of items in our programs, and we should strive to make them as readable as possible. For example, one of us, when younger, wrote a program to read a disk and called it `DRead`, which, when written using entirely one case was often misinterpreted.

Principle 4 *Spell out and capitalize words in identifiers.*

An informal convention for capitalization of identifiers in Java is provided in Appendix B (for *B*asics).

1.2   Variables and Constants

Java is a *strongly typed language*, which simply means that every data storage location that appears in a program must be *declared* and must have some *type*. This allows the compiler to anticipate the use of the data and to allow space in memory for it. It also allows the compiler to check that the usage of the data is consistent with the declared type. Compilers can then catch certain kinds of logical errors involving incorrect interpretations of data.

As we have mentioned, the *state* of our program is determined by the values of *variables* and *constants* within our programs. In this chapter we will see two types of values: *primitive types* and *objects*. While objects are the focus of any object-oriented language, the primitive types represent the simplest forms of data, including numbers and characters. For example, 7 is an integer value, while 7.0 is a floating point value and '7' is a character. Values are stored in the machine at particular locations associated with identifiers. It is convenient to think of these locations as boxes where values are stored. Some of these boxes always contain the same value—for example, `daysInWeek` is often an integer location that always holds 7. These are referred to as *constants*.

Edwin Hubble was also a lawyer and boxer.

It might not seem necessary for constants to have names, but occasionally it is necessary to change a constant. For example, *Hubble's Constant* is a constant that determines the rate at which the universe is uniformly expanding. Hubble estimated that this expansion causes any point currently a million light years distant to move away from us at a rate of 150 kilometers per second. Since Hubble's time, several significant corrections to the approximation of the constant have brought the rate down to a mere 20 kilometers per second. Any program, of course, that made use of dated values of Hubble's Constant should be changed. Naming constants helps to isolate these changes to a single point in the program—where the constant is defined.[2]

Variables keep track of portions of the state that potentially change as the program runs. For example, a program that simulates a swinging pendulum might have a variable that keeps track of the angle of the pendulum. The score of a video game, the digital odometer in your car, and the alarm setting in a digital watch are all examples of data that have the potential to vary and that must be stored in variables.

The design of programs, then, involves identifying those state values that describe what the program is doing. In order to adequately implement the program, we must account for the type of storage of all the different values that make up its state. The remainder of this chapter describes different types of data and how they are declared and used in Java computations.

1.3 Primitive Types

Java provides eight *primitive* data types that are used to perform basic calculations. These include several forms of integers and floating point numbers, characters, and booleans. Integers are used in numeric computations where fractional values may be ignored. Floating point values are used to represent numbers with potential fractional parts. Characters are used in the manipulation of textual information. Booleans are used to encode answers to questions, and ultimately help in making decisions.

1.3.1 Integers

The integer data types `int` and `long` are designed to express numbers without fractional parts. Integers are a natural data type to use when the value models something that can be counted. If, for example, you say "How *many* people

---

[2] As it turns out, this "constant" isn't really constant for other reasons—the rate of expansion of the universe changes with time.

are there in the telephone booth?" the word "many" is an indicator that the quantity should be stored as an integer.

The `int` type is used to represent integers that fall between -2147483648 and 2147483647. (An occasional reader will recognize these values as $2^{31} - 1$ and -2^{31}! These 2^{32} different values are stored in 32 bits. We'll soon see that a somewhat larger range of values can be stored within the 64 bits of a `long`.) An attempt to manipulate an integer value outside of the range of values for its type, for example:

```
int big  =  2147483648;
```

will result in a message from the compiler that looks something like:

```
declarations.java:12: Numeric overflow.
int big  =  2147483648;
             ^
```

```
1 error
```

Notice that when integer values appear within a program, they are typed without commas. Commas are a useful mechanism for humans to read values, but they provide little aid to computers.

A number of standard mathematical operators can be applied to integers. For example, '+', '−', and '*' (multiplication) are binary operators—they take a value on the left and right. They operate within each numerical type and give results of the same type, as we would expect. The division operator, '/', gives the integer part of the quotient; any remainder from the division is thrown out. When an expression is made up of several of these operations, they are evaluated as one might expect: any multiplications and divisions are computed first, from left to right, and then any additions and subtractions are computed, also from left to right. Thus, the number of seconds in $1\frac{1}{2}$ hours might be computed as:

```
60*60*3/2
```

The result, 5400, is the result of performing the multiplications first, followed by the division. Since the division computes an integer result, a similar expression

```
3/2*60*60
```

computes something completely different: 3 is divided by 2, yielding 1 (not 1.5), which is then multiplied by 60 twice, giving 3600. The strange behavior of division can be the source of errors if one does not think carefully about the ordering of the computation. The general rule of thumb is that operators produce results of the same type as they consume.

Exercise 1.1 *Sometimes the results of* `i/j` *are not what you might expect. Write one or more programs to compute* `5/(-2)`, `(-5)/2`, *and* `(-5)/(-2)`. *Explain the phrase "Integer division rounds toward zero."*

Operator	Prec.	Meaning	Assoc.	Applicable types
v++ v--	8	postincrement/decr.	—	alphanumeric
++v --v	8	preincrement/decr.	—	alphanumeric
!	7	logical not	right	boolean
* / %	6	alphanumeric	left	alphanumeric
+ -	5	addition, subtraction	left	alphanumeric
< <= >= >	4	ordered comparison	left	alphanumeric
== !=	3	equality test	left	all
&&	2	logical and	left	boolean
||	1	logical or	left	boolean
=	0	assignment	right	if precision not lost

Figure 1.3   The order of precedence for the most common operators. Higher precedence operators are evaluated first, unless indicated otherwise through the use of parentheses. Alphanumeric types include `int`, `long`, `float`, `double`, and `char` (which is automatically converted to an `int`).

The ordering of the computation of different operations is called *precedence*. Operators with higher precedence are performed earlier. The ordering of similar operations within an expression is called *associativity*. Most sequences of operators (but not all) are combined from left to right and are called *left associative*. A table of precedence and associativity for all Java operators is provided in Figure 1.3.

The precedence and grouping of the computation can be controlled through the use of parentheses: expressions within parentheses are always fully computed before they are used in any larger expression. Thus, we can make the computation of the number of seconds in $1\frac{1}{2}$ hours very explicit by adding parentheses:

```
(60*60*60*3)/2
```

One can, of course, use too many parentheses, obscuring the expression to the point where it is unreadable.

There are a number of unusual operations used on integers when programming. For example, the remainder that was thrown away during integer division can be computed using the *modulo* operator ('%'). The number of days left over in a year, when 52 weeks have been accounted for, is

```
365%7
```

or

1

since 365 divided by 7 is 52 with a remainder of 1. Notice that if a and b are positive (and nonzero[3]), then a%b is one of the b values between 0 and b-1.

Exercise 1.2 *Write a program to compute the (four) values of computing the remainder for operands that are various combinations of positive and negative numbers. What can you conclude?*

The result of this last exercise should demonstrate that it is possible to get remainders that are negative. The remainder of dividing integer a by integer b is always selected so that it makes up for what is lost in computing the quotient; in other words,

```
(a/b)*b + (a%b)
```

is always equal to a.

Exercise 1.3 *Verify this last statement by writing a program that prints the results of several typical cases.*

As we mentioned in the previous section, variables play an important role in keeping track of the state of a program. To declare a variable of type int we include a statement like

```
int i;          // frequently used as a counter
int j,k;        // two variables in a single declaration
```

Declarations

A declaration is used to reserve space in the computer to store a value, here an int. The declaration must appear before the variable is first used. Declarations are simple Java statements and, like all simple Java statements, must end in a semicolon (';').

A variable such as dowJones can be *assigned* a value by using the *assignment* '=', for example dowJones=20000. This causes the value of the expression on the right of the '=' operator (20000) to be stored in the memory associated with the variable (dowJones) on the left. The variable retains the value until it is assigned again. We have referred to the '=' as an operator. The result of this operator is the value assigned to the variable, and the entire assignment can be used as a value in another expression. Thus,

```
int myAge, yourAge;
yourAge = (myAge = 6);
```

assigns 6 to myAge and then later to yourAge. The '=' operator is also an example of a *right associative* operator: assignments on the right are performed before those on the left. Thus, the above expression is usually simplified as:

```
yourAge = myAge = 6;    // now we are six
```

---

[3] Mathematicians generally consider positive numbers to be nonzero. Computer scientists loosely consider zero to be positive as well.

The phrase "usually simplified" should be taken with a grain of salt, as these two assignments can almost always be replaced by the more obvious pair of statements:

```
myAge = 6;
yourAge = myAge;
```

If a value is not assigned to the variable, it should not be referenced, and Java will work hard to make sure that this initial assignment is performed. Generally, when the program starts up, all variables should be *initialized* by assigning them values you think will be most useful when you first need them. For example, you might reasonably want to initialize a variable `sum` that is used as a running sum to 0, or a variable `minutesLeftInGame` to 15. To facilitate the initialization process, variables may be initialized as part of their declaration:

*"How **many** minutes are left in the game?" (cf. page 19)*

```
int ourAge = 6;          // a perfect age...
```

Principle 5   *Initialize variables before they are used.*

Java considers constants to be a special type of variable that can be assigned exactly one value. That value is called its *final value*, and is usually indicated in its declaration by adding the `final` modifier:

```
final int max = 2147483647; // the largest Java integer
final int secondsInYear = 365*24*60*60; // secs in nonleapyear
```

Constants

The last example is interesting because it shows that the computer can be asked to *compute* the initial values for a variable. We could have performed this calculation on a calculator and then used the specific result to initialize the constant, but the computation serves to describe, in some sense, the interpretation of the value. In case we find ourselves moving to another planet, the computation can be easily changed.

We are now ready to consider the design of a simple program to compute the sum of the first five whole numbers. We will use two integers to keep track of the progress of our program. One integer, `i`, keeps track of the next value to be accumulated into the sum, and the other, `sum`, keeps track of the intermediate values of the ongoing computation.

ComputeSum

```
// Compute the sum of the first five natural numbers
public class ComputeSum
{
    public static void main(String args[])
    {
        int sum = 0;
        int i = 1;

        sum = sum + i;          // sum now equals 1
        i = i+1;                // i now equals 2
        sum = sum + i;          // sum now equals 3
```

```
            i = i+1;                // i now equals 3
            sum = sum + i;          // sum now equals 6
            i = i+1;                // i now equals 4
            sum = sum + i;          // sum now equals 10
            i = i+1;                // i now equals 5
            sum = sum + i;          // sum now equals 15
            System.out.println(sum);
        }
    }
```

This program shows the variables i and sum being reassigned over and over again. It represents a lot of programming effort to compute the sum of five numbers, the pair of statements sum = sum + i; and i = i+1; having to be typed in five times. Moreover, while it is clear how the program could be extended to compute the sum of the first 100 positive integers, nobody would want to do it. We will soon see that there are efficient ways to indicate the repetition of statements like these.

The range for int is large enough to handle almost all requirements. But for the relatively few occasions when one needs to represent an integer outside the range of int, a long type is provided. Declarations of this type are made in an analogous way:

```
    long national_debt;     // how *many* dollars?
```

Declarations

long integers require more memory space in the computer than int integers, and such integers' values are identified by appending an 'L' to the number. Integers between $-9223372036854775808L$ and $9223372036854775807L$ can be declared long. This range of values is extremely large. As we shall see later, the long type is needed to keep track of the time in Java, which is represented as the number of milliseconds since 1969.

There are some *idioms* that experienced programmers are fond of using. For example, the idiom sum += i is equivalent to sum = sum+i and is easier to type. The idioms sum -= i and sum *= i have similar meanings for subtraction and multiplication. Finally, the operation of *incrementing* or *decrementing* an integer variable by one (as above) occurs so frequently that the expressions i++ and i-- are used for that. If the variable is being used in an expression, the question arises as to whether the increment is performed before or after the value is used in the calculation. When using the *postincrement* operator, the ++ occurs *after* the variable, and the variable is increased by one *after* its value used. The *preincrement* form, ++i, increments the variable *before* it is used. With these in mind, the repeated statements in the above program could be written as the two statements i++ and sum += i. With these, the program looks like this:

idiom: a frequent, recognizable form

```
    // Compute the sum of the first five natural numbers
    public class ComputeSumWithIdioms
    {
        public static void main(String args[])
```

iPlus

```
{
    int sum = 0;
    int i = 1;

    sum += i;                       // sum now equals 1
    i++;                            // i now equals 2
    sum += i;                       // sum now equals 3
    i++;                            // i now equals 3
    sum += i;                       // sum now equals 6
    i++;                            // i now equals 4
    sum += i;                       // sum now equals 10
    i++;                            // i now equals 5
    sum += i;                       // sum now equals 15
    System.out.println(sum);
}
}
```

Just as with the other arithmetical operators, there are assignment short-hands for division ('/') and modulo ('%'), though their use is less obvious.

1.3.2   Floating Point Numbers

The German mathematician Leopold Kronecker once said *"God made the whole numbers; all the others are the work of man."*[4] Having made provision for declaring integers, we now must provide for the others! These include the fractional, or *rational* numbers such as $\frac{1}{2}$ and 0.25, as well as the *irrational* numbers such as π. If you find yourself saying, "This variable should indicate how *much* potassium should be added to the water," the word "much" should signal the need for the use of a floating point number.

To help us, scientists have developed a notation for expressing numbers, called *scientific notation*, that has the advantage of compactly expressing very large and very small numbers. Numbers are expressed in the form $a \times 10^n$, where a is a decimal and n is an integer. For example, light travels through vacuum at approximately $186282.4 = 1.862824 \times 10^5$ miles per second, or $983571056 = 9.83571056 \times 10^8$ feet per second. On the other hand, the distance light will travel in one *nanosecond*, which is defined to be $1/1000000000 = 1 \times 10^{-9}$ of a second, is approximately 0.983571056 feet or 11.802853 inches. (These physical constants are of some interest to computer scientists because the speed of light determines a lower bound for the time required for a signal to be sent between computers, say, on a network. Alternatively, the distance light or any *information* can be conveyed in a nanosecond bounds the speed of a computer of a given physical size.) Java uses an alternative form of scientific notation— with En standing for 10^n—to optionally describe floating point values. In Java, the sun travels northward across the equator approximately every 365.2422 or 3.652422E2 days.

Actually, Java falls slightly below the equator.

---

[4] *"Die ganzen Zahlen hat der liebe Gott gemacht; alles andere ist Menschenwerk."*

Variables that may assume `float` values are declared in Java like this:

```
float velocity = 1.86E5F;// speed of light in mps
float nano = 1.1785E1F;   // distance light travels in one nsec
```

Note that ordinary numbers of type `float` must have an 'F' or 'f' appended to them.

The numbers that can be represented by a `float` constant or variable can be as large as $\pm3.40282347E{+}38F$ and as small as $\pm1.40239846E{-}45F$, which is obviously sufficient for ordinary purposes. There is, however, a second type available for floating point numbers called `double`. These can be written with the same exponential notation, but constants of type `double` have an optional 'D' or a 'd' appended.

*"How **much** time is left in the game?" (cf. page 16)*

```
double pi = 3.14159265358979323E0D;
double daysInYear = 3.652422e2d;
double timeLeftInGame = 1.3;
```

There are, of course, arithmetical operators for real variables just as there were for the integer variables. These include '+', '-', '*', and '/'. (Here '/' produces the full quotient.) Even the modulo operator, '%', is available to compute the portion of a value unaccounted for by whole division.

Exercise 1.4 *How do you compute the value of the expression at the head of the chapter?*

It might just happen, of course, that a number declared as a `float` or `double` holds a whole number that could be used (without loss of precision) as an integer. The Java compiler will not recognize this fact unless it is prompted. We accomplish this by a method known as *casting*, by which a value that could be of two data types is converted from one to the other. The general syntax is[5]

$$(\langle type \rangle)\langle value \rangle$$

which takes ⟨value⟩ of some given type and transforms it into a value of type ⟨type⟩. Here is a little sequence of casts:

```
double r = 3.0E+2;      // r (300) is declared as double
float p;
int q;

q = (int)r;             // r is whole, so no information lost
p = (float)r;           // r is small, so no information lost
```

Some of this "casting about" is done automatically. For example, 2+3 will produce the integer 5, reflecting the fact that both of the operands are of type

---

[5] We use angle brackets to highlight logical components of a statement. The brackets are not included in the actual statement.

int. Java knows that integers are also floating point numbers and when it sees the expression 3+5.5, it casts 3 to type double before carrying out the operation of addition to produce the value 8.5. On the other hand, if it encounters 3.5+5.5, it views the sum 9.0 as a floating point number unless it is explicitly cast as an integer. Generally, in any case where the conversion *might* cause a loss of information, the computer is unwilling to perform the cast without being explicitly told.

Given floating point numbers, we can now perform a number of standard mathematical calculations. For example, to find the points where the quadratic equation $ax^2 + bx + c$ is zero, we can apply the quadratic formula:

$$\frac{-b \pm \sqrt{b^2 - 4ac}}{2a}$$

We need, of course, three constant values, a, b, and c. To perform this computation, however, it is necessary to compute the square root of a quantity. This can be accomplished using a method of the Math class, Math.sqrt. It takes a double value and returns the square root as a double. Here we see code that prints out the two roots of $x^2 - x - 1$:

```
final double a = 1.0;
final double b = -1.0;
final double c = -1.0;

System.out.println("Roots of "+a+"x^2+"+b+"x+"+c+": ");
System.out.println((-b+Math.sqrt(b*b-4*a*c))/2*a);
System.out.println((-b-Math.sqrt(b*b-4*a*c))/2*a);
```

The solution printed is

```
1.618033988749895
-0.6180339887498949
```

The first of these two values is the *golden mean*, a ratio that is commonly found in nature and used in art. A very good estimate of this value can be computed by dividing your height by the height of your belly button.

As another application, we consider the tuning of a musical scale. The ancients discovered that two pitches whose frequencies are in the ratio 2 : 3 have a particularly pleasing relationship. This is called a "perfect fifth." Thus, if a violin is tuned to an A^4 whose frequency is 440 cycles per second, a perfect fifth above is the E^4 string with a frequency of 660 Hz. Tuning of an instrument in a manner that maximizes the use of perfect fifths is called *Pythagorean tuning*. The 17th century, however, ushered in a slightly different tuning—called *equal temperament*—that fixed many problems with supporting a large variety of keys. In this system, two frequencies a semitone apart have frequencies in the ratio $1 : 2^{\frac{1}{12}}$. In this system, a fifth—which is 7 semitones away—would be slightly flat. We can figure out *how* flat by comparing the value of $(2^{\frac{1}{12}})^7$ with $\frac{3}{2}$. To help us, we will make use of the Math.pow method; it returns the result of raising

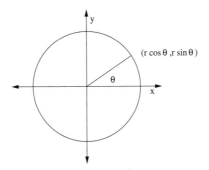

Figure 1.4   The location of a point on a circle of radius r centered at the origin.

its first parameter to the power of the second parameter. Our computation computes the frequency of a tempered fifth above A^4:

```
final double semitone = Math.pow(2.0,1.0/12.0);
final double temperedFifth = Math.pow(semitone,7.0);
// or combine as temperedFifth = Math.pow(2.0,7.0/12.0);
System.out.println(440.0*temperedFifth);
```

The output of this program

```
659.2551138257401
```

is so close to E^4 it is not noticeably flatter.[6] The tuning with equal temperament is generally considered a more versatile tuning of keyboard instruments, though studies show that concert violinists are more likely to depend on the use of Pythagorean tunings.

All of the common trigonometric functions are also part of the `Math` class of functions. They act on double values. One of the most useful facts from trigonometry describes a point on a circle of radius r. If the circle is plotted on the $x - y$ axes (see Figure 1.4), with its origin at $(0,0)$, the circle is made up of all of the points $(r \cos \theta, r \sin \theta)$ where θ is an angle measured in radians counterclockwise from the positive x axis. In Chapter 3 we will learn how to plot individual pixels with integer coordinates. Here, we will compute the integer coordinates for the location of the point at two-o'clock on a standard analog clock that has radius 100 inches:

```
// Compute the location of two-o'clock on an analog clock
public class Trig
{
```

Trig

----

[6] Of course, if the two versions of E^4 were played simultaneously—something not likely in a single tuning—one *would* be noticeably flatter.

```
public static void main(String args[])
{
    double theta = Math.PI/6.0; // PI/6 radians is 30 degrees
    final double radius = 100.0; // radius for the clock
    int x, y;

    x = (int)(radius * Math.cos(theta));
    y = (int)(radius * Math.sin(theta));
    System.out.println(x);
    System.out.println(y);
}
}
```

The computed x and y coordinates are:

```
86
49
```

The conversion of floating point to integers using casting truncates the value. The result is interesting since we expected a y coordinate of $100 \sin \frac{\pi}{6} = 100 \cdot \frac{1}{2} = 50$. "Roundoff" error in the `Math.sin` function caused the computed value to fall slightly below 50 (Java computed `49.99999999999999`). Thus, in this case the truncation is quite dramatic. We can avoid problems like this by rounding the value with `Math.round`:

```
x = (int)Math.round(radius * Math.cos(theta));
y = (int)Math.round(radius * Math.sin(theta));
```

`Math.round` computes a `long` result, so we are required to cast it if we wish to assign the value to an integer. The x and y coordinates computed by our revised program are:

```
87
50
```

It is interesting to note that, viewed from the y axis, two-o'clock falls midway between noon and three-o'clock! The entire program to plot a circle in a window can be found on page 82. We include in Appendix D (for *Documentation*) a listing of the other useful mathematical functions included in the `Math` class; you should browse through them now.

1.3.3   Characters

Most computer programs have some character-based data. The data type `char` provides for data values that consist of a single character—a single keystroke or symbol to be displayed on a screen. The values `'a'`, `'B'`, `'3'`, and `'&'` are all valid `char` values. The character values always appear between single quotes. Thus `'a'` refers to a character, while `a` might be the name of a constant or variable.

Character variables are declared and initialized just as we have come to expect:

```
char grade;
grade = 'A';
System.out.println(grade);
```

Character

which prints

```
A
```

Single characters are not as useful as you might at first think. It is usually a *string* of characters, like a word, that you want. We take up expressions on Strings a bit later.

What is perhaps most interesting about the characters is that they are ordered, with each assigned an ASCII (American Standard Code for Information Interchange) value—an integer to indicate its relation among the others. In this ordering, the lowercase letters appear in order near each other, the uppercase letters appear in order in a separate set of values, and the digits appear in such a way that the order of the ASCII values for the digits is the same as the order of the numbers they represent. We'll come to depend heavily on this later, in Chapter 4. We can see *what* that integer is by placing the character in position where an integer is useful. In fact, the operators and relations that we have learned about for integer data types all work with characters. This is because the char type is, essentially, a synonym for the int type. The program fragment

```
char firstLetter = 'a';

System.out.println((int)firstLetter);
System.out.println(firstLetter);
```

generates the output

```
97
a
```

This little program shows us that 'a' is represented in the computer by the code 97. (The full set of these ASCII codes can be found in Appendix B.)

Exercise 1.5 *What is printed when we include* System.out.println('a'+0); *in our Java program? How about* System.out.println('a'+'0');*?*

Some values of char represent characters that do not print a symbol on the screen, but cause some other action to be taken. For example '\n' represents a *newline* character and acts just like the RETURN key on a Macintosh or the ENTER key on a PC—it moves the cursor down to the beginning of the next line. While you must type the *two* characters '\' followed by 'n', this is interpreted by Java as a *single* newline character. This pair is called an *escape sequence* for a newline character. The other nonprinting characters and their escape sequences can be found in Figure 1.5.

Escaped character	Meaning	Escaped character	Meaning
\b	backspace	\f	form feed
\r	carriage return	\n	newline
\t	tab	\'	apostrophe
\"	quotation mark	\\	backslash

Figure 1.5   The escape characters of Java.

While single characters are useful, we cannot write

```
char negative = 'n''o';
```

To print out no we could write the equivalent pair of statements:

```
System.out.print('n');
System.out.print('o');
```

Strings of characters constitute a more useful nonprimitive data type that we
will consider shortly.

1.3.4   Booleans

There are many times in a computer program when it is necessary to have
the computer make a decision. These decisions are based, of course, on the
state of the program—the state of other variables at hand. The `boolean` type
allows the programmer to compute and store answers (`true` and `false`) from
decision-making questions. A typical instance is when you have a block of
statements that is to be executed fifty times. Every time the block is finished
executing, the program must ask the question *"Have I done it fifty times?"* and
take appropriate action. This is usually accomplished by defining an integer
variable, say `count`, that is to act as a counter. Each time the block is executed,
the counter is increased by one and the expression `count<50` is evaluated. This

George Boole: `boolean` expression evaluates to either `true` or `false`.
a 19th *century*   A common way to compute a boolean value is to perform a comparison as we
mathemati- saw above. All Java types may be compared using equality ('`==`') or inequality
cian. ('`!=`') tests, though these operators are usually only used on primitive types.
Each of these tests returns `true` when the condition holds (see Figure 1.6). For
numeric and character types where the values are *ordered*, we can verify the
ordering of two values using boolean *relations*: '`<`' (less than), '`<=`' (less than
or equal to), '`>=`' (greater than or equal to), and '`>`' (greater than). These
operations return `true` if the designated condition holds. One *unary* operator,
'`!`' (not) inverts the value of the boolean: `!true` is `false` and *vice versa.*
    So, given the declarations:

```
boolean result;
int a, b;
```

P	Q	!P	P==Q	P!=Q	P||Q	P&&Q
true	true	false	true	false	true	true
true	false	false	false	true	true	false
false	true	true	false	true	true	false
false	false	true	true	false	false	false

Figure 1.6   The results of applying various boolean operators on boolean values P and Q.

each of the following boolean expressions sets `result` to `true`:

```
// all of the following are true:
result = 42 == (41+1);  // same value: 42
result = 42 >= 42;
result = 'A' < 'B';     // 'B' falls later in alphabet
result = 'A' == 65;     // ASCII code for 'A' is 65
result = Math.sqrt(4.0) == 2.0; // no roundoff...yet
result = ((a/b)*b + (a%b)) == a;// always true
result = a == a;             // any value == itself
result = (a != a) == false;
result = !false;
result = true == true;       // they're the same
```

while the following set `result` to `false`:

```
// all of the following are false:
result = 42 != 42;              // these are equal
result = !(42 == 42);
result = 'a' == 'A';            // upper and lower are different
result = Math.sin(Math.PI/6) == 0.5; // roundoff error
result = !true;                 // false is "not true"
result = true == false;         // they're not the same
```

Some boolean operators require us to hit two keys on the keyboard (e.g., the '<=' is '<' followed by '='), but they are seen by the Java compiler as a single operation. One wants to be especially vigilant not to confuse the assignment operator '=' and logical equality '=='. The statement *"Let x equal 3"* is different than *"Is x equal to 3?"* The first changes x, while the second does not. We cannot have this ambiguity in our computer programs, so different symbols are used. Forgetting the second equal sign in '==' is one of the most common programming errors.

Simple boolean expressions can be combined into more complex expressions using the logical operators '||' (or) and '&&' (and). These binary operators take two boolean values and produce another. The 'or' operator returns `true` if either of the operands (or both) are `true`. The 'and' operator returns `true` if both operands are `true`. We can see, for example, if a value falls strictly between 100 and 200 by combining two tests:

```
boolean between = (100 < a) && (a < 200);
```

The result is `true` exactly when `a` is bigger than 100 *and* smaller than 200. By the way, it's possible to write a very complicated version of `false`, by a simple change:

```
result = (100 > a) && (a > 200);
```

It's not possible for an integer to be both less than 100 and greater than 200! We call these always-`false` expressions *fallacies*. Similarly, we can use the 'or' operator to make a *tautology*—a statement that is always `true`:

```
result = (100 > a) || (a < 200);
```

If you're thinking of an integer, it's undoubtedly either less than 200 *or* greater than 100. In general, we try to avoid complicating the work of interpreting a program by introducing fallacies and tautologies; it's better to either rethink our logic or simply assign the appropriate boolean value directly.

One common mistake in programs is to attempt to write the mathematical shorthand for our previous computation:

```
between = 100 < a < 200;
```

but careful inspection demonstrates what is really being computed is the following:

```
between = ((100 < a) < 200);
```

The first comparison generates a `boolean`, which is then compared to an `int`. It's meaningless to compare these two different types, so the expression is logically problematic. We must use the longer expression we saw before.

Exercise 1.6 *The exclusive or of two boolean values is* `true` *if exactly one of the values is true. What boolean operator can be used to compute exclusive or? (Hint: See the table in Figure 1.6.)*

One must be very careful in forming long or complicated boolean expressions to be sure they represent what is wanted. The compiler can't know what you want and will often compile mistaken expressions without a whimper if they are syntactically correct. Generally,

Principle 6 *Use parentheses to make explicit the order of evaluation.*

Of all of the data types, the `boolean` type is probably least familiar. A long boolean expression can often be simplified with a little work. For example, any equality test with `true` can be eliminated. Because `true` is the *identity* for the '`==`' operator, we can always rewrite `a == true` as `a`. Likewise, `a == false` can be written as `!a`.

Exercise 1.7 *How might we simplify* `a != true` *and* `a != false`*?*

Often the simplification of a complex boolean expression demonstrates we can simplify our logic elsewhere in our program.

1.3.5   Time

We now consider the use of a timer to measure time in our programs. There are many reasons why we might wish to use a timer. We might want to compare two different programs that produce the same results by different methods in order to choose the more efficient. We might have a program that does the same thing (such as sorting a list) on input data (a list) of varying lengths. Before using the program on a huge list of a million items, we might like to estimate how long it will take by timing the program on various short lists. We might see a pattern of running times that we could extrapolate to an estimate for the huge list. And sometimes it is just fun to see how long something takes! (How quickly can *you* double-click the mouse button?)

When we consider how to time a program, it becomes immediately clear that a wristwatch is not the appropriate instrument. The amount of time taken for human reaction in identifying the start and finish is so large, compared to the running time of small programs, that the error threatens to overwhelm what we are trying to measure. Fortunately, Java provides the components for constructing accurate timing instruments.

Every modern computer contains a very accurate clock. All we need is some way to "read" this clock and to interpret the results. There is a method provided in the built-in `System` class. Just as years might be counted from the beginning of the Christian era, the Java environment counts and reports time in milliseconds since the beginning of 1970. To calculate the running time of a program, we simply read the clock once at the beginning and once at the end of the program and subtract. For example, how long does it take to sum 1 million integers? We can find out with the following program

```
public class Timing
{
    public static void main(String args[])
    {
        int sum = 0;
        int i;
        long start, stop;

        start = System.currentTimeMillis();
        for (i = 1; i <= 1000000; i = i+1) {
            sum = sum + i;
        }
        stop = System.currentTimeMillis();
        System.out.println(stop-start);
    }
}
```

Timing

The number that appears is the number of milliseconds required to perform the million loops:

    793

Dividing this time by 1 million (the number of loops), we find that a single loop takes about 793 nanoseconds.

Exercise 1.8 *The previous timing included the time it takes to execute the loop. How could you run another experiment to help determine the time it takes to do just the* `sum = sum+i` *statement?*

We measured the length of time it takes to perform the statement within the loop as approximately 300 nanoseconds—the length of time it takes light to travel the length of an American football field. (At the time of this writing, this was measured as being about 50 times slower than an equivalent operation in a traditional language, C.) We can see, then, that even though we can directly measure times that are greater than a millisecond, repeating the experiment allows us to measure much smaller intervals of time with accuracy.

It is important to observe that the time is returned from `currentTimeMillis` using a `long`. We expect, however, that the difference will be a very short interval of time. The difference can be easily stored within an integer.

Exercise 1.9 *How long an experiment must we time before we are forced to store the elapsed time in a* `long`*?*

1.4   Object Types

Java is an *object-oriented* language, and as a result, much of its power is derived from the construction and manipulation of objects. While primitive data types are responsible for supporting much of the arithmetic in the language, objects are responsible for structuring or modeling higher concepts that are often found in modern programs. We will see, here, two examples of objects—strings and random number generators—that play important roles in the programs we write. Objects, however, involve a complexity that is greater than that found in primitive types, and so programmers must take more care in manipulating objects. Despite this "overhead," we will see over the course of this text that the introduction of objects in a language can ultimately *reduce* the complexity of programming concepts.

Before we investigate particular types of objects further, we must develop an appropriate model of what is actually happening when we declare an object in Java. Let us assume, for the purposes of illustration, that we have available to us `Balloon` objects; presumably, a `Balloon` models a real-world inflatable balloon. The identifier `Balloon` is the name of the *class* that describes all balloon *objects*. If our program manipulates three balloons, there are three *objects*, all of which are *instances* of the class `Balloon`. We can think of the class as a cookie cutter, and the individual balloons as the result of cutting out new instances from balloon material.

Object variables in Java do not directly hold objects. Instead, they hold *references* to objects. In our balloon analogy, the reference is like the string on the balloon. Sometimes the variable is referencing a balloon instance—the reference-string is actually tied to a particular balloon. At other times, the reference is `null`; the string is not attached to any balloon.[7] For this reason, we must not only declare the reference to the object, but explicitly tell Java to *construct* every object we use. This is accomplished with the unary **new** operator. It takes as its only operand the name of a class, along with any parameters that might be useful in initializing the object.

```
Balloon tweety = new Balloon(); // a new Balloon ref'd by tweety
Balloon woodstock = null;       // woodstock not referencing
```

As we can see, `tweety` references a new `Balloon` object, while `woodstock` does not. This operand to **new**—the class name with its list of parameters—is called a *constructor*. Again, we'll see more on constructors later.

The motivation behind these "references" and the explicit construction of objects is not difficult to understand. Objects are frequently complex and their interactions with other parts of the Java environment must be carefully controlled. Explicitly constructed objects make it possible to create new objects as needed, and not just at the beginning of the program.

Finally, we'll see more "dotted" notation as we consider objects in detail. For example,

```
woodstock = new Balloon();  // play with a new balloon
woodstock.inflate();        // call inflate method
woodstock.pop();            // balloon enters useless mode
```

calls two methods, `inflate` and (sadly) `pop`. These methods belong to and apply to the object `woodstock`. Calling `inflate` on `woodstock` does not affect `tweety`. Notice, by the way, we did, ultimately, have `woodstock` reference a newly constructed `Balloon`. If this had not been done, Java would have difficulties applying the `inflate` method, since there would have been no `Balloon` to inflate.

We now investigate two classes of objects that appear throughout the rest of the text—the `String` class and the `Random` number generator class.

1.4.1   Strings

A *string* is a sequence of symbols that is used to form words and messages. The `String` is our first real example of an *object*. `String` constants are indicated by a sequence of characters between double quotation marks (`"`). The following are all valid assignments to `Strings`:

We've seen Balloons...now Strings!

---

[7] We won't worry about this now, but it's actually possible to have two references to the same object.

```
String bean = "Kentucky Wonder";
String blankVerse = "";
String mustache = "must" + "ache";
```

The last example demonstrates the operation of *concatenation*, ('+'). The String "mustache" is the result of appending "must" and "ache". In fact, *any* value of any type may be concatenated with a String.

Exercise 1.10 *What do we get when we concatenate an* int *and a* String?

We will see more details about the manipulation of Strings in Chapter 5, but we provide one word of warning here: String variables are references to objects. This means that the '==' operator compares the *references*, not the Strings themselves. Instead, two Strings are compared by applying the equals method of one to the other. The result is a boolean that is true whenever the two Strings are exactly the same. Here is a simple example:

```
String front = "cove";
String back = "rage";
String result = front + back;

System.out.println(result == "coverage");
System.out.println(result.equals("coverage"));
```

The value of result is a new string, "coverage", which is the concatenation of "cove" and "rage". This result, however, is a reference to a String object that is *different* from a reference to the String constant, "coverage". Thus, the '==' comparison will yield false even though the two strings have the same value. The second comparison, using equals, does the work of actually comparing the two distinct strings to find that they are character-for-character identical.

1.4.2   Random Numbers

Recently, we were reminded by a pilot *"Please keep your seatbelts fastened: random turbulence is not easily predicted."* Indeed. Sometimes randomness needs to be modeled in programs. In games one or more cards are often drawn "at random" from a standard deck of 52 playing cards. Sometimes a "fair" six-sided die or a "fair" coin is tossed. Sometimes a letter or a character is drawn "at random." The words in quotation marks here are always meant to imply that the choices to be made are equally likely to occur and are unpredictable each time the game is played.

The basis for building in random behavior is usually a *pseudorandom number generator*. The generator is usually *seeded* with a starting number n_0 from which a sequence of seemingly random values $n_1, n_2, n_3, \ldots$ are generated. What properties characterize a sequence of truly random numbers is a subject of research and debate. (For example, if you toss a fair coin n times and observe k heads, then we would not expect that $k = n/2$ *exactly*, but we would also not expect k to differ from $n/2$ by very much.) In computers, the seed is most commonly taken from some rapidly changing and unrelated source such as the computer's internal clock. The sequence is then generated from a complicated formula, involving several of the preceding random values. Such a sequence cannot be truly random, because a computer can only represent a finite number of numbers, and the sequence must eventually begin repeating itself or *cycle*. The formulas are developed to ensure that such a cycle is very long, and one gets a sequence that is pseudorandom or very difficult to distinguish from random.

To use the Java random number generator, one needs to tell Java where to find it. This is done by loading or *importing* the `Random` class from the package `java.util`. The statement that accomplishes this comes right at the beginning of our first random number program:

```java
import java.util.Random;

public class RandomSample
{
    public static void main(String args[])
    {
        int n=6;        // random numbers will be from 1..n
        int value;      // value

        Random random = new Random();  // new generator
        value = random.nextInt();      // get a new random number
        value = Math.abs(value);       // throw away the sign
        value = value%n;               // random integer in 0..n-1
        value++;                       // result is between 1 and n
        System.out.println(value);
    }
}
```

RandomSample

This program uses an integer, n, that controls the range of possible values that can be produced. In this program the numbers come from 1...6 so they might be suitable for simulating a thrown die. Stepping through each of the statements, we first ask the generator to return the next random `int` in its sequence (from the call to the method `nextInt`). Since this integer might be negative, we take the absolute value (with `Math.abs`). The combination of these two statements generates nonnegative random integers. To limit the number of different values to n, we simply compute the remainder of the nonnegative value when divided by n. Since there are only n possible remainders, we have the correct number of different values, but they are between 0 and n-1. We must add 1 to ensure that the final value is found between 1 and n. Here, we compress our computations into a single statement used to compute the roll of a die:

```java
import java.util.Random;

public class Die
{
    public static void main(String args[])
```

Die

```
      {
            Random random = new Random();
            // roll a die:
            int side = Math.abs(random.nextInt())%6+1;
            System.out.println("the die is showing a "+side);
      }
}
```

The output when we ran it was:

```
the die is showing a 2
```

There wasn't much point in showing you the output we got when we ran the
program—yours has a one in six chance of being the same! We will later see
how to have n read from the keyboard during each run of the program.

We can also simulate the drawing of a card from a deck:

Card

```
Random random = new java.util.Random();
int drawn;

// normalize to 52 outcomes,
// and add 1 to get a random integer 1..52
drawn = java.lang.Math.abs(random.nextInt())%52+1;

System.out.println("the card drawn is number " + drawn);
```

with output

```
the card drawn is number 5
```

The output here is nowhere near so satisfying as with the die. We are simply
told the number of the card drawn, and we have to interpret that information:
imagine the cards all laid out in a row, each suit increasing from the Ace to the
King, and the suits laid out in the order clubs, diamond, hearts, and spades.
Card number 5 is the five of clubs. Card number 33 is the 7 of hearts, etc.

Exercise 1.11 *Modify the program to print the card's face value (1...13), followed by the number of the suit (clubs are 1, spades are 4).*

Unfortunately, we cannot simulate drawing two cards (or a poker hand) from
a deck because the cards drawn are not independent. (There are only 51 cards
available for the second draw.) But we can expand our die-throwing simulation
to the case of two dice. The result of each of the two throws is independent of
the other:

Dice

```
import java.util.Random;

public class Dice
{
      public static void main(String args[])
```

```
        {
                Random random = new Random();
                int side1, side2;

                side1 = Math.abs(random.nextInt())%6+1;
                side2 = Math.abs(random.nextInt())%6+1;

                System.out.println("the first die is showing a "+side1);
                System.out.println("the second die is showing a "+side2);
        }
}
```

with output

```
    the first die is showing a 4
    the second die is showing a 3
```

1.5 Chapter Review

Computers are capable of computing a great number of different things. Because the domains of computation are so varied, the types of data that are supported in modern programming languages like Java are just as varied. In this chapter, we have seen that Java supports computations using primitives: integers, floating point numbers, characters, and booleans. Java, being object-oriented, also supports references to objects. Understanding the distinctions between primitive types and objects plays an important role in understanding the capabilities of Java to represent abstract types of data.

- Every variable in a Java program is associated with a type. This association is called a declaration, and helps the compiler determine the correct usage of the variable in the program.

- Primitive data types have a specific range of values. Attempts to assign values outside this range generate errors while compiling or running your program.

- Objects are accessed through references. References usually either are null or refer to an object constructed by the new operator.

- Different types have different operators. Some operators have different meanings when applied to different data—for example, the '/' operator performs integer division on integers, and full division on floating point values.

- Primitive values can be assigned to each other if it is clear that no precision is lost. Otherwise, data of one type can be explicitly converted to data of another type using *casting*.

Problems

1.1★   What would be an appropriate data type for variables that represent each of the following:

   a. The number of students in your computer science class.

   b. The mean (average) number of students per class in your school.

   c. The distance in centimeters from the earth to the moon, measured to the closest centimeter.

   d. The total number of gifts mentioned in the song "The Twelve Days of Christmas."

   e. Whether a person qualifies to legally purchase beer in your state.

   f. The grade you expect to receive in this class. (Disregard +'s and −'s.)

   g. Whether you have a younger sister.

1.2   Consider a program that attempts to represent a lottery device that contains 26 uniquely numbered balls within a jar. After a drawing, 6 balls are removed. Write declarations for each of the following variables or constants:

   a. The number of balls initially loaded in the lottery jar.

   b. The largest number drawn.

   c. The average value drawn.

   d. Whether or not a 3 was drawn.

   e. The probability that two numbers drawn are the same.

   f. The letter associated (using a traditional alphabet code: `A`= 1, etc.) with the last number drawn from the jar.

1.3★   Every occurrence of the phrase `X == X` can be replaced by `true`, and every occurrence of the phrase `X != X` can be replaced by `false`. Explain why this is the case.

1.4   Suppose `y` is a boolean variable representing whether you have a younger sibling, `s` indicates whether you have a sister, and `n` indicates the number of siblings you have. Write out exact interpretations of the following Java boolean expressions:

   a. `!y`

   b. `!s`

   c. `n==0`

d. `(!s) && (n > 0)`

e. `(n==1) && y && s`

f. `(n==1) && ((!y) || (!s))`

g. `s && (!s)`

h. `y || (!y)`

1.5★   If `hours` represents time, measured in hours, write an expression for `hours` measured in seconds.

1.6   If `millis` represents time measured in milliseconds, write an expression for `millis` measured in hours.

1.7★   If `millis` represents time measured in milliseconds, write a series of statements that break the time into the equivalent combination of days, hours, minutes, seconds, and milliseconds.

1.8   If `temp` represents the temperature in degrees Fahrenheit, write an expression that expresses `temp` in degrees Celsius.

1.9   If `temp` represents the temperature in degrees Celsius, write an expression that expresses `temp` in degrees Fahrenheit.

1.10★   The average speed of the planet Earth about the Sun is 66400 miles per hour. How far does the Earth move in one nanosecond? Write (or modify) a program to determine this answer.

Knuth suggests the use of "kilobyte (KB)" for 1000 bytes and "large kilobyte (KKB)" to describe 1024 bytes.

1.11★   How long (in inches) is a "micromile"?

1.12   When measuring the number of bytes on a disk drive, the units of kilobyte are often used. This is a slight misuse of the prefix "kilo," which traditionally means 1000. Instead, a kilobyte is $1024 = 2^{10}$ bytes. A megabyte contains 2^{20} bytes. How many are there? A gigabyte contains 2^{30} bytes. How many are there? (A terabyte contains approximately 10% more bytes than one might expect!)

1.13★   Write a program to compute and print 150 factorial—the product of the numbers 1 through 150. (Hint: Use a `double`.)

1.14   Using only one variable (for assignment), multiplication, and the number 2, write no more than 4 short expressions to compute 2^{256}. Using a fifth statement, print out only the units place, computed from the variable. (Extra: what's the units place of $2^{(2^{256})}$?)

1.15★   Nikolay Rimsky-Korsakov's *Flight of the Bumblebee* is composed of 114 bars of (mostly) 16th notes in $\frac{2}{4}$ time. The composer suggests playing the piece *vivace*; at this speed, there are 144 quarter notes in a minute. Assuming no changes in tempo, how long does the bumblebee fly about the swan? Assuming a violin plays each 16th note (nearly true), and that during each note, the bow travels 2 inches (an educated guess), how many feet does the bow travel during the piece? What is the average speed (in miles per hour) of the bow?

1.16⋆   The Birthday Paradox states that, if one writes a program to print out only 23 independently selected random numbers between 1 and 365, there is a 50% chance that there will be a duplicate number in the list. (The analogy stems from collecting 23 random people in a room: it is more likely that two will share a birthday than not.) Write a program to print 23 random numbers. Describe (but do not implement) how you might develop a boolean variable that is `true` exactly when there are two similar values in the list. (We will learn how to implement this in Problem 7.15.)

1.17   If you are a native of our moon, you will know there are 14 possible lunar birthdays (leap years occur 2 out of 5 years, but we'll ignore that). How many moon-children must you have in a room before you can guarantee a 50% chance of a duplicate birthday? Write a program (involving a `while` loop) that determines this value. In contrast, there are approximately 377 possible Martian birthdays. How many Martians are necessary to demonstrate the Birthday Paradox?

Chapter 2

The Element Package

> *"Simplicity is mastery of the complex."*
> —Sweets Edison

ONE OF THE SUCCESSES OF JAVA is that it claims *platform independence*. One of the difficulties of Java is that, in an attempt to address everyone's needs, the system is overly complex for introductory programmers. In this chapter, we discuss an approach to looking at Java that stresses the *elements* of programming. These elements are stable, but not exhaustive. What you learn here about Java will be sufficient to program, but will not provide you all the specific details of complex programming styles and techniques.

To insulate us from the (necessary, but annoying) trends of Java style, we have provided the `element` package, a collection of pieces of software that will make this book and its lessons more lasting.[1] It is composed of two main components: a `ConsoleWindow`, for communicating textually, and a `DrawingWindow`, for communicating graphically.

A *package* is a collection of related software components. It might consist, for example, of parts of an astronomical calculator, or a collection of tools for building pinball machines. This package consists of several Java classes. Most of the examples of this book make use of classes from the `element` package. The easiest way to make Java use this package is to simply include all of the element software. This is accomplished with the line:

```
import element.*;
```

FirstConsole

The word `element` indicates the name of the package, while the asterisk means *all* of the classes within the package. The remainder of this chapter will be spent experimenting with the classes that are imported by this statement.

2.1 The Console Window

At one time, the only way that computers communicated with their users was through a special typewriter-like device called the *console*. Typically, the console consisted of a *keyboard* and a *typewriter*. These devices are, of course, different in their purpose. The keyboard allows the user to type information

---

[1] This software is freely available from McGraw-Hill at `http://www.mhhe.com/javaelements`. We encourage you to pick it up. More specific details of the software discussed in this chapter may be found in Appendix E.

Figure 2.1   The initial view of the `ConsoleWindow`.

into the computer and is, therefore, an *input device*. The typewriter (or, in more modern times, the monitor) is a device for presenting information to the user and is, thus, an *output device*.

The `ConsoleWindow` class from the `element` package allows us to communicate through the keyboard and monitor. Initially, it is necessary for us to *construct* a `ConsoleWindow` object. This is accomplished with the following statement:

```
ConsoleWindow c = new ConsoleWindow();
```

The variable `c` is a reference to a `ConsoleWindow`. Recall that, initially, a reference doesn't refer to anything. An assignment similar to the one above forces `c` to refer to a new `ConsoleWindow`. Once constructed, a new `ConsoleWindow` appears on the screen. Its appearance is similar to that shown in Figure 2.1. Once the window is displayed, we will see it is possible to read information from the console and write output to the window. From this point in the text onward, programs that communicate textually with the user will use the console window from the element package, and we will declare the variable `c` as a reference to that window.[2]

Once a console window is constructed, the programmer has access to three "streams" that allow the programmer to communicate with the outside world—the user. The fields `in` and `out` are similar to those made available by the `System` class, while `input` provides an improved (more *user-friendly*) interface to the `in` stream.

2.1.1   Output Streams

As we have seen earlier, communication from the program to the user often occurs by placing text, numbers, and other information in the console window. This process is called `printing`. The main mechanism we will use for printing

---

[2] We have chosen the identifier `c` for brevity, but invite you the reader to use a longer, more descriptive identifier should you so desire.

to a Java `ConsoleWindow` is to call the `print` and `println` methods of the `out` stream. Every type of data in Java can be printed in a `ConsoleWindow`:

```java
import element.*;

public class Printing
{
    public static void main(String args[])
    {
        ConsoleWindow c = new ConsoleWindow();

        c.out.print("Watson, come here!");
        c.out.println("  I want you!");
    }
}
```

Printing

Notice that each of these statements is a method call. Thus `c.out.print` tells the output stream `c.out` that *it* is to print the indicated line. Here, `c.out` is the *object* (an output stream) and `print` is the *method*.

We recall, here, the difference between two types of `c.out` method calls. The first, the `print` method, causes `Watson, come here!` to be printed on the screen. The location of the output cursor—the location of the next character to be printed—follows immediately after the exclamation point ('`!`'). The following `println` method call follows on with the phrase `I want you!`. Unlike the `print` method, `println` appends a *newline* to the end of the printed output, causing the current output position to be placed on the next line. Here's the entire output:

```
Watson, come here!  I want you!
```

The quotation marks about the phrases are the standard double quotes. If desired, we can modify the two historic lines above, and attribute them as we see here:

Notable words!

```java
c.out.println("''Watson, come here!"+"  I want you!''");
c.out.println("\t\t-Alexander Graham Bell");
```

This generates the output

```
''Watson, come here!  I want you!''
                -Alexander Graham Bell
```

PrintLine

Notice the difference between double quotation marks—used to delimit strings— and pairs of apostrophes (or pairs of *quotes* as opposed to *quotation marks*)— used to print about quotations. The first line is another example of concatenation of strings. The two strings `"''Watson, come here!"` and `"  I want you!''"` are glued together to make one long string. Concatenation of string values is useful if the string you wish to print is too long to be typed on one line, or if it is the result of concatenating strings from many sources.

Concatenation: feline conviction.

The second line makes use of escape characters. Here, the backslash ('\')

Flag: the
signal used by
a boat or
train's
signalman.

escapes from normal processing and signals or *flags* the next character to be interpreted specially. The \t indicates we want to insert a tab. (A full table of escape characters appeared in Figure 1.5 on page 24.) If the double quotation mark is to be included in strings, it should be escaped.

Data other than strings can be printed in a similar manner. For example, the following prints out information about someone's age:

Age

```
ConsoleWindow c = new ConsoleWindow();
double ageInYears = 12.5;

c.out.println("I can't believe you're "+ageInYears+" years old!");
c.out.println("(That makes you about "+
                          (ageInYears*365.25)+" days old!)");
```

The result is to print a line that is the concatenation of a string, and *the string representing* a double. Whenever Java encounters a nonstring object in a place where a string seems necessary, it generates a string representation of the object on-the-fly. Here, on the first line, we see Java converts the double to the four character string, "12.5". The second line demonstrates the use of parentheses to force the mathematical computation before the concatenation operator turns the result into a string. This is an important observation, as many Java programs that make use of the concatenation operator generate unexpected (but correct) results (see Problem 2.4).

2.1.2   Input Streams

In the ConsoleWindow there are two streams—in and input—for reading input from the keyboard. The more primitive stream in is less suitable for day-to-day programming, and so we focus on the *filtered* input stream, input.[3]

Suppose we are interested in writing a program whose behavior is similar to the age computation of the last section, but whose initial age is read from the keyboard. Here is how we might accomplish this:

AgeInput

```
import element.*;

public class AgeInput
{
    public static void main(String args[])
    {
        ConsoleWindow c = new ConsoleWindow();
        c.out.println("How old are you?");
        double ageInYears = c.input.readDouble();

        c.out.println("I can't believe you're "+ageInYears
```

---

[3] More details about the in stream may be gleaned from any Java reference manual but, again, it is usually unnecessary.

```
                              +" years old!");
                c.out.println("(That makes you about "+(ageInYears*365.25)
                              +" days old!)");
        }
    }
```

The first `c.out` line prompts the user to type in an age. The program then calls the `readDouble` method, and reads the initial value for the **double** variable, `ageInYears`. The next two statements print two lines of messages, using concatenation of strings and values of **double** expressions. The conversation, all found in the `ConsoleWindow`, appears as follows:

```
How old are you?
38
I can't believe you're 38.0 years old!
(That makes you about 13879.5 days old!)
```

In general, several pieces of information are read from the keyboard during the run of a program. The `ReadStream` object, `c.input`, provides access to many methods that allow the user to read in Java primitive values. Because there is often intervening white space (spaces, tabs, carriage returns) between data values presented at the keyboard, the `ReadStream` skips any white space that might appear before the data. The `ReadStream` also has a number of other features that are described in detail in Appendix D (for *Documentation*).

As a larger example of the use of the `c.input` object, we investigate a program that carefully reads several types of information about a person's swimming workout. The input is typed on several lines, and includes their name, number of laps they swam, and the time it took to swim those laps:

```
import element.*;

public class Swim
{
    public static void main(String args[])
    {
        final double SECONDS_PER_HOUR = 60.0*60.0;
        final double FEET_PER_MILE = 5280.0;
        final double FEET_PER_METER = 39.37/12.0;
        final int    POOL_SIZE = 50;
        final double FEET_PER_LAP = POOL_SIZE*FEET_PER_METER;
        ConsoleWindow c = new ConsoleWindow();
        String first, last;
        int laps, minutes, seconds;
        double hours, distance, lapTime;

        c.out.println("What are your first and last names?");
        first = c.input.readString();
        last = c.input.readString();
```

Swim

```
          c.out.println("Thanks, "+first+".");
          c.out.println("How many "+POOL_SIZE+
                          " meter laps did you swim?");
          laps = c.input.readInt();

          c.out.println("How long did it take you "+
                          "(in minutes and seconds)?");
          minutes = c.input.readInt();
          seconds = c.input.readInt();

          // Now compute total number of seconds and number of hours:
          seconds = seconds + 60*minutes;
          hours = seconds/SECONDS_PER_HOUR;

          // Now compute average lap time:
          lapTime = seconds/(double)laps;
          c.out.println("It took you, on average, "+lapTime
                          +" seconds per lap.");

          // Compute the total distance, in miles
          distance = laps*FEET_PER_LAP/FEET_PER_MILE;
          c.out.println("Your average speed was "+(distance/hours)
                          +" miles/hour.");
          c.out.println("You swim about "
                          +Math.round(SECONDS_PER_HOUR/lapTime)
                          +" laps per hour!");
      }
  }
```

This program is fairly long, but careful inspection reveals that it is not that
complex. Most of the statements perform input or output, and the remaining
computations are typical of calculations one might perform with a calculator.
Notice the use of constant values to facilitate the readability of the program. In
a well-written program, most of the constants other than 1 and 0 are named.

Here is how the program appears when it is run:

```
What are your first and last names?
Ray Tracer
Thanks, Ray.
How many 50 meter laps did you swim?
34
How long did it take you (in minutes and seconds)?
37 28
It took you, on average, 66.11764705882354 seconds per lap.
Your average speed was 1.691629933678421 miles/hour.
You swim about 54 laps per hour!
```

Notice that the programmer has a firm idea of what input should be provided
and how it will be formatted. Deviations from the required format will lead to
errors and are likely to cause the program to stop or compute the wrong results.

Some interesting conversion between double and integer values is accomplished during the computation; it is useful to follow the computation along to see how our choices of data type facilitate the computation.

2.2   The Drawing Window

Not all input and output is accomplished textually. For example, those who play video games understand that input and output can be accomplished using the mouse, trackball, and high speed video output. Like the `ConsoleWindow`, the `DrawingWindow` is an object that allows the programmer to communicate with the user. Instead of textual communication, however, the `DrawingWindow` allows the programmer to communicate graphically. The input device is the mouse, and the output is the graphics of the window. The `DrawingWindow` facilitates a type of graphics interface that is similar to that found in the complex graphics packages that come with Java. The design of the `DrawingWindow` graphics is also motivated by toolkits found on traditional programming environments. Let's investigate the various features of the `DrawingWindow`.

2.2.1   Pixel-Oriented Graphics

Windows on most computers are rectangular collections of colored dots called *pixels* (from *picture elements*). Modern displays allow the display of thousands of colors using hundreds of thousands or millions of pixels. From afar the coordinated painting of these pixels can be used to form various types of graphics: line drawings, text, buttons, pictures, and so on. Programming languages that allow the direct manipulation of computer graphics allow the user to *address* these pixels directly through a coordinate system not unlike the two dimensional *Cartesian coordinate system* we use in high school mathematics. Each pixel (or, informally, *point*) is given a pair of integers called x and y. The x-coordinate describes the column of the pixel from the left side of the containing window, while the y-coordinate describes the row of the pixel, as measured *downward* from the top of the window.[4] Considering Figure 2.2, we see that in a default window, the top-left coordinate of the window has $(x, y) = (0, 0)$, and that points along the right side have $x = 200$. Points along the top edge all have $y = 0$, while those along the left edge all have $x = 0$.

2.2.2   Drawing

Drawing in a `DrawingWindow` is not all that different from painting on a canvas: one picks a color and paints the color onto the screen. As with programs in general, some care is necessary in planning your attack on a picture:

Principle 7   *Later drawing usually obscures earlier work.*

---

[4] This seems rather unusual, until we realize that most computer applications are responsible for displaying text—from left to right, and from top to bottom.

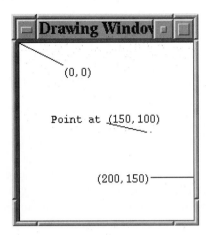

Figure 2.2 The coordinates of some interesting points in a window.

When drawing line art, the computer keeps track of a special point, the *current position*. This point is, essentially, the point over which a virtual pen resides. One can set this point by telling the computer to move to a particular location. For example, the statements

```
DrawingWindow d = new DrawingWindow();

d.moveTo(100,100);
```

Tutorial   construct a new DrawingWindow, d,[5] and move the pen over the point $(100, 100)$, the center pixel in the drawing window. No mark is left on the canvas, but the *state* of the drawing window has potentially changed. To make a mark, we can draw a line. Suppose, for example, we now execute

```
d.lineTo(50,0);
```

the result is a line from the center upwards and to the left. The line extends from the current position to the point specified. Once the line is drawn, the destination endpoint becomes the current position. In this way, we can draw fairly complex shapes.

Exercise 2.1 *What commands would you use to draw a square?*

Sometimes, it is useful to move the pen *relative* to the current location of the pen—that is, to move the pen by specifying how far it should be moved in

---

[5] Again, we will consistently use d throughout this text, for brevity; the reader may wish to develop a more descriptive name for the DrawingWindow reference commonly found in graphical programs.

each direction, and not by directly specifying the destination. The relative pen movement and line drawing commands are `move` and `line`, respectively. Thus, to perform the same drawing of a line, we use

```
d.moveTo(100,100);
d.line(-50,-100);
```

By using relative commands, you can draw entire pictures relative to a central point. This program draws an X at the location read in from the keyboard:

```
import element.*;

public class XMarks
{
    public static void main(String args[])
    {
        ConsoleWindow c = new ConsoleWindow();
        DrawingWindow d = new DrawingWindow();
        int centerX, centerY;
        final int RADIUS = 10; // size of the cross

        c.out.println("Enter the coordinates of the X:");
        centerX = c.input.readInt();
        centerY = c.input.readInt();

        d.moveTo(centerX, centerY);   // move to center
        d.move(-RADIUS,-RADIUS);      // move northwest
        d.line(2*RADIUS,2*RADIUS);    // draw to southeast
        d.move(0,-2*RADIUS);          // move to northEast
        d.line(-2*RADIUS,2*RADIUS);   // draw to southwest
    }
}
```

XMarks

Exercise 2.2 *Given only the commands we have seen so far, how would you draw a single point? (Hint: Drawing a line always draws at least one endpoint.)*

2.2.3   Drawing Objects

To facilitate our use of the drawing window, the `element` package provides a number of graphical primitives as Java objects. For example, one means of drawing a point on a screen is to use the `Pt` (point) object. This object, like any other in Java, must be explicitly constructed by the programmer. When you construct a `Pt`, you provide its coordinates. The coordinates describe where the point is located in a target window. Thus, the following draws the point located at $(100, 100)$:

```
DrawingWindow d = new DrawingWindow();
Pt p = new Pt(100,100);
d.draw(p);
```

DrawPoint

Figure 2.3   The point $(100, 100)$ in the drawing window.

The output of this program is shown in Figure 2.3.

Another way to do the same thing is to combine the two statements involving the point into one:

```
DrawingWindow d = new DrawingWindow();
d.draw(new Pt(100,100));
```

The difference is that after the point is used in the latter example, it may not be reused. In the first program, the `Pt` variable may be used several times without going through the process of reconstructing the object each time. Since assigning the value to a variable doesn't take much time and provides more of a hint of the purpose of the object, it's also slightly more readable.

Finally, we note that the above examples asked the `DrawingWindow` to draw an object. We can reverse the request and ask the object to *draw itself* on the `DrawingWindow`:

```
DrawingWindow d = new DrawingWindow();
Pt p = new Pt(100,100);
p.drawOn(d);
```

While all of these methods are equivalent, it is nice to have the choice of modes of expression. Programming languages, like human languages, can be improved by careful thought about expression.

Principle 8   *Program with a reader in mind.*

The `Pt` object, like most other objects in the **element** package, has methods for both *accessing* and *setting* the various parameters of the object. The *accessor* methods take no parameters (e.g., `p.x()`) and return the desired value.

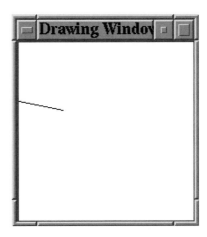

Figure 2.4   A line from $(50, 75)$ to $(-75, 50)$ that extends off the drawing window.

The *mutators* take a single new parameter value (e.g., `p.x(10)`). This ability to modify the state of an object allows for even more flexibility in deciding when to create new objects or modify existing ones.

Line segments are also `element` objects. To specify a line segment, one only needs to specify the two endpoints—either as two `Pt` objects or as the four coordinates that determine the points. The following program draws a line from $(50, 75)$ to $(-75, 50)$:

```
Line l = new Line(50,75,-75,50);
d.draw(l);
```

Notice (see Figure 2.4) that one of the endpoints is not actually located within the drawing window. Java simply "clips" the line to the portion that is visible.

Tutorial

2.2.4   The Mouse

While drawn graphics in a window provide output, the *mouse* serves to provide input. At any time, the mouse is pointing at a pixel, and its buttons are either pressed or not pressed. In the `element` package, one provides graphical input by pointing to interesting locations within the window, or by pressing buttons at important times. In this section, we consider the simple manipulations of the mouse.

Imagine: the Output Mouse

Since the position of the mouse is often useful as input, it is reasonable to ask the drawing window where the mouse is with respect to the upper-left corner of the window. The `getMouse` method of the `DrawingWindow` allows the programmer to retrieve the current mouse location. For example, the following program prints the starting location of the mouse, and then draws a line from the origin to the current mouse position:

MouseLine

```
import element.*;

public class MouseLine
{
    public static void main(String args[])
    {
        ConsoleWindow c = new ConsoleWindow();
        DrawingWindow d = new DrawingWindow();
        Pt destination = d.getMouse();

        c.out.println("Drawing from origin to "+destination);
        d.moveTo(0,0);            // move pen to origin
        d.lineTo(destination);  // draw from origin to destination
    }
}
```

The value of the d.getMouse() method call is a new Pt object that can be used
anywhere a user-constructed Pt object can be used. We see, for example, that
Pt objects can be used as a parameter to the lineTo method. They may also
be used in the moveTo method. Clearly, the mouse is acting as an input device
here. Unfortunately, the mouse position when the program starts is probably
not ideal: as the program starts up you might not have the mouse in the position
you want (for example, you might have been placing the drawing window in the
correct position).

To help synchronize the Java program and the user's mouse positioning, we
can use the mouse buttons. The element package assumes that you have a
mouse with at least one button, although many well-dressed mice have three
or more. When you want to wait for the mouse to be pressed, you can use the
awaitMousePress method of the drawing window. The program simply idles or
sleeps until an appropriate mouse button is pressed. At that point (excuse the
pun), the program awakens and the method finishes. The result of this method
call is the point where the mouse was pressed and can optionally be assigned to
a Pt reference. Here's a modified version of our mouse program that makes use
of the awaitMousePress and the timing methods considered in the last chapter:

MouseTime

```
import element.*;

public class MouseTime
{
    public static void main(String args[])
    {
        ConsoleWindow c = new ConsoleWindow();
        DrawingWindow d = new DrawingWindow();
        Pt destination;
        long startTime, stopTime;

        c.out.println("Press the mouse!");
        startTime = System.currentTimeMillis();
        destination = d.awaitMousePress();
```

```
            stopTime = System.currentTimeMillis();
            c.out.println(destination);
            d.moveTo(0,0);
            d.lineTo(destination);
            c.out.println("It took you "+(stopTime-startTime)+
                        " milliseconds");
        }
    }
```

Notice that when we print out the number of milliseconds we use string concatenation ('+') and subtraction of long integers ('-'). The parentheses here
help Java (and us) remember that these two operations do not work on the
same class of data. If the parentheses were missing, the start time would be
concatenated to the initial string, and then Java would attempt to subtract the
stop time from the string—clearly something that should be avoided!

A similar command, awaitMouseRelease allows Java programs to wait until
the mouse is released in the drawing window. The two commands may be used
together to draw arbitrary lines:

DrawLine

```
import element.*;

public class DrawLine
{
    public static void main(String args[])
    {
        ConsoleWindow c = new ConsoleWindow();
        DrawingWindow d = new DrawingWindow();
        Pt pressPoint, releasePoint;

        c.out.println("Press the mouse, "
                    +"drag out a line, and release!");
        d.awaitMousePress();
        pressPoint = d.getMouse();
        d.awaitMouseRelease();
        releasePoint = d.getMouse();
        d.draw(new Line(pressPoint,releasePoint));
    }
}
```

You can now see the mouse's line of attack!

2.2.5   The Two-Dimensional Drawing Objects

If you look at your computer carefully, you'll soon see that drawing everything
with points and lines would be an unsatisfying task. Windows and menus, for
example, are drawn on solid rectangles. If Java knew how to directly draw
rectangles, then our graphical tool set would be richer. Let's consider, then, the
more complex objects found in the element package.

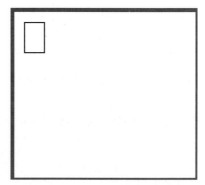

Figure 2.5   A `Rect` object painted with the `draw` method of the `DrawingWindow`.

The `Rect` Object

On computers rectangles are most often drawn with their sides parallel to the sides of the screen. In the `element` package, you can draw rectangles with the help of the `Rect` object. In Java a rectangle is specified by its upper-left coordinate and its width and height. (There are, of course, many other ways that a rectangle could be specified, but this is perfectly satisfactory for our use.) As with all objects in Java, we need to construct a copy of the object before it can be used. Once constructed, it can be passed to the `draw` method of the `DrawingWindow` as were the `Pt` and `Line` objects previously. The following draws a rectangular frame that is 20 units wide and 30 tall. Its upper-left corner is at location $(10, 10)$ in `DrawingWindow` d:

DrawRect

```
import element.*;

public class DrawRect
{
    public static void main(String args[])
    {
        DrawingWindow d = new DrawingWindow();
        Rect cornerRect = new Rect(10,10,20,30);

        d.draw(cornerRect);
    }
}
```

The result is the window shown in Figure 2.5. To simplify the way `Rect`s are specified, we can use other combinations of points and integers. For example, you can specify a rectangle with the top-left corner and a width and height, or you can specify two corners with two points. The following code allows the programmer to draw a rectangle on the screen much as we drew an arbitrary line with the mouse:

```
import element.*;

public class MouseRect
{
    public static void main(String args[])
    {
        DrawingWindow d = new DrawingWindow();
        Pt pressPoint, releasePoint;
        Rect box;

        d.awaitMousePress();
        pressPoint = d.getMouse();          // one corner
        d.awaitMouseRelease();
        releasePoint = d.getMouse();        // another
        box = new Rect(pressPoint,releasePoint);

        d.draw(box);
    }
}
```

MouseRect

Playing with this program, you will realize that it doesn't matter which way that the mouse is dragged out; the rectangle is the tightest rectangle that encompasses the points of press and release. It is important to distinguish this behavior from that of the point-and-two-integer version—there, the point is always interpreted as the upper left.

To fill in a rectangle, we use the `fill` method of the `DrawingWindow`. Each of the pixels that reside on or within the frame is drawn on the screen. Similarly, the `clear` method allows the rectangle to be erased from the screen.

A rectangle that is often of interest is the rectangle that describes the bounds of the drawing window. We can ask the drawing window for a copy of that `Rect` with the `bounds` method. Given this, we can see that the following method would erase all the pixels of the `DrawingWindow d`.

```
d.clear(d.bounds());
```

ClearScreen

Since the drawing window can be constructed to be various sizes, the ability to ask the drawing window its actual size makes our programs more robust, should we decide to change the window's dimensions.

Once a `Rect` object is constructed, we may use various methods to ask it about itself, or to modify its current state. For example, the coordinate associated with each side of the rectangle can be determined by using the `left`, `right`, `top`, and `bottom` accessor methods. Given a `Rect r`, the following code (thoroughly) describes it, including its width, height, and center point (the average x and y coordinates):

RectInfo

```
import element.*;

public class RectInfo
{
    public static void main(String args[])
    {
        ConsoleWindow c = new ConsoleWindow();
        DrawingWindow d = new DrawingWindow();
        Pt corner1, corner2;
        Rect box;

        c.out.println("Click mouse at opposite corners of rect.");
        d.awaitMousePress();
        corner1 = d.awaitMouseRelease();
        d.awaitMousePress();
        corner2 = d.awaitMouseRelease();
        box = new Rect(corner1,corner2);
        d.draw(box);
        c.out.println("left    = "+box.left()
                    +" right   = "+box.right());
        c.out.println("top     = "+box.top()
                    + " bottom = "+box.bottom());
        c.out.println("width   = "+box.width()
                    +" height = "+box.height());
        c.out.println("center = "+box.center());
    }
}
```

Example output from this program would be:

```
Click mouse at opposite corners of rect.
left    = 41 right   = 154
top     = 11 bottom = 90
width   = 113 height = 79
center = <Point: (97,50)>
```

Once a Rect is constructed, it is also possible to change its state with any of several mutator methods. For example, the left method takes a single parameter and shifts the rectangle so that its left side is at the coordinate specified. The dimensions of the rectangle do not change. The following program constructs a 10 by 10 rectangle whose bottom right is at the point of a mouse press:

```
import element.*;

public class SetRect
{
    public static void main(String args[])
    {
        final int SIZE = 10;     // dimensions of box
```

```
        DrawingWindow d = new DrawingWindow();
        Rect box = new Rect();
        Pt press;

        // construct SIZExSIZE rectangle
        box.width(SIZE); box.height(SIZE);

        // now, paint a box with lower right at point of press
        press = d.awaitMousePress();
        box.right(press.x());
        box.bottom(press.y());
        d.fill(box);
    }
}
```

The rectangle is first constructed to be the correct shape, and then its bottom and right sides are aligned with the mouse. To change the dimensions of the rectangle, `width` and `height` can be used to resize the rectangle about its center. `center` can be used to recenter the rectangle about a new point. We will see more use for these methods in later chapters.

Sometimes it is convenient to build buttonlike objects. This may be accomplished by drawing a `Rect` on the screen and pressing the mouse within the `Rect`. We can test whether a point is in a `Rect` using the `contains` method. This method returns `true` if the point is contained within the rectangle. In the following short game, the computer secretly selects a rectangle and waits for the user to guess the location by clicking the mouse. The program then prints whether or not the mouse was clicked in the computer-imagined rectangle:

```
import element.*;
import java.util.Random;

public class LoopTheMouse
{
    public static void main(String args[])
    {
        DrawingWindow d = new DrawingWindow();

        // construct a randomly placed rectangle
        final int SIZE = 50;
        Rect target = new Rect(0,0,SIZE,SIZE);
        Random generator = new Random();
        int centerX =
            Math.abs(generator.nextInt()) % d.bounds().width();
        int centerY =
            Math.abs(generator.nextInt()) % d.bounds().height();
        target.center(new Pt(centerX,centerY));

        // wait for the mouse to be pressed
        Pt mouse = d.awaitMousePress();
```

LoopTheMouse

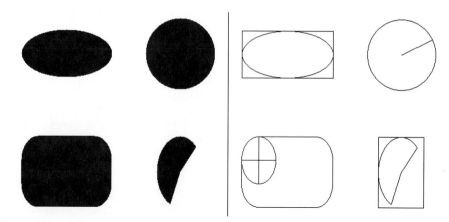

Figure 2.6 On left, various filled shapes available in the `element` package: the `Oval`, the `Circle`, the `RoundRect`, and the `Arc`. On right, the important features that must be specified for each of the graphical objects.

```
    // now draw rectangle and check for hit
    d.fill(target);

    ConsoleWindow c = new ConsoleWindow();
    c.out.println("Mouse in the target? "
                    +target.contains(mouse));
}
}
```

Notice that the center of the rectangle is selected randomly from the pixels displayed within the current drawing window.

Exercise 2.3 *Describe how one might test to see if a line segment is entirely within a rectangle.*

Other Complex Objects

Rectangles are not the only complex objects that may be drawn. There are, in addition, ovals, arcs, circles, and rounded rectangles (see Figure 2.6). It is even possible to manipulate text.

The `Oval` is the largest ellipse that can be inscribed in a rectangle. We specify the `Oval` in the same way that a `Rect` is specified—by specifying the bounds of the containing rectangle. If we replace the `Rect` of a rectangle-based program with an `Oval`, the program runs exactly the same, but the shape drawn on the screen is an ellipse.

To draw circular objects, we can use either a "square" oval (one whose width and height are equal) or element's `Circle` type. The circle is specified by a center point and a radius. Here, for example, are the commands that drew the solid `Circle` in Figure 2.6:

```
final int XCENTER = 150;
final int YCENTER = 50;
final int RADIUS = 30;

Circle sampleCircle = new Circle(XCENTER,YCENTER,RADIUS);
d.fill(sampleCircle);
```

FillShapes

Once constructed, the `Circle` can be drawn, filled, and erased in a manner similar to `Rect` objects.

The `RoundRect` is a marriage between a `Rect` and an `Oval`. The Round-Rect is constructed by drawing a `Rect` whose corners are portions of an `Oval`. The shape of the oval is determined by two parameters, the *corner width* and *corner height*. In the extreme, if the corner width and height are zero, the `RoundRect` looks like a rectangle. If the corner width and height are equivalent to the width and height of the bounding rectangle, the object becomes an `Oval`. When constructing a `RoundRect`, we specify the corner width and height as the final parameters of the method. We drew the filled `RoundRect` of Figure 2.6 with the commands:

```
final int RECT_WIDTH = 80;
final int RECT_HEIGHT = 60;
final int CORNER_WIDTH = 30;
final int CORNER_HEIGHT = 40;

RoundRect sampleRoundRect =
    new RoundRect(10,120,RECT_WIDTH,RECT_HEIGHT,
                  CORNER_WIDTH, CORNER_HEIGHT);
d.fill(sampleRoundRect);
```

Exercise 2.4 *Are buttons on your computer represented by rectangles or round-ed rectangles? If rounded rectangles, is it possible to press the button by pressing* outside *the button, but within the* inside *of the bounding rectangle?*

In the `element` package, each of the graphical objects supports a `contains` method that checks to see if a point is contained within the boundary of the shape.

The `Arc` object allows a programmer to draw a pie-shaped part of an oval. Its construction requires the definition of a bounding rectangle, along with two pieces of information—the start angle and the sweep of the arc. The start angle is measured in degrees counterclockwise, where zero degrees points from the center to the right. The sweep is specified as the number of degrees to rotate counterclockwise while sketching the arc. In the filled `Arc` of Figure 2.6, the starting angle was 45 degrees, and the sweep was 200.

The last object we consider in the `element` drawing package is the `Text`. It is formed by specifying—as with `print` and `println`—any string or object along with a pair of integers that locate the lower-left coordinate of the text in the window. Once constructed, the `Text` object can be treated much like other graphics objects: `left`, `top`, `right`, `bottom`, `width`, and `height` accessors can be used to locate the edges of its bounding rectangle, and it can be moved about by updating the sides or center point. The following sequence of code prints the string `inside a box` inside a box:

DrawText

```
Text t = new Text("inside a box");
t.center(d.getMouse());
d.draw(t);
d.draw(new Rect(t.left(),t.top(),t.width(),t.height()));
```

draws the following interesting picture:

inside a box

A description of all the features of the various objects can be found in Appendix E (for *E*lements).

2.2.6   Color and Pen Mode

While not absolutely necessary, color enhances the output of most computer programs. Only a decade ago, most computer monitors were capable of displaying black and white or, at best, shades of gray. Today, color monitors abound, and most can display millions of colors simultaneously. In this chapter, we discuss two aspects of color control in detail: color and pen mode.

Before we consider these details, we reconsider the model for applying paint on the screen. First, the methods named `fill` and `clear` give the impression that the processes are inherently different. In fact, a better model is to imagine a double ended crayon—one end we draw with, and the other end we erase with *by drawing with the color of the canvas*. The drawing color is the *foreground* color, and the erasing color is the *background* color. By manipulating these two colors and by using `draw`, `fill`, and `clear` in creative ways, we can have our programs generate some interesting shapes that might not immediately seem possible.

Next, just as there are a variety of colors that may be displayed, there are an equal variety of *color models*. Although these models are important, modern programming environments like Java allow us to *abstract away*[6] the details of the particular color model used. To make use of the Java color mechanisms, we

---

[6] Something that is *abstract* has few specified details. The process of *abstraction* is to remove all but the essential details. In our laziness, we use "abstract away" to make obvious that we are not considering some of the more unnecessary and annoying details. We (happily) avoid them here.

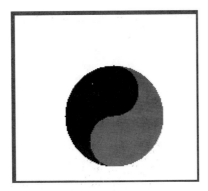

Figure 2.7   An example of drawing with two colors.

must import the `java.awt.Color` class from Java's AWT (*Abstract Windowing Toolkit*) package:

```
import java.awt.Color;
```

ColorDemo

Once imported, the `Color` class defines the values of various common colors: `Color.white`, `Color.gray`,[7] `Color.black`, `Color.red`, `Color.green`, `Color.-blue`, `Color.yellow`, `Color.magenta`, and `Color.cyan`. We can use these color objects to refill the drawing and erasing sides of the pen. To change the color of the `fill`s, we use the `DrawingWindow`'s `setForeground` method. Symmetrically, the `clear` side of the pen is refilled with `setBackground`. Here, for example, is a program to draw the picture shown in Figure 2.7:

One filling goes a long way.

```
// draw mystic symbol
d = new DrawingWindow();
// draw half-gray, half-black circle
d.setForeground(Color.black);
d.fill(new Arc(50,50,100,100,90,180));
d.setForeground(Color.gray);
d.fill(new Arc(50,50,100,100,-90,180));
// add upper and lower discs
d.setForeground(Color.black);
d.fill(new Oval(75,50,50,50));
d.setForeground(Color.gray);
d.fill(new Oval(75,100,50,50));
```

Clearly, the application of paint in this particular order has allowed us to draw shapes that are not immediately obvious with the primitives found in

---

[7] The poets have long debated the spelling of this shade, but programmers of Java (which is adamant in its way) remember to "make w*ay* for gr*ay*."

Figure 2.8   A bull's-eye drawn from concentric rings.

the `element` package. We can simplify the code a bit more by loading both the foreground and background colors and using both the `fill` and `clear` methods to apply the two different colors of paint.

```
// draw mystic symbol
d = new DrawingWindow();
d.setForeground(Color.black);
d.setBackground(Color.gray);
// draw half-black (fill), half-gray (clear) circle
d.fill(new Arc(50,50,100,100,90,180));
d.clear(new Arc(50,50,100,100,-90,180));
// add upper and lower discs
d.fill(new Oval(75,50,50,50));
d.clear(new Oval(75,100,50,50));
```

To us, it seems less obvious which methods are drawing different parts of the figure. Still, the use of alternative background pen colors can be useful when drawing and erasing on a background that is not white.

Let's now consider how we might draw Figure 2.8, but in red. Here, it helps if we don't consider each of the rings or *annuli* as a separate object, but, instead, a series of concentric red and white circles. So, we draw the larger circles first, and the smaller circles last, overlapping them as we go along:

Bullseye

```
import java.awt.Color;
import element.*;

public class Bullseye
{
    public static void main(String args[])
    {
        DrawingWindow d = new DrawingWindow();
        Oval o = new Oval(50,50,100,100);
        d.setForeground(Color.red);
        d.fill(o);
        o.extend(-10,-10);
        d.clear(o);
        o.extend(-10,-10);
```

```
        d.fill(o);
        o.extend(-10,-10);
        d.clear(o);
        o.extend(-10,-10);
        d.fill(o);
    }
}
```

We're painting a single oval several times. In between each `fill` or `clear`, we move each side *in* 10 pixels toward the center by `extending` it *outward by* -10. Since we alternate filling and clearing, we get alternating red and white areas. Changing the foreground and background colors of this program will change the two colors of the bull's-eye.

By default, the foreground and background colors are `Color.black` and `Color.white`. In addition, we think of the foreground and background pens as *painting* their pixel color on the screen; essentially, the color is copied from the pen to the window, overwriting the previous pixel color. In the default "black-and-white" mode, it is possible to make use of a special drawing method, called *inverting*. In this mode, whenever black color would normally be painted on the screen, the color of the pixel—black or white—is flipped to white or black. To understand this, let's take a look at a modified version of the bull's-eye drawing program that paints a black-and-white picture with only `fill` methods:

Invert-
Bullseye

```
import element.*;

public class InvertBullseye
{
    public static void main(String args[])
    {
        DrawingWindow d = new DrawingWindow();
        Oval o = new Oval(50,50,100,100);
        d.invertMode();        // flip black and white
        d.fill(o);             // paints black
        o.extend(-10,-10);
        d.fill(o);             // clears to white
        o.extend(-10,-10);
        d.fill(o);             // paints black
        o.extend(-10,-10);
        d.fill(o);             // clears to white
        o.extend(-10,-10);
        d.fill(o);             // paints black
    }
}
```

The figure drawn is shown in Figure 2.8. If, however, the `d.invertMode()` line were removed, it would draw a single filled circle. Again, by default, the screen is in normal painting mode, as though we had typed `d.paintMode()` as soon as we constructed the window.

An interesting property of inverting mode is that, in this mode, anything drawn twice disappears from the screen. We will see, in the next chapter, how this feature might be used to construct simple animations. For now, we depend on remembering:

Principle 9 *Inverting a drawing an even number of times makes it disappear.*

2.3 Chapter Review

The `ConsoleWindow` and `DrawingWindow`—classes from the `element` package— provide a simple and portable mechanism for experimenting with input and output in Java. They provide the following features:

- Input of primitive data types is accomplished with the input `ReadStream`.

- The `ConsoleWindow` supports output of the primitive data types using the out stream.

- The `DrawingWindow` supports drawing of simple lines with the methods `moveTo` and `lineTo`.

- Absolute methods like `moveTo` and `lineTo` move to specific coordinates, while the relative methods `move` and `line` draw *relative* to the current position of the pen.

- The `DrawingWindow` supports shapes like `Pt`, `Line`, `Rect`, `Circle`, `Oval`, `Arc`, and `RoundRect`. `Text` objects support general writing in the `Draw-ingWindow`.

- All shapes may be drawn with the `draw` method, erased with the `clear` method, and painted as filled objects with `fill`.

- Normally, paint is applied to the screen, but inverting paint can be selected with `invertMode`. The normal mode can be recovered with `paintMode`.

- Paint should be applied from back to front; items inverted twice disappear.

Problems

2.1   How many different ways can you draw a square?

2.2★   How would you compute the points of a regular pentagon of radius r?

2.3   What happens when you call the `ConsoleWindow` method `println` with no arguments? Can this be distinguished from calling the `ConsoleWindow` method `println` with an empty string (`""`).

2.4★   The following statements may be wrong, or may be correct and print something. Indicate which are illegal, and for legal statements, indicate the exact text printed.

```
ConsoleWindow c = new ConsoleWindow();
c.out.println(1+2);            // line a
c.out.println("1"+"2");        // line b
c.out.println("1"+2);          // line c
c.out.println(""+1+2);         // line d
c.out.println(""+(1+2));       // line e
```

2.5   Write a program that draws the famous Müller-Lyer illusion, shown below. The lengths of both horizontal lines are the same. Ideally, the ends should be drawn with *relative* drawing commands.

2.6⋆   Write a program to draw the following picture of "cow lips":

2.7   Write a program that draws the König-Necklace illusion, shown below. (The tops of all the circles are colinear.)

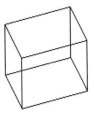

2.8   Write a program that draws the cube shown below:

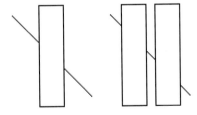

2.9⋆   Write a program that draws the Poggendorff illusion, shown below. (Note that there are two obscured diagonal lines.)

2.10   Write a program that draws the Kanizsa illusion, shown below. (A little trigonometry will be required.)

2.11   Write a program that draws the following vase (or is it a pair of faces?).

2.12★   The `DrawingWindow` provides two methods `hold` and `release`. `hold` stops the updating of the screen during drawing commands, while `release` performs an immediate and complete update of the window. Why might these methods be useful?

2.13★   Write a program to individually paint the 10000 pixels in a 100×100 pixel square (you'll have to read up on loops in Chapter 3). How long, in milliseconds, does it take to draw these points? Now, perform the drawing of the pixels between `hold` and `release` methods. How long does it take to paint this square using this method?

2.14   Write code to time the length of a double-click of a mouse. How fast can you double click the mouse?

2.15★   The `element` package does not directly support drawing filled triangles. Describe an approach to filling a triangle using other `element` primitives.

2.4 Laboratory: A First Experience with Java

Objective. To write a first program within the Java environment.

Discussion. Learning Java is like learning a musical instrument: it requires practice, practice, practice. Solving problems in the text and stepping through labs will help you gain experience programming.

Intro

In this lab we'll start the Java programming environment and enter a pre-written program. Even though we don't yet know many features of Java, the program can be easily understood with a little effort. When we're finished entering the program, we'll make some changes and observe their effects on the running program. When we're finished, we will have learned how to start and stop the programming environment, how to enter programs, and how to make them run.

Procedure. The goal of this program is to start the programming environment, enter a program, make it run, save the program, and exit the environment. We will assume that you have access to a programming environment and its documentation.

We first need to enter the following program:

```java
// Lab 1: Experimenting with console and drawing windows.

// This next line incorporates all the features of Java Elements
// including the console window and drawing window.
import element.*;

public class Intro // this name should also be the name of the file
{
    public static void main(String args[])
    {
        // the following lines "declare" the resources we need
        DrawingWindow d = new DrawingWindow();
        ConsoleWindow c = new ConsoleWindow();
        Pt p;

        // we now ask the user to press the mouse, and wait
        c.out.println("Press the mouse in the drawing window.");
        p = d.awaitMousePress();

        // the mouse is now pressed, and p is the point of press
        // we draw that point on the screen
        d.draw(p);
        d.draw(new Circle(p,10));
        p = d.awaitMouseRelease();

        // the following two lines print as one.  Why?
        c.out.print("Thanks!  You pressed at ");
        c.out.println(p);
```

```
// in general, your programs may need these lines
// to make the system pause:
c.out.println("Press the mouse to stop the program.");
d.awaitMousePress();

// this statement abruptly "kills" the program.
// usually we will let the program finish more naturally.
System.exit(0);
    }
}
```

Please make sure you enter the program *exactly* as you see it here. Those statements that begin with double slashes are comments—they're important, but if you make changes to them it will not change the way the program runs.

This program, you will observe, waits for the mouse to be pressed and released. The location of the mouse press is drawn on the screen and is printed in the console window. That's it!

1. You should make or *compile* your program. During this process of translating Java into a computer-readable representation, the computer checks to make sure that your *syntax* or program structure is correct. If any errors are reported, you should compare the code above with the code you have typed into the computer. If there are differences near the point of error, they should be fixed and the program should be recompiled. If you don't understand an error, relax. Many error messages in Java take a little experience to understand. Scan your program a little more carefully, and then, if necessary, seek assistance.

   If your program had no errors, you are lucky indeed!

2. Once the program is compiled, it can be *executed* or *run*. Tell your environment to run the program. Two windows should appear. You should experiment with dragging the windows about, and resizing the windows. Can you place the console and drawing windows side-by-side?

3. Carefully noting where you're pressing, press the mouse in the drawing window. The exact coordinates of this point will be printed in the console window. The point is drawn and circled so you can see the association between the point and its coordinates.

4. Once the program runs correctly, you should consider the thought questions at the end of this lab. Some of the questions may cause your program to break. Don't worry! Retyping in the original code should make things work again.

5. At some point in this process, print your program. Save the printout: it represents an interesting moment in your life you may wish to reflect on later!

6. Save your program and leave the environment. At this point, you might start the environment up again. Can you get your saved program to run again?

Thought questions. Consider the following questions as you complete the lab:

1. What happens when you press the mouse at one point and release it at another: which point is the one circled? How do you think you might change your program to circle the other point?

2. What is the difference between `c.out.print` and `c.out.println`? What happens when you change the `print` statement to read `println`.

3. The `System.exit(0);` statement essentially caused your program to kill itself. What happens if you remove the statement? What happens if you insert it in the middle of your program?

4. How do you think you could change the radius of the circle? Experiment with your program to see if your assumptions are correct.

5. What happens if you put the comment characters before a valid statement? How might this be useful?

6. Have you told your family you're a programmer? (You should!)

2.5 Laboratory: A Simple Drawing Program

SimpleDraw

Objective. To play with some of the features of the `element` package.

Discussion. In this lab we enter a prewritten program that allows us to experiment with the features of the `element` package. The program with which we will be experimenting allows us to draw a single "curve" in the drawing window. This may seem a little simplistic, but there are many things to be learned even from scribbling on a computer's screen.

Here is the program we will start with:

```java
// Lab: Experimenting with interaction in the drawing window.

import element.*;
import java.awt.Color;

public class SimpleDraw
{
    public static void main(String args[])
    {
        DrawingWindow d = new DrawingWindow(200,400);
        Pt mouse;
        final int radius = 2;
        Circle nib = new Circle(0,0,radius);

        d.setForeground(Color.red);
        d.awaitMousePress();

        while (d.mousePressed())
        {
            mouse = d.getMouse();
            nib.center(mouse);
            d.fill(nib);
        }
    }
}
```

First, this program does not use a `ConsoleWindow`. Increasingly, programs in today's world are graphically oriented. Instead, we use the `DrawingWindow` referred to by `d`. Skipping down we see there is the loop

```java
while (d.mousePressed())
```

Strictly speaking, we don't know about loops, but this one is simple: it executes the `getMouse`, `nib.center`, and `d.fill` methods as fast as possible, as long as the mouse button is being pressed. In fact, all of the external evidence of the program running is the result of executing those three statements: the program simply draws circles at each point.

Procedure. Enter, run, and modify the `draw` program:

1. Start your programming environment and type in the above program.

2. Compile and run the program. When the program begins to run, the drawing window appears. With a curve in mind, press the mouse and sketch out the curve with the mouse down. When you let go, the program should stop.

3. Run the program and draw your curve by moving the mouse fast. You should see the individual circles that make up the curve. This is a physical representation of the very short length of time it takes for Java to execute one iteration of the loop! If your machine is faster, the circles will be closer together and the curve will be smoother.

4. Change the `radius` declaration so that it has the value 5. This allows you to draw with a thicker pen.

5. Change the program so that the nib is a thin rectangle whose center point is `mouse`. (Hint: You will have to declare a `Rect` of the appropriate dimensions and frequently `center` it at `mouse`.).

6. Experiment further with changes to the program (see below), remembering to save your program at the end.

Thought questions. Consider the following questions as you complete the lab:

1. What happens if you put a `d.invertMode()` at the top of your program and change the foreground color to `Color.black`? (Since black is the usual color, you can just comment out the `setForeground` command.)

2. What happens if you use *relative* mouse commands (like `move` and `line`) after having moved *absolutely* to the point `mouse`? Is it possible to have, for example, a slanted nib for italic calligraphy?

3. How would you get the compter to report (say, in a console window), the number of points drawn?

4. How would this help you determine the average length of time it takes for Java to draw a `Circle` at the point `mouse`?

5. What happens if you type `main(args)` as the last line of your program?

2.6 Laboratory: Draw Your Favorite Mascot

Objective. Gain experience with building a Java program from scratch.

Discussion. In this lab we will focus on constructing an entire program from scratch. Every aspect of its *design* will be decided by you. The general goal is to draw an image of your favorite mascot. One of the authors sheepishly submitted this picture of a horned member of the bovine family:

(It looks better in purple.) It is interesting to note that even though the `element` package is limited to drawing primitive shapes, the end result is a picture with fairly complex components. Thus, we're not interested in realism, but a demonstration of your skills with manipulating the various shapes with different colors and pen modes.

From this lab forward, you will find it useful to develop a *design* before you start writing Java. In this case, it's most useful to sketch your picture on graph paper, keeping in mind that all of the features of the picture must be drawn with fairly simplistic primitives. The graph paper also helps to easily locate important points within your artwork as you generate the supporting Java code. Word to the wise: Program design can be done without computers; programming cannot.

Procedure. Carefully follow the steps below while developing your picture:

1. Sketch a picture of your mascot on graph paper. Use the graph paper to orient your picture within the drawing window. Remember that each feature drawn on the paper is translated into one or more Java statements! Keep things simple at first; add detail later.

2. Identify the order in which features must be drawn. Remember that paint applied early on is obscured by paint applied later. Practicing artists will find this a natural step. The rest of us must develop this skill with care.

3. For each feature of your mascot, declare a graphical object that describes that feature. Whenever possible, use constants (values declared `final`) to locate these objects in the drawing window. For example, you may define a constant `noseY` that locates the height of the center of the nose. If the nose needs to be moved later, you can modify the value of `noseY` in one place.

4. Draw, fill, and clear objects as necessary to complete your image. If you use color, don't forget to import `java.awt.Color` to make use of predefined colors. Also, remember that if you use an inverting pen, you must only invert black and white pixels. The result of inverting colored pixels is not easily predicted.

5. If you're comfortable with looping constructs, you can optionally add a repeated feature—blades of grass, stars, etc.

6. Take pride in your work. Sign your name at the bottom with a `Text` object and save your program.

Thought questions. Consider the following questions as you complete the lab:

1. It appears the bovine's jowls were drawn with a `draw` command. The outline of the head, however, was drawn with an oval and not an arc. How *were* the jowls drawn?

2. How are our bovine horns drawn?

3. How is our bovine's cap drawn?

Chapter 3

Conditions and Loops

> *"He pointed to the ground in front of him.*
> *'What do you see there?'*
> *'Tracks,' said Piglet. 'Paw-marks.'*
> *He gave a little squeak of excitement.*
> *'Oh, Pooh! Do you think it's a—a—a Woozle?'*
> *'It may be,' said Pooh.*
> *'Sometimes it is, and sometimes it isn't....'"*
> —A. A. Milne

As we have observed to this point, the process of *sequential execution* of the statements of a Java program involves (1) interpreting the current statement and (2) moving to the next instruction. In the programs we have seen so far, the next statement is the one that follows; most of our examples have been *straight-line* programs. Clearly, if a program is to take any lengthy amount of time to execute, we cannot depend on providing large numbers of statements in long, straight-line programs.[1] This chapter considers how the *flow* or *locus of control* can be changed through an explicit decision-making process. We will first consider the `if` statement—the main decision-making statement—and then the wide variety of *looping* statements that allow programs to spend potentially infinite amounts of time repeatedly executing a finite number of statements.

3.1 The `if` Statement

The easiest conditional statement is an `if` statement. It has a very simple form:

> `if (`⟨condition⟩`)` ⟨statement⟩

Here the ⟨condition⟩ must be a boolean expression that evaluates to `true` or `false`. Then the ⟨statement⟩ must be a Java statement. It is more likely that it will be a *block* of Java statements, enclosed in curly braces (`{}`). Such a block is like "shrink wrap"—when multiple statements need to be used where only a single statement is allowed, curly braces surround zero or more statements to make a single *compound statement*. When the computer encounters an `if` statement, it first evaluates the ⟨condition⟩. If ⟨condition⟩ is `true`, the ⟨statement⟩ is executed. If ⟨condition⟩ is `false`, then ⟨statement⟩ is not executed, and Java continues execution with the statement that follows.

---

[1] This actually is not clear, as we'll see in the Chapter 6, on recursion. For the moment we'll find this assumption useful.

As an example, the following statement reacts to input provided from the keyboard:

Noah

```
c.out.print("You have "+cowInventory+" cow");
if (cowInventory != 1)
{
    c.out.print('s');
}
c.out.println("!");
```

This program fragment prints out phrases like

```
You have 1 cow!
```

if `cowInventory` is 1, but, in other cases, it prints the plural form:

```
You have 101 cows!
```

In many graphics programs, it is useful to perform checks based on the state of the mouse. If, for example, the mouse is pressed, we can see if it is pressed within a rectangular region that represents a button. Here, for example, we check to see if the point of press, `pressPoint`, is within a rectangle representing a button for quitting the program, `quitButton`:

```
Pt pressPoint;
String answer;
Rect quitButton = new Rect(10,10,20,30);
d.draw(quitButton);
    ...
pressPoint = d.awaitMousePress();
if (quitButton.contains(pressPoint))
{
    c.out.println("Type yes, if you're sure.");
    answer = c.input.readLine();
    if (answer.equals("yes"))
    {
        System.exit(0);
    }
    c.out.println("Whew!");
}
```

In the middle of an application, the program is waiting for a press of the mouse. If the point of press, `pressPoint`, is within the `quitButton` (a rectangle), the user is possibly trying to quit the application. Only in that case do we ask for verification. If the string we read is `"yes"`, then we exit without ceremony. If, however, the quit button was pressed *but* the verification response was not `"yes"`, the computer would print `Whew!` and continue on. Two things are subtle here. First, the `if` statements are *nested*. The braces are usually aligned to highlight this nested relationship. The inner `if` statement is only considered if the outer `if` is true. Second, `System.exit` is a method that stops the program. While the `Whew!` statement would normally be executed after the `if`, it cannot be reached if the answer was `"yes"`.

Exercise 3.1 *Experiment with this program fragment. What happens if you accidentally enclose the boolean condition in braces, '{}', instead of parentheses, '()'?*

Sometimes the need for nested if's can be eliminated by the use of a single if with a more complicated condition. The two statements

```
if (n%2==0) // if n is even
{
    if (n%3==0) // and if n is divisible by 3
    {
        ⟨statement1⟩
    }
}
⟨statement2⟩
```

are equivalent to the somewhat leaner

```
if ((n%2==0) && (n%3==0)) // if is divisible by 2 and 3 (or 6...)
{
    ⟨statement1⟩
}
⟨statement2⟩
```

Similar constructions are often possible whenever two or more simple if statements are tightly nested.

Exercise 3.2 *Is it possible to write a program fragment similar to the quit button example that does not have nested if statements? (You may introduce a new variable, but it's not necessary.)*

3.2 The if-then-else Statement

A second form of if statement is useful when one of *two* different statements is to be conditionally executed. It has the form

```
if (⟨condition⟩)
    ⟨statement1⟩
else
    ⟨statement2⟩
```

As with the if statement, ⟨statement1⟩ is executed when the ⟨condition⟩ is true. If, however, the ⟨condition⟩ is false, Java executes ⟨statement2⟩. For example, the following program checks for pairs of cows:

Pairs of bovine?

```
if ((cowInventory % 2) == 0)
{
    c.out.println("Noah, you have an even number of cows.");
} else {
    c.out.println("WARNING: cows aren't in pairs.  Get another.");
}
```

Exactly one of the two `println` statements is executed; which one depends on whether the size of Noah's cow inventory is even or odd.

Notice that the distinction between the two forms of the `if` statement is the word `else`. When there is doubt, the `else` belongs with the closest `if` that does not yet have a matching `else`. For example, the code

Sphinx

```
if (d.mousePressed())
    if (riddleButton.contains(d.getMouse()))
        c.out.println("What walks on 4 legs, then 2, then 3?");
    else
        c.out.println("You missed the button and a great riddle!");
else
    c.out.println("Hello?  Anyone there?");
```

If the mouse is pressed and is in the riddle button, a riddle appears in the console window. If the mouse is pressed, but not in the button, the user is chided for missing the button. If the button is not even pressed, the program wonders if the user is responsive.

When another alignment of `else` statements must be forced, it can be accomplished with the judicious use of braces:

Numbers

```
if ((n % 2) == 0)
{
    c.out.println("Number is even.");
    if (n == 2) c.out.println("(and prime!)");
}
else
    c.out.println("Number is odd (and possibly prime)");
```

Here, the `else` is forced to provide the alternative statement for the first `if`, since the second `if` is nested inside a compound statement.

3.3   The `while` Loop

Now that we have the concept of making a decision based on the state of the variables of the program, it is possible to *iteratively* execute statements, forming a *loop*. The first form of the loop, arguably the simplest, is called the `while` loop. It has the general form

> `while (⟨condition⟩) ⟨statement⟩`

As with the `if` statement, Java begins by evaluating the boolean ⟨condition⟩. If the ⟨condition⟩ is `false`, the loop stops executing (or is *terminated*). The interesting case is when the ⟨condition⟩ is `true`. The `while` loop then executes ⟨statement⟩. The hope is that the ⟨statement⟩ will have some effect on the computer that will possibly change the value of the ⟨condition⟩. Once the ⟨statement⟩ is executed, Java returns to evaluating the condition, and the loop is potentially executed again. This process continues until the ⟨condition⟩ is no

longer met. Of course, it is possible that the ⟨condition⟩ is always **true**; the
loop would, then, never terminate. We call such a loop an *infinite loop*.

The following **while** loop prints numbers from 3 down to 1:

```
counter = 3;
while (counter > 0)
{
    c.out.println(counter);
    counter--;
}
```

Loops

The effect of this statement is exactly equivalent to the test-less code:

```
counter = 3;                    // counter is 3
c.out.println(counter);
counter--;                      // counter is now 2
c.out.println(counter);
counter--;                      // counter is now 1
c.out.println(counter);
counter--;                      // counter is now 0
```

The four tests of the **while** loop have no effect on **counter**, of course. The test
simply checks to see if the two statements need to be further executed.

We should note that the second program fragment runs slightly faster because the tests are not necessary in straight-line code. The **while** version spends
a portion of its time testing. The difference is that the **while** loop is flexible,
and has the potential to run a varying number of times, depending on the conditions of variables (e.g., **counter**) in the program. The straight line code, of
course, must be recompiled to have a different effect.

To further demonstrate that a **while** loop executes a variable number of
times, we observe the following loop that waits for the mouse button to be
pressed:

```
while (!d.mousePressed());
```

Assuming **d** is a **DrawingWindow**, the **mousePressed** method checks to see if
the mouse is pressed in the drawing window. If it is pressed, it returns **true**,
which is then inverted, due to the logical negation ('**!**'), and the loop halts. If
the mouse button is not pressed, it executes the *empty statement* '**;**'. This is a
statement that does nothing! The programmer simply wants the computer to
test the mouse until the button is pressed. This technique is called *polling*.

Clearly, the condition of the **while** loop is **false** when the loop is finished
and the next statement is taken up. In this case, the mouse button must be
pressed, because if it weren't, then the loop would not have finished. In the
while loop that down, we know that the value of **counter** must finally be zero.

It's also important to realize that the **while** loop may *never* actually execute
its subordinate statement. For example, if we changed our mouse code to do
the following:

```
while (!d.mousePressed())
{
    target = 42;
}
c.out.println(target);
```

we would never be sure that `target` was 42 at the end. If the mouse is pressed before the loop was executed, then we never would get to execute the assignment to `target`. This is particularly upsetting if `target` was never initialized! We can make use of this notion in the following principle:

Principle 10 *Use the* `while` *loop to do something* zero or more times.

3.4   The `do-while` Loop

Recalling that the `while` loop first evaluates its ⟨condition⟩ statement, we see the utility of what we'll call the `do-while` loop. The `do-while` loop has the form:

```
do
{
    ⟨statements⟩
} while (⟨condition⟩);
```

This loop first executes the ⟨statements⟩, and then evaluates the ⟨condition⟩. The `do-while` loop, like the `while` loop, continues to execute the ⟨statements⟩ as long as the ⟨condition⟩ evaluates to `true`. The most obvious difference is that in the `do-while` loop, the ⟨statements⟩ are executed at least one time—even if the ⟨condition⟩ was *never* `true`. The `do-while` loop

```
do
{
    target = 42;
} while (!d.mousePressed());
```

always has the effect of setting `target` to 42. Understanding this point is important.

Principle 11 *Use the* `do-while` *loop to do something* at least once.

A frequent use of the `do-while` loop is to read in a value that is constrained in some manner:

```
do
{
    c.out.println("I'm thinking of a number between 1 and 100");
    c.out.println("What do you think it is?");
    guess = c.input.readInt();
} while ((guess < 1) || (guess > 100));
```

Here, it is necessary to attempt reading in the guess at least once—the program needs a guess. If the guess isn't in the appropriate range, then the demand for an appropriate value is repeated.

The following program fragment keeps track of the point where the mouse is pressed (if it isn't pressed already):

```
do
{
    releasePoint = d.getMouse();
} while (!d.mousePressed());
```

The effect of this is similar to `awaitMousePressed`.

3.4.1 Example: A Drawing Program

We can combine several of the loops that we've seen so far to construct a program that draws (not unlike Laboratory Program 2.5). The program begins by waiting for the mouse to be pressed. Once pressed, the mouse is carefully tracked from the point of press to the point of its ultimate release. The program makes use of the fact that the `element` package keeps track of the current position at all times:

```
DrawingWindow d = new DrawingWindow();
Pt mouse;                   // the last known position of mouse
while (!d.mousePressed()); // wait for the mouse to be pressed
mouse = d.getMouse();
d.moveTo(mouse);            // current position now at mouse start
while (d.mousePressed())
{
    mouse = d.getMouse();
    d.lineTo(mouse);        // draw to next mouse location
}
System.out.println("Done!");
// assertion: mouse is released
```

DrawLoop

In this program fragment, the first `while` loop is responsible for waiting until the mouse button is pressed and the `mousePressed` method returns `true`. After this loop, we can be sure that the mouse is pressed, so we immediately move our "pen" to the location of the mouse press. Of course, no mark is made in the window at this point. The next loop, however, will cause marks to be left on the screen as the mouse travels: the loop quickly evaluates the `mousePressed` method and finds it `true`, finds the location of the mouse, and draws a line from the current position (the end of our scribble) to the mouse. This drawing of line segments continues as long as the mouse button is pressed.

Exercise 3.3 *What happens if the mouse button is pressed and released without actually moving?*

Exercise 3.4 *What would happen if the mouse button, for some reason, were released quickly enough so that the second loop never executed its subordinate statement? (This is a possible, though unlikely, event on a reasonably fast and "undistracted" computer.)*

Exercise 3.5 *This program draws one curve. How might you modify the program to allow the artist to draw, say, five curves?*

Douglas Hofstadter made popular a form of mirror drawing where the drawing is *rotationally symmetric*. Here, for example, is a rendering of the word "Java" that appears the same when this page is rotated 180 degrees:

We can convert our previous program to facilitate drawing this type of picture. Each line segment drawn by the above program would be reflected through the center of the window. The resulting drawing looks the same right side up as well as upside down. Here's our approach:

Mirror

```
DrawingWindow d = new DrawingWindow();
int width = d.bounds().width();   // window width
int height = d.bounds().height(); // and height
Pt current, next;                 // points

d.awaitMousePress();     // drawing starts with mouse press

current = d.getMouse(); // move pen to initial location
while (d.mousePressed())
{
    next = d.getMouse();          // get next mouse position
    d.moveTo(current);            // draw the "right" image
    d.lineTo(next);

    // the "mirrored" points are the same distance
    // away from bottom and right sides;
    // draw line between them
    d.moveTo(width-current.x(),height-current.y());
    d.lineTo(width-next.x(),height-next.y());

    // current point is basis for next line segment
    current = next;
}
```

There are a number of important things to notice here. First, we have substituted the polling loop in the previous program with `d.awaitMousePress()`. These statements are identical in effect. It also makes the purpose of the "code" a little more obvious. Next, we cannot depend on the `element` package to keep track of *two* different current points, so we must do this explicitly. Here, `current` is the point in the upright image, while `next` is where the pen moved to in the upright image, and becomes the next value of `current` when Java has drawn both images. Again, this program only allows the user to sketch one curve, but there may be two curves in the image, due to reflection.

Exercise 3.6 *Modify the mirror drawing program to exhibit reflective left-right symmetry, as well as up-down. Each movement of the mouse causes four line segments to be drawn.*

3.4.2 Example: Syracuse Numbers

Here is an interesting mathematical function: suppose you have a value x. If x is even, the function returns $\frac{x}{2}$. If x is odd, the function returns $3x + 1$. If we iteratively apply this function to numbers larger than 1, mathematicians believe the sequence of values eventually returns to 1.[2] We can write a program that tests this hypothesis on numbers typed in at the keyboard:

Syr

```
ConsoleWindow c = new ConsoleWindow();
int x;

c.out.println("Enter a number to be iteratively mapped"
              +" using the Syracuse function.");
do
{
    c.out.println("(Please make sure it is greater than 1.)");
    x = c.input.readInt();
} while (x <= 1);

c.out.print(x);
do
{
    if ((x % 2) == 0) x = x/2;
    else              x = 3*x+1;
    c.out.print("->"+x);
} while (x != 1);
c.out.println();
c.out.println("Our hypothesis is true for this value!");
```

Here, we use two different `do-while` loops. Both of these loops depend on the development of a sentinel value. In the first loop, we demand a value that is *Sentinel: a guard.*

---

[2] At the time of this writing, this hypothesis is an open question from number theory.

greater than one. In the second loop, we demand a value of x that is exactly one. In both cases, we execute the loop at least once.

Here is what the output looks like if we type in the number 27:

```
Enter a number to be iteratively mapped using the Syracuse function.
(Please make sure it is greater than 1.)
27
27->82->41->124->62->31->94->47->142->71->214->107->322->
161->484->242->121->364->182->91->274->137->412->206->103->
310->155->466->233->700->350->175->526->263->790->395->
1186->593->1780->890->445->1336->668->334->167->502->251->
754->377->1132->566->283->850->425->1276->638->319->958->479->
1438->719->2158->1079->3238->1619->4858->2429->7288->3644->
1822->911->2734->1367->4102->2051->6154->3077->9232->4616->
2308->1154->577->1732->866->433->1300->650->325->976->488->
244->122->61->184->92->46->23->70->35->106->53->160->80->40->
20->10->5->16->8->4->2->1
Our hypothesis is true for this value!
```

We have, incidently, not found any numbers for which this program does not halt.

Exercise 3.7 *How might the second loop change if the first loop allowed the value of* x *to be 1?*

Notice that this is an example of a program that may or may not terminate. Given the right value—perhaps a long-sought value that never returns to 1—the program's loop would never terminate![3] The subtlety of understanding of the mathematical problem has directly translated into a subtlety of understanding the *behavior* of a computer program.

Exercise 3.8 *How would you change the program to verify the hypothesis, say, for the first 1000 numbers? It should print only one thing at the end:* The hypothesis is true! *(By the way, how long should you wait to determine that the hypothesis is false?)*

3.5   The for Loop

Many programs involve loops that have the form (1) initialize *loop control* variables used in the condition, (2) test the condition before executing the subordinate statement, and (3) within the subordinate statement, "increment" the control variables. To emphasize the particular form of the looping method, Java provides a for loop. The syntax of the for loop is as follows:

> for (⟨initialization⟩; ⟨condition⟩; ⟨increment⟩) ⟨statement⟩

---

[3] At least it would not terminate due to the success of the test x!=1. If the loop were infinite, it *might* ultimately reach values that were too large to be represented by an integer. It also, of course, might stumble across a loop of values that does not include 1.

Here, ⟨initialization⟩ is a list of expressions (usually a single assignment) that
is evaluated exactly once—before the loop is executed. The ⟨condition⟩ is evaluated at the top of the loop, before the subordinate ⟨statement⟩. The loop
terminates when the ⟨condition⟩ evaluates to `false`. If the ⟨condition⟩ is `true`,
then the ⟨statement⟩ is immediately executed. Before returning to evaluate the
⟨condition⟩, the ⟨increment⟩ expression list (usually another assignment) is evaluated. In readable `for` loops, the ⟨initialization⟩, ⟨condition⟩, and ⟨increment⟩
portions of the loop are all cast in terms of a single control variable.

Suppose we are interested in computing the average (the arithmetic mean)
of a sequence of `n` integers. Here is how it might be done:

Average

```java
import element.*;
import structure.*;

public class Average
{
    public static void main(String args[])
    {
        ConsoleWindow c = new ConsoleWindow();
        int i, n;
        double sum = 0.0;
        double average;

        c.out.println("Enter a positive integer:");
        n = c.input.readInt();

        for (i = 1; i < n+1; i++)
        {
            sum += c.input.readDouble();
        }
        average = sum/n;
        c.out.println("The average is "+average);
    }
}
```

In this example the variable `i` (which has already been declared) is initialized
to 1. This is the value it will have throughout the first execution of the loop.
The variable `i` can be used in calculations within the loop (as we have done
here), but it is poor style to change the value within the loop. The boolean
expression `i < n+1` will be evaluated before each execution of the loop. If it
evaluates to `true`, the summation will be executed, followed by the increment of
`i`. The loop then continues by reevaluating the condition. When the condition
first evaluates to `false`, execution moves on to the first statement after the `for`.

Exercise 3.9 *What value does* `i` *have when the program is finished?*

Principle 12 *The* `for` *loop is best used when counting or iterating a specific
number of times.*

3.5.1   Example: Drawing a Circle

We now return to the process of drawing a circle. There are obviously a number of ways of doing this; however, in this case, we will draw the circle by drawing hundreds of points. To determine positions of the points drawn, we sweep around the circle, evenly placing each of the n points r pixels away from the center of the drawing window. As we saw in Chapter 1, the position is $(r\cos\theta + x_c, r\sin\theta + y_c)$, where $0 \le \theta \le 2\pi$ and (x_c, y_c) is to be the center of the circle. Here is the program:

DrawCircle

```
import element.*;

public class DrawCircle
{
    public static void main(String args[])
    {
        DrawingWindow d = new DrawingWindow();
        // draw a circle with these parameters:
        final double RADIUS = 90.0;
        final int CENTER_X = 100;
        final int CENTER_Y = 100;
        // number of points to draw:
        final int N = 500;
        // current point information:
        int i;
        double theta, x, y;

        for (i = 0; i < N; i++)
        {
            theta = i*Math.PI*2.0/N;
            x = RADIUS*Math.cos(theta)+CENTER_X;
            y = RADIUS*Math.sin(theta)+CENTER_Y;
            d.draw(new Pt((int)Math.round(x),(int)Math.round(y)));
        }
    }
}
```

Notice that we know ahead of time that there will be exactly N points drawn, so it is useful to use a for loop to count these out. The angle, $\theta = \frac{2\pi i}{n}$, is a double value that is computed each time through the loop.

An alternative way to determine the points to be drawn is to draw all the points that are a particular (angular) distance apart. We accumulate, over the course of the program, a total angle that is used to locate the points. In this case, we use a for loop, though a while loop might be just as readable:

Draw-
IncrCircle

```
import element.*;

public class DrawIncrCircle
{
```

```
public static void main(String args[])
{
    DrawingWindow d = new DrawingWindow();
    // draw a circle with these parameters:
    final double RADIUS = 90.0;
    final int CENTER_X = 100;
    final int CENTER_Y = 100;
    // approximate number of points to draw:
    final double dTheta = 1.0/RADIUS;
    // current point information:
    double theta, x, y;

    for (theta = 0.0; theta < 2*Math.PI; theta += dTheta)
    {
        x = RADIUS*Math.cos(theta)+CENTER_X;
        y = RADIUS*Math.sin(theta)+CENTER_Y;
        d.draw(new Pt((int)Math.round(x),(int)Math.round(y)));
    }
}
}
```

Observe that we compute `dTheta`, the angle between neighboring points, as `1.0/RADIUS`. Since, for small angles, the angle (in radians) is approximately the distance spanned by the angle, this value of `dTheta` will draw pixels that are about one pixel apart around the circumference of the circle. Any closer and duplicate points might be drawn; any farther apart and holes would appear in the circle. Of course, a coarser circle can be drawn by joining successive points with short lines.

3.6 Loop Independence and Elegance

The determination of the appropriate type of loop is not a science but an art form. We have attempted, in the principles outlined above, to provide guidelines for using each of the three main types of loops. In fact, in this section, we show that any of the three loop forms can be used to write all of your loops! In some cases, however, we will see that this versatility comes at the cost of, perhaps, introducing more code, or more obscure code. Recognizing loops that are particularly obscure can help in reorganizing your code to be more readable.

Observation 3.1 *Every* do-while *loop may be replaced with a* while *loop.*

It is easy to see how this is done. Without loss of generality, suppose we have a do-while loop of the following form:

```
do
{
    ⟨statements⟩
} while (⟨condition⟩);
```

If we use a `while` loop with the same ⟨statements⟩, then the ⟨condition⟩ might initially be `false`, and the ⟨statements⟩ would never be evaluated. To ensure that the ⟨statements⟩ are evaluated at least once, we simply "cut and paste" a copy of the statements above the loop:

```
⟨statements⟩
while (⟨condition⟩) ⟨statements⟩
```

This form of the `while` loop augmented with a copy of the subordinate statements is equivalent in every way save, perhaps, the *elegance* of the solution. Since the `while` form has two copies of a group of statements while the equivalent `do-while` has only one, the `do-while` is preferred for this type of evaluation. If you see a `while` loop with the form shown above, it is simpler to state it as a `do-while`.

Our second observation is the opposite of Observation 3.1:

Observation 3.2 *Every* `while` *loop can be replaced by a* `do-while` *loop.*

This observation is nearly as simple. To simulate the statement

```
while (⟨condition⟩) ⟨statement⟩
```

with a `do-while`, we need only make sure that the ⟨condition⟩ is evaluated before the ⟨statements⟩ of the `do-while`. We use an `if` statement to help us out:

```
if (⟨condition⟩)
{
    do
    {
        ⟨statement⟩
    } while (⟨condition⟩);
}
```

The `if` statement used here is often called a *guard*. It guards against us accidentally executing ⟨statement⟩ when it wouldn't have been executed in the `while` loop. Clearly, this is a satisfactory but ugly alternative to the `while`. If you observe the use of an `if` statement guarding a `do-while` loop with the same ⟨condition⟩, that code is usually more succinctly stated as a `while` loop.

Since we can replace the `while` with the `do-while` *and* the `do-while` with the `while`, the two loops are *equivalent*. Java would be just as *powerful* if we had only one of these loops, but perhaps less *elegant*.

The `for` loop and the `while` loop are so related that we can make the following observation:

Observation 3.3 *The* `for` *and the* `while` *loops are equivalent.*

To demonstrate this, of course, it is necessary for us to show (1) the `for` loop can be replaced by a `while` and (2) the `while` loop can be replaced by a `for`. First, without loss of generality, if we have a `for` loop of the following form:

```
for (⟨initialization⟩; ⟨condition⟩; ⟨increment⟩) ⟨statement⟩
```

This can be replaced with an equivalent `while`:

```
⟨initialization⟩
while (⟨condition⟩)
{
        ⟨statement⟩
        ⟨increment⟩
}
```

Indeed, when the control portion of `for` loops becomes overly complex, these loops are often converted to `while` loops. The advantage to the `for` loop is that the ⟨initialization⟩ section of the loop becomes a part of the loop itself, making the code easier to read.

The reverse situation is almost trivially true. The `while`

```
while (⟨condition⟩) ⟨statement⟩
```

can be replaced by

```
for (;⟨condition⟩;) ⟨statement⟩
```

The combination of all of these observations allows us state that

Observation 3.4 *All loops in Java are equivalently expressive.*

This is important. It is the first sign that we can make statements about the expressive power of languages. This is one of the first steps toward proving that all *languages* are, in fact, computationally equivalent. Your father, who knows how to program in languages of the past, was able to write all the same programs you can but, given the evolution of computer languages, perhaps less elegantly.

3.7   Why Infinite Loops Cannot Be Identified

Anyone spending much time writing programs involving loops undoubtedly has written some loops that never terminate; these loops "hang" the machine and have to be interrupted. These *infinite loops* are often (but not always) an indication of problems with programming logic. It would be useful if your compiler could identify such loops and warn the user of a potential error in programming logic.

One approach might be to keep a list of infinite loops and to explicitly check for loops of these forms. For example:

```
while (true);

do { } while (!false);

for (;X==X;);
```

Infinities

(As we have seen in the previous section, each of these may be written in each of the other loop forms.) The difficulty is that infinite loops can be made arbitrarily complex:

```
while (!!true);

while (!!(!!true));

while (!!(true == (!!true)));

while (System.currentTimeMillis() > 10);
```

In essence, there are too many ways that a really smart (or dumb!) programmer can encode loops that never terminate. If, for example, we developed a Java compiler that claimed it could detect infinite loops, we could write a program that, given our new-found knowledge of the compiler, could express a more subtly cast infinite loop that the compiler could not possibly detect.

A considerable portion of the study of what computers *can't* do is related to Gödel's proofs on the incompleteness of proof systems to prove theorems in mathematics. Some other surprising results include:

- There is no general method that determines whether two programs behave similarly on similar inputs.

- There is no general method that determines whether a program stops on a particular input.

This last problem—the *halting problem*—is, perhaps, the most famous and startling result of computer science. We will have to put up with (and not *just* for the moment) the fact that compilers cannot assure us that there are no logic errors in our programs. To ensure that, we must depend on constructing our programs with care.

3.8   The switch Statement

Sometimes it is necessary to write several nested if statements that determine the course of action of a Java program, based on the value of a variable that takes on any of a small number of different states. For example, the following program prints out a different word, depending on the character read from the keyboard. (Our editors have requested we show you only a portion of this program because it is so long and tedious to read!)

ABCs

```
ConsoleWindow c = new ConsoleWindow();
char letter;

c.out.println("Type an uppercase letter and");
c.out.println("I'll print a cattle breed that comes to mind.");
```

```
do
{
    letter = c.input.readChar();
} while (letter < 'A' || letter > 'Z');

// many choices:
if (letter == 'A')
{
    c.out.println("A is for Angus.");
}
else
{
    if (letter == 'B')
    {
        c.out.println("B is for Boran.");
    }
    else
    {
        if (letter == 'C')
        {
            c.out.println("C is for Corriente.");
        }
        else
        {
            if (letter == 'D')
            {
                c.out.println("D is for Droughtmaster.");
            }
            else
            {
                if (letter == 'E')
                {
                    c.out.println("E is for Eringer.");
                }
                else
                {
                    if (letter == 'F')
                    {
                        c.out.println("F is for Freiburger.");
                    }
                    else
                    {
                        // several cases omitted...
                    }
                }
            }
        }
    }
}
```

An uppercase letter successfully read from the keyboard is first checked against
'A', then 'B', then 'C', and so forth, until the letter entered is found among
the cascading ifs. Once found, the name of a cattle breed is printed, and the
large nested if is finished:

```
Type an uppercase letter and
I'll print a cattle breed that comes to mind.
F
F is for Freiburger.
```

Not shown is a final else that handles those letters that have no associated
breeds:

```
Type an uppercase letter and
I'll print a cattle breed that comes to mind.
Q
I know of no breed that begins with Q.
```

Obviously, writing code like this is difficult to keep track of and is unsightly.
Furthermore, when a 'Z' is entered, it must be checked against every letter
before 'Z' before the phrase is printed.

A useful alternative statement is the switch statement. It has the following
general form:

```
switch (⟨value⟩)
{
    case ⟨constant 1⟩:
    case ⟨constant 1'⟩:
      ⟨statements 1⟩
      break;
    case ⟨constant 2⟩:
      ⟨statements 2⟩
      break;
          ... // other cases omitted
    case ⟨constant n⟩:
      ⟨statements n⟩
      break;
    default:
      ⟨default statements⟩
      break;
}
```

When the switch statement is encountered, the value ⟨value⟩ is used to determine which statements within the switch are to be executed. If, for example,
⟨value⟩ is equal to either of the fixed values ⟨constant 1⟩ or ⟨constant 1'⟩ then
the statements ⟨statements 1⟩ are executed. Each distinct action is handled by a
particular set of statements, and the cases that trigger the actions immediately
precede the action statements. If no case matches, then the default case is selected, and the ⟨default statements⟩ are executed. We have placed the default
statement at the end, but it may appear any place within the switch; it may be

more readable, for example, to have it appear as the first case. An important
part of the `switch` statement is the use of the `break` statement to finish execution of a case. When the `break` statement is encountered during execution,
the closest-containing `switch` statement is finished and exited, and execution
continues with the statement following the `switch`. (The `break` statement can
be used to prematurely exit a `while`, `do-while`, or `for` loop as well.)

We can now rewrite the complex nested `if` statement of the cattle breed
program as a `switch` statement:

SwitchABCs

```
// many choices:
switch (letter)
{
  case 'A':
    c.out.println("A is for Angus.");
    break;
  case 'B':
    c.out.println("B is for Boran.");
    break;
  case 'C':
    c.out.println("C is for Corriente.");
    break;
  case 'D':
    c.out.println("D is for Droughtmaster.");
    break;
  case 'E':
    c.out.println("E is for Eringer.");
    break;
  case 'F':
    c.out.println("F is for Freiburger.");
    break;
      // several cases omitted...
  case 'Z':
    c.out.println("Z is for Zebu.");
    break;
  default:
    c.out.println("I know of no breed that begins with "+letter+".");
    break;
}
```

As we can see, the switch statement provides a cleaner presentation of the
different cases. For example, the `default` case handles all of the values that
have no associated breed names, and that is a little more obvious here. The
main advantage of the `switch`, however, is in the speed at which it can be
executed. Internally, Java can make use of the fact that each of the `case` values
is constant, thus avoiding the repeated comparison of values. Instead, the entry
of a value 'Z' causes the `switch` to branch immediately to the appropriate
code. In this application, which needn't run quickly, the advantage is not at all
obvious, but in heavily used `switch` statements, the speedups can accumulate
and, in some cases, lead to significant increases in speed.

In some applications, the switch can be used to select a small number of
statements using a larger number of case values. For example, the following
code assigns daysInMonth the number of days in a particular month:

Month

```
ConsoleWindow c = new ConsoleWindow();
int month, year, daysInMonth;
boolean leapYear;

c.out.println("Enter a month and year.");
c.out.println("I'll print the length of the month.");

month = c.input.readInt();
year = c.input.readInt();

// figure out leap year (works for years 1901-2099)
leapYear = false;
if (year%4 == 0) leapYear = true;

switch (month)
{
  case 4:              // "Fourth,
  case 11:             //    eleventh,
  case 9:              //    ninth,
  case 6:              //    and sixth,
    daysInMonth = 30;  // Thirty days to each affix;
    break;
  default:
    daysInMonth = 31;  // Every other thirty-one
    break;
  case 2:              // Except the second month alone."
    if (leapYear) daysInMonth = 29;
    else daysInMonth = 28;
    break;
}
c.out.println(month+"/"+year+" has "+daysInMonth+" days.");
```

We've structured this switch statement to model a Quaker verse that parallels
the more common rhyme that is often used to remember the lengths of months:

> Thirty days hath September,
> April, June, and November;
> February has twenty-eight alone,
> All the rest have thirty-one;
> Excepting leap year,—that's the time
> When February's days are twenty-nine.

This switch demonstrates that the cases need not be in any particular order,
and that the default may be placed at a location other than at the bottom. One
must be vigilant in making sure the break statements appear after the code

associated with each case. Forgetting to include the `break` statement causes
Java to fall through to the next case. For example, if the `break` found on the
default case were left off:

```
default:
  daysInMonth = 31; // Every other thirty-one
case 2:              // Except the second month alone."
  if (leapYear) daysInMonth = 29;
  else daysInMonth = 28;
  break;
```

BadMonth

The program, which should assign 31 to `daysInMonth`, instead behaves as follows:

```
Enter a month and year.
I'll print the length of the month.
1 2000
1/2000 has 29 days.
```

Because the `break` is missing from the `default` case, it assigns first 31, then 29,
to `daysInMonth`.

We have seen that `switch` statements are useful for handling different be-
haviors for different values of integers and characters. Because of the difficulty
in representing arbitrarily precise floating point values, it is not possible to
have `switch` statements that have floating point cases. Also, because there are
only two boolean constants, the `switch` statement based on boolean values can
always be replaced by an equally effective `if` statement.

3.9   Chapter Review

Most interesting programs make decisions based on the state of the program's
variables. These decisions are associated with control statements, including the
`if`, `while`, `do-while`, and `for`. We learned, in particular,

- Braces ({}) are used to "shrink wrap" multiple statements to be used in
  a place where only one is allowed.

- The `if` statement conditionally executes a statement. An alternative form
  provides for an alternative statement.

- The `swith` statement is used to distinguish between a large number of
  different cases based on constant values.

- The `while` loop is used when you need to do something zero or more times.

- The `do-while` loop is used when you need to do something at least once.

- The `for` loop is used when you are logically incrementing or counting.

- The `break` statement can be used to prematurely escape the tightest enclosing `while`, `for`, or `switch` statement. Its use is essential in making the `switch` statement work correctly.

- All loops are effectively equivalent.

- Infinite loops cannot always be detected.

Problems

3.1   Our computation of a leap year on page 90 is fairly limited. Write a program that reads in a year and carefully identifies and prints out whether or not it is a leap year. The rules for leap years are as follows:

- Any year not evenly divisible by 4 is not a leap year.

- Any year divisible by 4 is a leap year, *unless* one of the rules that follow applies.

- Any year divisible by 100 is not a leap year, *unless* the rule that follows applies.

- Any year divisible by 400 is a leap year.

Make sure you test your program carefully.

3.2⋆   Why would a `switch` statement not be useful in the solution to Problem 3.1?

3.3   Write a program that draws this checkerboard:

3.4   Write a loop to solve each of the following problems:

- As long as the mouse button is pressed, write lines saying `Let go!` on the screen.

- Read in integers until a sentinel (0) is read.

- Read in characters until a whitespace is encountered.

- Read in all whitespace characters that immediately follow from an input stream.

- Read in all alphanumeric characters that immediately follow, from an input stream.

- Sum up the first few positive integers until the mouse button is pressed.

- Sum up at most the first 1000000 integers, as long as the mouse button is pressed.

3.5   Write one or more loops to solve the following problems:

a. Print a 10×10 multiplication table.

b. Print a lower-triangular multiplication table (only entries such that the row number is greater than or equal to the column number).

c. Print entries of a 10×10 multiplication table, but only if the product is greater than 50.

3.6⋆   On a particular day at the stock market, there were **a** advancing stocks and **d** declining stocks. These numbers may be quite large. Write one or two loops that determine a best ratio of two integers, each of which is less than 20, that best approximates the ratio **a:d**.

3.7   Indicate what the following program does and then rewrite it using a while loop:

```
for (i = 1; i <= n; i *= 2)
{
    System.out.println(i);
}
```

3.8⋆   Indicate what the following program does and then rewrite it using a do-while loop:

```
for (d = 0; n != 0; d++)
{
    n /= 10;
}
System.out.println(d);
```

3.9   Draw the checkerboard of Problem 3.3, but use two **Rect** objects, each drawn exactly four times. (Use offsets, inversion, and loops.)

3.10   Write a program that draws the picture on the following page. (Hint: It is not that different from Problem 3.9.)

3.11⋆ Can a `for` loop be used to replace an `if` statement? If so, indicate how you might rewrite:

```
if (d.mousePressed()) c.out.println("Let go!");
```

3.12   Write a program that draws this interesting picture:

3.13   Recall that the points on a circle of radius r are $(r \cos \theta, r \sin \theta)$. With this information, draw this picture:

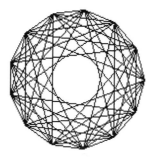

3.14   Write a program that prints the factors of a number n.

3.15   Write a program that prints the prime factorization of n. (Recall the prime factorization is a list of primes whose product is n.)

3.16⋆ Write a program to compute whether or not a small number (< 1000000) is *prime*. Recall that a prime number has exactly two positive factors—one and itself. A suitable method is to check all the possible witnesses to the number being composite—all the potential factors of n.

3.17   Write a program to determine the greatest common divisor of two values. If a or b is 1, then the greatest common divisor is 1, and if $a = b$, then that value is the greatest common divisor. If $1 < a < b$, the greatest common divisor of a and b is also the greatest common divisor of $b - a$ and a.

3.18   Write the program of Problem 3.6 in such a way that the integers are relatively prime (they don't share any common factors other than one; i.e., their greatest common divisor is 1).

3.19   Write a program to draw the following picture. The pixel (x, y) is painted black exactly when x and y are relatively prime; in other words, their greatest common divisor is 1.

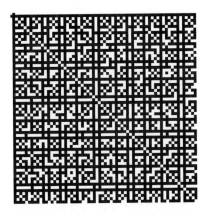

3.20   Write a program to print out all *perfect* numbers that are less than 10000. A perfect number, n, is one whose positive factors (other than itself) sum to n.

3.21   Write a program that, in the drawing window, draws the path of a point on the perimeter of a circle that rolls along the top edge of the drawing window.

3.10 Laboratory: Baby, Crab, and Cone Puzzle

Objective. To use booleans, conditional statements, and loops to help solve a classic puzzle.

Discussion. In this lab, we develop a program to validate potential solutions to a classic puzzle[4] recast as Mama's puzzle of the baby, crab, and cone. As the story goes, Mama headed off to the ice cream shop on a hot summer day with her delightful baby and pet crab. On the way she crossed a river with the aid of a ferry boat that, rowed by herself, could carry one other. A little thought demonstrates that this was no minor obstacle—it required three trips in the ferry to get everyone across (the crab, it seems, was no great swimmer). By the time she got to the shop, she was clearly ready to make a purchase.

Having purchased the largest cone possible, Mama set back toward home with all in tow: baby, crab, and cone. At the river, however, she faced a dilemma: in what order should she row everyone across in the ferry? The difficulty was that since only one of the baby, crab, or cone could be ferried across (it must have been a *huge* cone), two must be left behind. Unfortunately, if the baby was left unattended with the crab, violence of some form would surely ensue. If the baby was left with the cone, it would overindulge. Thus, each trip of the ferry had to be made with care, making sure that the baby was never left with either of the other two on the same shore.

To facilitate Mama's journey, you are to write a planning program of sorts that allows the harmless simulation of the various possibilities. We have in mind a program with output similar to the following:

```
Welcome to the Puzzle of the Baby, the Crab, and the Cone.

One hot summer day, Mama crossed the river to the left
bank to take a break from programming and buy an ice cream.
She brought her baby and her pet crab.  On the return
she came to the river and was faced with a dilemma: how
could they all cross without disaster?  The ferry holds
Mama and just one other item.  The problem is that
  * if the baby is left with the cone, it spoils its dinner.
  * if the baby is left with the crab, the crab bites the baby.
Please help Mama make her journey across the river!

Mama is on the left.
The baby is on the left bank.
The crab is on the left bank.
The cone is on the left bank.
Who would you like Mama to cross with?
(type 0 for no one, 1 for baby, 2 for crab, or 3 for cone)
2
```

---

[4] The farmer's puzzle of the chicken, fox, and the corn.

```
Mama crosses the river with her pet crab.
Oh no! The baby ate the ice cream.
We'll have to stop and help Mama and her family.
Undoubtedly, she'll need your help again.
```

As you can tell, the program keeps track of the location of each of the parties, perhaps by a boolean. After describing the state of the situation, the facilitator is asked to determine who rides in the ferry with Mama. As Mama leaves shore, the various lethal conditions are checked for and the simulation is potentially terminated. If, however, everyone eventually makes it to the destination (here, the "right bank"), the puzzle is solved. A good program would point out that the solution might have been faster if more than seven moves were required.

Procedure. This is a complex program, so the following steps should be considered in the *design* of your program. Once designed, the program is more easily coded:

1. Identify all the variables that will be needed. Variables help to keep track of the state of the program. If something must be remembered, it must be accounted for as a variable. For example, it might be useful to keep track of the number of times the ferry has crossed the river.

2. For each variable, identify its type, and if necessary, its initial value. This should complete your declarations.

3. Break the program down into several sizeable pieces. It's not important to know immediately how each piece is implemented, but it is necessary to identify logically distinct portions of the program. For example, the instructions must be written at the beginning, the results at the end, and in the middle it is necessary to print the location of all the participants. There may be other parts, as well.

4. Identify those parts of the program that are part of a conditional or looping construct, remembering the features that distinguish each of the loop types.

5. Our informal design is completed if a reasonable person can follow the logical states of the program without doing anything that seems contrary to the imagined execution of the program.

6. Armed with a design, it is now possible to implement each of the logical components in Java. It is often the case that the design has to be augmented to take into account the finer details. As you implement each of the logical components of the program, you may find it useful to test to see if the program works as expected. For example, you run the program to see if the instructions and initial state are printed correctly. The intermediate steps also help to ward off any unforeseen problems as early as possible.

7. Once completed, test your program thoroughly. Does it work in short simulations (as we have just seen)? Does it work when you follow the optimal solution? Does it work, even if Mama makes far too many trips? What happens if the number 4 is provided as input to the question?

8. When completed, sit back, take pride in your work, and save your program.

Thought questions. Consider the following questions as you complete the lab:

1. In your finished program, are there any unnecessary variables?

2. Are there any statements that don't get executed?

3. Return to this code a couple of days later. Are there improvements you can see after this fresh view of your code?

4. If crabs liked ice cream (they don't), could the puzzle be solved? (You should assume Mama eats neither the crab nor the cone in transit.) If so, how? If not, why?

5. Suppose there were four players (include, say, a cat). What is the simplest set of rules that makes Mama cross the river the most times before success? (It must be solvable.)

6. How might you implement this program graphically?

Chapter 4

Methods

"'What hasn't come here, come! What's here, stay here!'
... If you buried a marble with certain necessary
incantations, and left it alone a fortnight, and then opened
the place with the incantation he had just used, you would
find that all the marbles you had ever lost had gathered
themselves together there, meantime, no matter how widely
they had been separated."
—Mark Twain

THE ORGANIZATION OF LARGE PROGRAMS TAKES CONSIDERABLE PLANNING. Indeed, the construction of nontrivial programs involves the collaboration of large numbers of components, usually associated with different logical functions or distinct objects within the program. In Java this collaboration depends heavily on the use of *methods*.

4.1 The Method

Consider the structure of the following programming tasks:

- The computation of a list of the first million primes. It is clear that one component of the program is to compute whether a single number is prime.

- The hypothetical video game version of Ring-the-Gack.[1] The drawing of the Gack and the throwing of rings might be isolated in dedicated logical units.

- The construction of a word processor. The management of a "help window" is a logically isolated portion of the program.

- The launching of the space shuttle. The preflight testing is accomplished (at some level) by a single logical entity. It itself might be composed of several subcomponents.

In each of these tasks, some features appear logically isolated. Even though we may not know how they might be programmed, we can be confident that the supporting code is similarly isolated within the program.

Principle 13 *The structure of the program should model the structure of the problem.*

---

[1] Made popular by Dr. Seuss in *One Fish, Two Fish*.

```
prog          public static void maine(String args[])
              {
                   ...
              }


private static int fix(double d)          public static int mini()
{                                         {
     ...                                  }
}

              public static void main(String args[])
              {
                   ...
              }
```

Figure 4.1   The logical view of a program `prog` containing four methods. The `fix` method is declared for `private` use and is not accessible outside of the program. The `main` method matches the form needed to run a general computation.

In most programming languages, the *method* or *procedure* or *function* is used to organize code that performs a specific, well-documented task. The organizational method of identifying the logical components of a large process and placing each in its own procedure is called *procedural abstraction*. We will see other forms of abstraction in later chapters, but procedural abstraction is the most basic form found in most programming languages, and we will focus on it here.

We have actually already seen an example of a method—the `main` method. Let's look at it in more detail. Whenever an application runs (see, for example, the various methods of the application represented by Figure 4.1), the Java environment locates the `main` method and executes its instructions in order. You can test this by writing a program with different two methods: `main` and `maine`. When the program is run, the only instructions executed are those that are found within the `main` method.

The declaration of the `main` method always appears as follows:

Functions

```
public static void main(String args[])
```

The keyword `public` tells Java that this method is available for use outside of the containing class definition. In particular, it makes it possible for the Java environment to *call* the `main` method to cause your program to run. If the method were not `public`, it would be declared `protected` or `private`, making it impossible for the Java environment to reference it. For the moment, we will only consider methods declared `public`.

The keyword `static` signals that this method is always accessible. When the program starts, the `main` method may be called. In fact, the method may be called any time during the run of the program. Later we will make use of *dynamic methods*—methods that are available only in particular circumstances. Again, we currently focus on methods declared `static`.

The keyword `void` indicates that, once completed, this method leaves nothing behind. It may seem strange that we might produce something at the end of a program, but other methods—the method that computes the square root of a number, for example—are designed to produce values to be used in expressions. We will loosely refer to these value-producing methods as *functions*, and non-value producing methods (such as `main`) as *procedures*. If your mother knows how to program, there's a good chance she'll know what you mean if you write home and say, "I wrote my first procedure," but you might expose a Java-induced generation gap if you quip: "I wrote my first *method!*" In any case, we'll discuss both methods that produce values and those that don't in this chapter.

The identifier `main`, obviously, is the name of the method you're writing. Strictly speaking, its full name is prefixed by the name of the class that contains the method. In most cases, the class name can be avoided, but in some cases (like `Math.sin`) Java considers it sinful to drop the prefix. We'll see the precise reasoning for this later, but you should be aware of the possibility now.

Between the parentheses, we have a list of zero or more *parameters*. Parameters describe the data or resources needed from a method's environment before the method can run. Parameter declarations take a form similar to the declaration of variables. Multiple parameters are separated by commas. In `main` we have one: an array (indicated by the brackets, `[]`) of `String` values. This is simply a list of `String`s from the environment that might be useful to our `main` method.

All `main` methods must be declared in precisely this manner. If you should drop or change a keyword, the Java environment will be confused: it is looking for a procedure with one specification or *interface* but does not find it because the method provided is slightly different. The components of the interface that help the environment select the method determine its *signature*: its name and its parameter types (in `main`, a single array of `String`s). Deviation from the norm—no matter how acceptable elsewhere—is not tolerated in Java. In particular, in Java it is not possible to declare a function and a procedure with the same signature.

As another example of the declaration of a method, we consider the declaration of the `cos` function in the `Math` class. Its declaration is

```
public static double cos(double theta)
```

The designers of the `Math` class were interested in providing the use of the cosine function for *everyone* to use, so it is declared `public`. The function is available at all times, so it is declared `static`. The function requires a single value—`theta`, a double describing the angle in radians—and returns a `double` value between -1.0 and 1.0. The `sin` function has a similar declaration, though, obviously, its name is `sin`.

The drawing method, `lineTo`, is a procedure associated with the `Drawing-Window` class. Unlike the methods we have seen so far, it is only available when there is a `DrawingWindow` to work with. Its behavior, then, is *dynamic*. Its declaration is

```
public void lineTo(int x, int y)
```

The `void` indicates that `lineTo` doesn't return a value (in the same way that `cos` returns a value); its effect is to cause a line to be drawn in the associated drawing window.

Over the next few sections, we will consider declarations of static methods (e.g., `main` and `cos`). First, however, we consider a simple mechanism for developing documentation of our methods.

4.2   Some Comments about Comments

In this text, we will make significant use of *preconditions* and *postconditions*. The precondition is a statement of what must be true for a procedure to correctly accomplish its task. In the `main` methods we have seen, the precondition of the method might ensure that `Strings` were passed to the array `args`. The postcondition is something that will be true when the precondition is met *and* the method completes execution. Nearly every procedure has a precondition, and all procedures have a postcondition. (If there was no postcondition, then the procedure would not change the state of the machine, and the procedure couldn't be said to have done anything. Even the worst programmer is unlikely to write such a procedure—on purpose!) Our use of pre- and postconditions throughout the remainder of the text helps to promote better documentation of our programs. To the extent that we provide these simple pieces of documentation, we improve the utility of our code.

Principle 14 *Pre- and postconditions provide an easy method for formalizing your documentation.*

4.3   Procedures: The Valueless Methods

The *procedure*, or `void` method, provides a mechanism to *encapsulate* or *abstract* or *hide the details of* a particular process. For example, we might wish to write a procedure that simply waits for one second. It would appear as follows:

Timer

```
public static void wait1second()
// post: pause for one second
{
    long now = System.currentTimeMillis();
```

```
        long then = now + 1000; // one second (in milliseconds)
        while (System.currentTimeMillis() < then)
        { } // do nothing!
    }
```

It is clear that this procedure incorporates some rather unsavory details: the system clock measures time in milliseconds, and the process of waiting involves looping until the system clock reads "a second later." To call or *execute* or *invoke* this procedure, we type its name followed by an empty parameter list:

Waiting in loops: computer loitering

```
    public static void main(String args[])
    {
        wait1second();
    }
```

The parameter list is empty because this process—the process of waiting a single second—does not depend on any values provided by the user. What is the effect of running such a procedure? The computer appears to pause one second. (We say it *appears* to pause because there's no external indication that the procedure is actually working hard "spinning its wheels" repeatedly asking the system for the current time in milliseconds since 1969.)

With a mind to making our procedure more versatile, we might ask: Can we pause *an arbitrary* number of seconds? Sure! Here's how we cast this:

```
    public static void waitNSeconds(int number)
    // pre: number >= 0
    // post: pause for number seconds
    {
        int i;
        for (i = 0; i < number; i++)
        {
            wait1second();
        }
    }
```

Here, we say that **number** is a *formal parameter*. It holds the place for the quantity that represents the number of seconds to wait. This number is clearly referenced in the calculations that follow. We loop **number** times (whatever that value might be) calling **wait1second** each time.

The variable that controls this looping, **i**, is a *local variable*. It maintains a reasonable value as long as the method is *active*—that is, as long as it hasn't executed all of its statements. We'll return to local variables in a moment.

Observe that if we don't know what the value of **number** is, we can't run this method. It's necessary, then, for us to "nail down" this number *before* the method is invoked. That's the role of the *actual parameter*. We specify the actual parameter when we call the procedure:

Timer

```
    waitNSeconds(60/5);
```

In this case, the computer will pause at that instruction for a fifth of a minute, or 12 seconds. Any expression, as long as it results in an `int`, is suitable as the *actual* parameter for this single parameter method. This process—the *passing* of an actual parameter to the formal parameter—serves to initialize the values of the method's formal parameters before the method is run.

Try this!   By the way, passing a `double` to the above method—that expects an `int`— would definitely cause problems!

Exercise 4.1 *Write a method that can wait a number of seconds, specified as a* `double`.

In Java all parameters are *passed by value*. That means that the actual parameters passed may be any computed value and, if a variable is passed to the method, the variable's value cannot be directly changed by the method. This is an important observation, and one that explains a behavior that might otherwise be considered strange. Here, for example, are the methods of a program that *Warning:* appears (at first blush) to print out the sum of the first n integers:
broken code!

SumUp

```
public static void main(String args[])
{
    int n, sum;
    ConsoleWindow c = new ConsoleWindow();

    sum = 0;
    n = c.input.readInt();
    sumUp(n,sum);
    c.out.println(sum);
}

public static void sumUp(int n, int total)
// pre: total is zero
// post: total is the sum of integers 1 through n
{
    int i;
    for (i = 1; i <= n;  i++)
    {
        total += i;
    }
}
```

However, when we type 10, instead of printing 55, the sum is reported as 0. Unfortunately, even though the total is being computed in the formal parameter `total`, the final value of `total` is not assigned back to `sum` when the `sumUp` method finishes. We must depend on the use of value-producing methods (functions), which we discuss in the next section. Notice that `sumUp` has a local variable `i`. Its value is available to be referred to in expressions in the `sumUp` method while the method is running, but it is "recycled" when the method finishes. In essence, the variable *only exists while the* `sumUp` *method is running*. A side effect

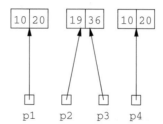

```
Pt p1 = new Pt(10,20);
Pt p2 = new Pt(19,36);
Pt p3 = p2;
Pt p4 = new Pt(10,20);
```

Figure 4.2   Four references to three `Pt` objects. On the left, declarations of four references; on the right, a picture describing the relation between the references. References `p2` and `p3` refer to the same object, and are affected by each other's modifications. References `p1` and `p4` refer to distinct objects with similar values; there is no interaction between the two.

---

of this result is that the method `main` may not refer to the variables declared within `sumUp`. In addition, it is not possible to refer to the variables in the `main` method from the `sumUp` method. Of course the *values* of the local variables may be indirectly *passed* as actual parameters to methods, but methods may not directly *modify* them.

When we work with nonprimitive types, the relation between actual and formal parameters is somewhat more difficult to interpret. First, we recall that objects in Java are *referred to* by *references*. When we declare a variable of nonprimitive type, we are actually only declaring a reference to an object. Later, if necessary, a reference to a new object is constructed by the `new` operator. Usually this reference is assigned to a variable. In this way, the object referenced must be distinguished from the reference itself. For example, it is quite easy to arrange for several references to refer to the same object (see Figure 4.2).

We can use this feature to allow us to modify objects that we pass between methods. Here, for example, we pass a reference to the `DrawingWindow` to a method:

```
public static void drawHashAt(DrawingWindow d, Pt center)
// pre: d is a valid drawing window, center is a valid point
// post: draw a hash mark centered at center in drawing window d
{
    d.moveTo(center);     // move to center of hash mark
    d.move(-10,0);   // move left
    d.line(20,0);    // draw horizontal axis
    d.move(-10,-10); // move up
    d.line(0,20);    // draw vertical axis
}
```

Hash

The method makes use of the reference `d` to draw on the screen, modifying the contents of the `DrawingWindow`. The formal and actual parameters are

distinct references to the same object. The method draws a hash mark in the
`DrawingWindow` referred to by its parameter. Clearly, there are lasting results
of calling this procedure. A program that allows you to place hash marks at
various places on the drawing window might be written as follows:

```
public static void main(String args[])
{
    DrawingWindow d = new DrawingWindow();
    Rect stop = new Rect(0,0,10,10);
    Pt pressPoint;
    d.draw(stop); // a button for stopping
    d.setForeground(Color.red);

    while (true) // potentially infinite
    {
        pressPoint = d.awaitMousePress(); // mouse is now down
        if (stop.contains(pressPoint)) break; // leave loop
        drawHashAt(d,pressPoint);
        d.awaitMouseRelease();                 // mouse is now up
    }
    System.exit(0);
}
```

*An excellent
example of a
potentially
infinite loop.*

The program paints red hash marks each time the mouse is pressed on a pixel.
Pressing the mouse in the `stop` rectangle stops the program.

In our final example, we write a procedure to assign $(0,0)$ to a point. Our
first example attempts this by making the reference `p` point to a new `Pt`, which
is located at $(0,0)$.

Origin

```
public static void origin(Pt p)
// post: no change; p is a reassigned formal parameter
{
    p = new Pt(0,0);
}
```

```
public static void main(String args[])
{
    ConsoleWindow c = new ConsoleWindow();
    Pt q = new Pt(10,66);
    origin(q);
    c.out.println(q);
}
```

Unfortunately, this does not have the desired effect. The reference `p` is changed
by this method (it now points to a new point; see Figure 4.3), but because `q`
initializes `p` as a value parameter, q's new value is not updated when `origin`
completes. Thus, the program causes the original value to be printed:

```
<Point: (10,66)>
```

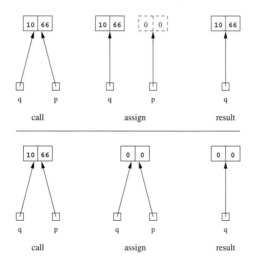

Figure 4.3 Above, in `origin` the result of assigning a new `Pt` to a formal parameter. Below, in `origin2` the result of assigning a new value to an existing reference.

This happens because reference to the point is being changed, not the point itself. This change is lost once the `origin` method is finished.

The correct way to modify the object is to use the `Pt` mutator methods, `x` and `y`. In this version of the method, the object to which `p` refers (the same object to which `q` in the calling program refers) has its state modified—*not* its reference:

```
public static void origin2(Pt p)
// pre: p is not null
// post: p's value is (0,0)
{
    p.x(0);
    p.y(0);
}
```

Because the primitive types of Java (`int`, `double`, etc.) are not maintained by references, it is impossible to have a procedure effect a permanent change to the state of a primitive variable.

4.3.1 Example: Drawing Tools

While Java excels at drawing simple objects, it is often the case that our programs are constructed from more complex sequences of drawing commands that appear in several places. For example, clearing the drawing window and drawing a regular polygon are operations that are useful to graphical programs, but require complex sequences of statements. Here, we construct a few methods that are of general use in our programs.

Our first example is a method to clear the drawing window. This method requires only a reference to the drawing window (there may be multiple drawing windows in a program). Since no other information is needed, we know that only this one parameter must be passed to the procedure. For this method to be useful, we must declare the method `public` and `static` (it can be used anytime). Its signature, then, is

```
public static void clearWindow(DrawingWindow target)
```

Tools

The process of clearing the window involves asking the drawing window for a description of its boundary, and then erasing that portion of the window. Adding pre- and postconditions, we have the following method declaration:

```
public static void clearWindow(DrawingWindow target)
// pre: target is a valid drawing window
// post: target is erased
{
    Rect boundary = target.bounds();
    target.clear(boundary);
}
```

To make use of this method, we simply add this code to any program that wishes to make use of the method. Calling the method, then, is simply a matter of passing the appropriate drawing window to it.

```
clearWindow(d);
```

Since `clearWindow` requires a drawing window as its parameter, we can pass it our usual window for drawing, `d`.

Next, suppose we're interested in drawing a regular polygon with n equal sides. To locate it on the screen, we must specify a number of important parameters: the drawing window, the center of the polygon, the "size" or radius of the polygon (measured from the center to one of its vertices), and the number of vertices. In addition, it may be necessary to indicate an angle to one of the vertices—in this way, it's possible to draw, say, a square at any angle desired. Given all of these pieces of information, we can develop the signature of the method:

```
public static void drawPoly(DrawingWindow d,
                    Pt center, double radius,
                    int n, double degrees)
```

We believe it may be convenient to express the angle in degrees, and the radius as a floating point value. To help document this, we provide the following pre- and postconditions:

```
// pre: d, center is not null, radius >= 0,
//      n > 2, 0 <= degrees < 360
// post: a regular polygon is drawn on d, centered at center
//       with radius radius and n sides; one point makes
//       angle measuring degrees with the positive x axis
```

Since we have specified our offset angle in degrees and the trigonometric functions require radians, we must be careful to convert to radians. The process of actually drawing the polygon involves drawing n lines between $n + 1$ points. (The first point is the same as the last.) Since we have a specific number of iterations in mind, it's useful to use a `for` loop to control the drawing:

```java
double offsetRadians = degrees/180.0*Math.PI;
double theta;
int x,y;
int vertexNumber;

for (vertexNumber = 0; vertexNumber <= n; vertexNumber++)
{
    // angle of vertex (initial is offsetRadians)
    theta = 2*Math.PI/n*vertexNumber + offsetRadians;
    // compute location of vertex
    x = (int)Math.round(center.x() + radius*Math.cos(theta));
    y = (int)Math.round(center.y() + radius*Math.sin(theta));
    if (vertexNumber == 0) d.moveTo(x,y);
    else                   d.lineTo(x,y);
}
```

Notice that when we call the polygon drawing routine, the only change that takes place is the image drawn on the screen. The routine itself does not generate a value.

Not all methods in Java, of course, are valueless. Many times it is useful to be able to write methods that perform complex calculations that may be used later in expressions.

4.4   Functions: Value-Producing Methods

On occasion, the computation of some value is so complex it is useful to be able to encapsulate the process in a method. There are many obvious examples: getting the state of the mouse button, computing the value of the sine function, approximating π to n decimal places and selecting a random integer. Each of these tasks is potentially parameterized by one or more values (sine demands an angle, the calculation of π must know the number of decimal places to be computed), and each *returns* a quantity that is useful as part of some greater computation. Such methods are called *functions*.

Functions are simply methods that are declared to return a non-**void** value. The purpose of the function is to compute the ultimate value and then return it

Functions

as the result using the `return` construct. Here, for example, is a function that computes the square of an integer:

```
public static int square(int n)
// post: returns the square of the value n
{
    return n*n;
}
```

We can use this function anyplace that the square of an integer is needed. For example, it appears in the quadratic formula and in the computation of distances between points.

Exercise 4.2 *Write a function that computes the distance between two points.*

Here is simple code that computes the sum of the squares of integers between 1 and n.

```
public static int sumOfSquares(int n)
// pre: n >= 0
// post: returns the sum of squares of values between 0 and n
{
    int sum = 0;   // intermediate result
    int i;
    for (i = 1; i <= n; i++)
    {
        sum = sum + square(i); // calls our square function
    }
    return sum;
}
```

The important line is the computation of the sum. It calls the `square` function on `i` and gets back the square of `i`. This is accumulated into the running total. Notice that this last piece of code is, itself, a function. It calls the square function in the computation of sum of the sequence.

Exercise 4.3 *Can you write the `sumOfSquares` function without a loop?*

Notice, also, that nothing is printed out. The action here is the return of a computed value. Even though we might call each of these functions a number of times, there is no indication that anything is ever printed. This is a difficult concept—the computer is working here, even though it may not appear so on the outside.

Principle 15 *Functions don't generate output.*

Functions, of course, are capable of returning complex objects as well. For example, this method returns the `Pt` that is opposite the point `p` in the drawing window `d`. It could have been used as part of the program that draws rotatable art (see page 78):

```
public static Pt opposite(DrawingWindow d, Pt p)
// pre: p is a valid point, d is a valid window
// post: returns the point that is opposite of p in d
{
    int windowRight = d.bounds().right();
    int windowBottom = d.bounds().bottom();
    Pt oppositeP = new Pt(windowRight-p.x(), windowBottom-p.y());
    return oppositeP;
}
```

Notice that we compute the value of a function and then return it on the last line of the function. This is a convention and is not required by Java. The reader would do well to adopt this habit. Avoiding this allows you to write Java methods that have errors because they do not return values, or they return unexpected values.

Principle 16 *Return a result on the last line of a function.*

To see how we might use this function, we can recast the curve drawing program of page 78 using our `opposite` function. The use of the `opposite` function makes this loop considerably more readable:

```
Pt current, next;              // points

current = d.getMouse();        // initial location
while (d.mousePressed())
{
    next = d.getMouse();       // get next mouse position
    d.moveTo(current);         // draw the "right" image
    d.lineTo(next);

    d.moveTo(opposite(d,current)); // draw mirrored segment
    d.lineTo(opposite(d,next));
    current = next;
}
```

As one last example, we consider a function that selects a random integer (using a particular generator) between lower and upper bounds:

```
public static int rand(int low, int high, Random gen)
// pre: low <= high
// post: returns uniformly random value v, low <= v <= high
{
    return (Math.abs(gen.nextInt())%(high-low+1))+low;
}
```

The `Random` generator is an instance of the `java.util.Random` object discussed in Chapter 1.

Grayscale

4.4.1   Example: Color Functions

The Abstract Windowing Toolkit (AWT) of Java provides access to each of the several million colors that are available to programmers that use color monitors. To make use of color in Java, it is useful to import the `Color` class from Java's AWT:

```
import java.awt.Color;  // must be imported to include Color
```

One method of specifying colors is to indicate the intensity of red, blue, and green (hence, the color model's acronym RGB) that are to be included in the color to be mixed. Intensities range from 0.0 (no color contribution) to 1.0 (this color used at full intensity). Thus, intense red has an RGB triple of $[1, 0, 0]$, while intense blue is represented by $[0, 0, 1]$. Magenta—the color achieved by mixing red and blue—is represented by an RGB triple of $[1, 0, 1]$. A darker magenta is $[0.5, 0, 0.5]$.

Various intensities of gray are achieved by setting the RGB components to equal values. Thus $[0, 0, 0]$ is black (no intensity), and $[1, 1, 1]$ is white (full intensity). The values in between provide various gradations in the intensity of the shade.

To create a new color for use in Java, we need only construct a new `Color` object whose parameters are the red, green, and blue intensities, specified by `float` parameters. Thus, to create a foreground color of pink, we can construct a new `Color` that is part way between red $[1, 0, 0]$ and white $[1, 1, 1]$.

```
d.setForeground(new Color((float)1.0,(float)0.85,(float)0.85));
```

In general, the construction of specific colors is difficult, but we can use our knowledge of the RGB color model to build a simple function to generate shades of gray for use in our drawings. The only parameter to this method is the intensity of the gray we desire, and the result is a new `Color` reference. An obvious name for our function would be `gray`:

```
public static Color gray(double intensity)
// pre: 0 <= intensity <= 1.0
// post: returns a gray with indicated intensity level (1.0=white)
{
    return
      new Color((float)intensity,(float)intensity,(float)intensity);
}
```

Of course, the use of `double` values is somewhat preferred in Java (since floating point constants are `double` by default), so it is most useful if the function takes a `double` value and casts it to the required `float` intensities. This hiding of the difficulties of constructing a new `Color` is one of the main features of the use of methods. When we use the `gray` method, we needn't think about the RGB color model or the peculiarities of the way that colors are constructed. Here, for example, we fill in the drawing window with hundreds of lines, each of which is shaded with a different intensity of gray:

Figure 4.4 The contents of the drawing window after drawing several hundred vertical lines with increasing intensities of gray.

```java
public static void main(String args[])
{
    DrawingWindow d = new DrawingWindow();
    int i;

    // draw vertical lines, each with a fixed gray color
    // that varies from left (black) to right (white)
    for (i = 0; i < d.bounds().width(); i++)
    {
        d.setForeground(gray(i*1.0/d.bounds().width()));
        d.moveTo(i,0);
        d.lineTo(i,d.bounds().height());
    }
}
```

The result is the image shown in Figure 4.4.

Exercise 4.4 *Write a method* intense *that takes two parameters—a* Color *and an "intensity"—and returns a* Color *between black and the indicated color, depending on the intensity. (Hint: See Appendix D to find learn more about the* getRed, getBlue, *and* getGreen *methods of the* Color *class.)*

4.4.2 Example: Parameterized Functions

Physicists, of course, are used to parameterizing functions that describe many physical phenomena. The function might, for example, describe the position or velocity of an object over time, or the potential energy of a pendulum might be parameterized as a function of the angle of the pendulum. These types of functions are easily expressed in languages like Java.

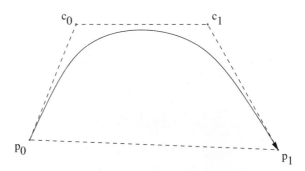

Figure 4.5   The model of the Bézier curve. Curve leaves p_0 and toward c_0 and enters p_1 from c_1. The curve never leaves the dashed quadrilateral.

For our example, we will make use of a more graphically oriented parameterized curve: the *Bézier* curve. Imagine we wish to draw a smooth curve from point p_0 to p_1. This could, of course, be accomplished by moving the pen from one intermediate point to another. We can parameterize these points p in terms of an independent variable, $0 \leq t \leq 1$, where $p(0) = p_0$ and $p(1) = p_1$.

To help define the curve we wish to draw, we might provide two other *control points* c_0 and c_1 (see Figure 4.5), that, along with p_0 and p_1 describe a quadrilateral $p_0 - c_0 - c_1 - p_1$. We imagine that the pen leaves from p_0 along the edge $p_0 - c_0$ with velocity proportional to the length of $p_0 - c_0$, and that it arrives at p_1 along the edge $c_1 - p_1$ with velocity proportional to the length of that edge. The Bézier curve is described by a parameterized weighted average of the coordinates of points p_0, c_0, c_1, and p_1:

$$p(t) = (1-t)^3 p_0 + 3(1-t)^2 t c_0 + 3(1-t)t^2 c_1 + t^3 p_1$$

A little inspection demonstrates that when $t = 0$, $p(t) = p_0$, and when $t = 1$, $p(t) = p_1$. Still, this computation is not so simple that it is immediately obvious, so we should ideally write—once—a Java function to perform this calculation.

Our task, then, is to implement p as a function of t. Additional information is, of course, needed: p_0, c_0, c_1, p_1 must also be passed along. Here is the start of the declaration for a function that generates the points of a Bézier curve (we'll call this function `bezierPoint` so that its purpose is obvious):

Bezier

```
public static Pt bezierPoint(Pt p0, Pt c0, Pt c1, Pt p1, double t)
// pre: p0 and p1 are endpoints, c0 and c1 are control points
//      0 <= t <= 1
// post: returns the point along the Bezier curve determined
//       by p0, c0, c1, p1, and t
```

First, we observe that the function performs the indicated calculation on the x and y coordinates of the point independently. Thus, we break down the computation as two ugly computations—one for x and another for y:

```
double omt = 1.0-t;
double x = omt*omt*omt*p0.x()+
           3*omt*omt*t*c0.x()+
           3*omt*t*t*c1.x()+
           t*t*t*p1.x();
double y = omt*omt*omt*p0.y()+
           3*omt*omt*t*c0.y()+
           3*omt*t*t*c1.y()+
           t*t*t*p1.y();
return new Pt((int)Math.round(x),(int)Math.round(y));
```

To simplify the calculation, we precomputed the value of $1 - t$ and stored it as `omt` (one minus `t`). There are other optimizations that might make this calculation run even faster, but the clarity of the relationship between the Java and the mathematical function might be sacrificed.

Exercise 4.5 *Ok. Don't worry about the clarity! What is the minimum number of operations (additions, subtractions, and multiplications) needed to perform these calculations? You may use as many intermediate variables (e.g., omt) as you feel are necessary.*

Exercise 4.6 *Since arithmetic operations are the main thing that slows the computation down, reducing their number (see the previous exercise) should make this function run faster. How might you test this hypothesis?*

To plot the curve, we draw line segments between a small number of points that are known to be on the parameterized curve. Notice how the `bezierPoint` function does not actually get evaluated at the endpoints, because we know these are p_0 and p_1:

```
public static void bezier(Pt p0, Pt c0, Pt c1, Pt p1)
// pre: p0, c0, c1, p1 all not null
// post: draws smooth curve from p0 toward c0, to p1 from c1
{
    int cnt = 10;
    int i;
    d.moveTo(p0);
    for (i = 0; i <= cnt; i++)
    {
        d.lineTo(bezierPoint(p0,c0,c1,p1,i*(1.0/cnt)));
    }
}
```

It is surprising how few line segments are actually necessary to make the curve appear smooth (see Figure 4.6).

An excellent treatment of the Bézier cubics can be found in Donald Knuth's manual describing *Metafont*, a language for designing computer generated type faces.[2]

---

[2] The type face used in this book was generated by Metafont. It employs the tell-tale u-turn tail on the 'a' and 't'.

Figure 4.6 A child's art challenge: start by drawing five curves with the `bezier` method. What do you see?

4.4.3   Predicates: Methods That Perform Tests

Predicates

Considering the number of control statements in Java that demand a boolean value, it is useful to be able to write functions that return boolean values. Examples of this technique include testing to see if a number is prime or perfect, or to check for the similarity of two colors. Here we consider the test to see if one value falls between two others, that is: given parameters a, b, and c, whether or not $a \le b \le c$. The solution to this is nearly as straightforward as writing the mathematical expression:

```
public static boolean between(double a, double b, double c)
// post: returns true iff a <= b <= c
{
    return (a <= b) && (b <= c);
}
```

Recall that comparison operators (including `<=`) return boolean values; thus, it is not meaningful to compute `a <= b <= c` since this would result in comparing a boolean value (the result of `a <= b`) to a double (`c`).

Sometimes, one will see an equivalent function

```
public static boolean between(double a, double b, double c)
// post: returns true if a <= b <= c
{
    if ((a <= b) && (b < c)) return true;
    else return false;
}
```

The astute reader will note that the `true` is returned when the condition is `true`, and `false` is returned when the condition is `false`. Either way, the value returned is the value computed in the condition. It is simpler and more readable to return the condition directly.

We can also write functions that are useful for manipulating character values. These are often used when reading and converting characters from the keyboard.

Each of these makes use of the fact that in all character sets the characters 'a' through 'z' and 'A' through 'Z' appear contiguously and in order.

Contiguously: adjacently.

Our first function tests to see if a character passed in is a lowercase letter:

```
public static boolean isLower(char c)
// post: returns true if c is a lowercase letter
{
    return ('a' <= c) && (c <= 'z');
}
```

Notice that this looks surprisingly like the between function we wrote earlier. We can write a slightly different between function that works on characters instead:

```
public static boolean between(char a, char b, char c)
// post: returns true if a <= b <= c in the ASCII ordering
{
    return (a <= b) && (b <= c);
}
```

Since it has a different signature than our between function that accepted three doubles, the identity of the function to be called can always be determined by inspecting the types of the parameters. This useful *overloading* of the name between is called *polymorphism*. In essence, there is a single abstract function, between, that apparently considers the relations of many types of data.

We now can use this between function to help us write functions like isLower. Let's expand our repertoire with an isUpper function:

```
public static boolean isUpper(char c)
// post: return true if c is an uppercase letter
{
    return between('A',c,'Z');
}
```

Wow! The power of composing methods is becoming clear.

4.4.4 Character-Returning Methods

We can extend our understanding of the meaning of upper- and lowercase letters realizing that if the uppercase letters are in order and contiguous, and the lowercase letters are in order and contiguous, the distance (in terms of encoding) is constant between corresponding upper- and lowercase letters. Here is a function that converts uppercase letters to lowercase:

```
public static char toLower(char c)
// post: if c is an uppercase letter, it is converted to lowercase;
//       otherwise, c is returned untouched
{
    int position;
```

Converter

```
        if (isUpper(c))
        {
            position = c - 'A';        // position of c in uppercase
            c = (char)('a'+position);  // corresponding lowercase
        }
        return c;
    }
```

This function is somewhat tricky. Notice, first, that if a letter is not uppercase, it is not modified by the function. If it is an uppercase letter, the letter's ASCII value (an int) is shifted by the difference between an uppercase letter and its equivalent lowercase letter. The difference is computed in a manner that subtracts off "uppercaseness" and adds back on "lowercaseness." Since the letters begin as uppercase letters, they must end in lowercase. Nowhere is the specific offset actually used. If a specific value had been used, problems would result if the order of the encoding was changed from ASCII to some other standard.

Exercise 4.7 *Write a method that converts a lowercase letter to uppercase.*

Exercise 4.8 *Write a method that swaps 'a' for 'z', 'b' for 'y', and so on.*

Here is an example of how our toLower function might be used to convert all the characters of the input to lowercase:

```
public static void main(String args[])
{
    ConsoleWindow c = new ConsoleWindow();
    while (!c.input.eof()) // while there's input
    {
        while (!c.input.eoln()) // for every character on a line
        {
            char ch = c.input.readChar();
            c.out.print(toLower(ch));
        }
        c.input.readln();   // read end-of-line mark
        c.out.println();    // write an end-of-line mark
    }
}
```

This program makes considerable use of the text-oriented methods of the Read-Stream class. The method eof is a function that returns true when the next character on input indicates the end of input (usually a control-D), while eoln returns true exactly when the end of a line is encountered (usually accomplished by pressing carriage return). Finally, the readln method reads any characters remaining on the line (in our case, there won't be any), and it then consumes the end-of-line mark. Clearly, as all of the characters are read in, they are converted to lowercase (if necessary) and then the transformed characters are written to the output.

4.5   Evaluating the Effectiveness of Methods

After designing a number of methods, it is often useful to reconsider each and identify ways in which it might be improved. Here are some things to be considered when evaluating the effectiveness of your method design:

1. Purpose. The logical purpose of a method should be simple. If it cannot be described succinctly in a single, sufficiently abstract postcondition, the function should be reconsidered. It's unusual, for example, for the purpose of a method to be described by a compound sentence.

2. Length. If the logical description of a method is a single sentence, its implementation should be no more than, say, a dozen statements. Any longer method can be broken into a larger number of smaller methods that call each other.

   A rule for patents: Concept must be described in a single sentence.

3. Functions versus Procedures. Functions return values that are used in expressions. Procedures generally perform complete actions. Functions can always be written neatly to return their values on the last line of the function.

4.6   Classes: An Encapsulation Mechanism

Having looked at the way in which methods help to contain the unsightly details of the processes they support, we are now in a position to understand one of the purposes of a *class*. In Java, classes are used to group and manage the details of related methods. For example, the class `java.lang.Math` contains simple mathematical and trigonometric functions. In a similar way, when we construct a simple program, we write a single class that contains all the methods that support the running of our program. So far, this collection consists of the mandatory `main` procedure, along with all of the methods that `main` calls, along with all the methods those methods call, and so on. We can think of classes as being some sort of "computational glue" or "shrink wrap" that binds related computing resources together. When all the necessary methods have been written, they are glued together by the definition of a single class. That class is our program.

Classes, themselves, are contained within *packages*. The classes that support this book, for example, all fall within the `element` package. The `Math` class mentioned above resides within the `java.lang` package. The name of the package is, in most environments, loosely interpreted as the name of a path through a directory or folder hierarchy that leads to the location where the class is stored, but we stray into the gray details of particular implementations.

Most programmers write classes that sit inside a current project or folder. We term this the *default package*. All classes within the default package are automatically imported, so it is possible that a single program can be composed of a number of methods stored in a number of classes. In a video game, we might imagine that one class contained all the methods that supported the on-screen graphics, another class might manage the scoring facilities, and another might support an input device like a trackball. Loosely speaking, those items that are declared as `public` within a class are visible to other classes— public methods of one class within the default package can be invoked by the methods of another. Declaring these entities `private` within the class makes it impossible to access these components from outside the class. For example, while we might be interested in allowing programmers to access the `bezier` function, it might be considered unnecessary to allow programmers to directly access the `bezierPoint` method. Declaring `bezierPoint private`, we can be sure that it will not be accessible by methods of other classes. Within the class, however, `private` methods are fully accessible (`bezier` can access a `private` `bezierPoint` method). It becomes clear, now, why the `main` method—which is called by the Java environment from outside its class—must be declared `public`: declaring it otherwise makes it impossible to run!

4.6.1 Static Instance Variables

We have seen in nearly all of our functions and procedures that it is possible to declare local variables. This makes one think: *Is it possible to have variables that are not local, but "global"?* The answer is a guarded *Yes*.

This is how it is accomplished. Just as methods can be declared within the containing class, we may declare `static` "instance" variables as well. Instance variables are not declared as part of any method. Instead, they usually appear near the top of the body of the class definition. Since they are declared `static`, these variables are available during the entire run of the program. We usually initialize them early in the `main` procedure so that methods within the class can make use of them as soon as possible.[3] The types of variables that are declared globally are those features that describe, at all times, the state of the program. If, however, there is a point in the program where one of these variables does not seem necessary to describe the state of the machine, it should be made a local variable in a method and passed to other methods as necessary.

In many of the more complex programs of this text, the `DrawingWindow` (`d`) and `ConsoleWindow` (`c`) are used by most of the methods that make up the program. Since these windows describe, in some sense, the outward appearance of the program, we will choose to declare them as `static` instance variables. These "global" variables are initialized once within the `main` method, and are accessed directly in any method that needs to perform textual or graphical input or output. Here, for example, is a rewrite of our mirror-drawing program that uses a static instance variable, `d`, for the drawing window:

Scribble

```
import element.*;
```

---

[3] It *is* possible to initialize them directly where they are declared, but to ensure they are initialized in a particular order, we suggest they are initialized within methods.

```java
public class Scribble
{
    static DrawingWindow d;

    public static Pt opposite(Pt p)
    // pre: p is a valid point
    // post: returns the point that is opposite of p in d
    {
        // note reference of static instance variable, d
        int windowRight = d.bounds().right();
        int windowBottom = d.bounds().bottom();
        return new Pt(windowRight-p.x(), windowBottom-p.y());
    }

    public static void draw()
    // pre: mouse is down
    // post: draws mirrored curve until mouse is released
    {
        // note reference of static instance variable, d
        Pt current, next;
        current = d.getMouse();          // initial location
        while (d.mousePressed())
        {
            next = d.getMouse();         // get next mouse position

            d.moveTo(current);           // draw the "right" segment
            d.lineTo(next);
            d.moveTo(opposite(current)); // draw mirrored segment
            d.lineTo(opposite(next));    // simplified: not passing d

            current = next;
        }
        // mouse is released
    }

    public static void main(String args[])
    {
        d = new DrawingWindow();

        while (true)                     // draw forever
        {
            d.awaitMousePress();         // while mouse pressed
            draw();                      // draw mirrored curve
        }
    }
}
```

The disadvantage to having global variables within a class is that the methods that make use of the variables become less easily copied for use in other classes. It becomes less feasible to to cut and paste methods between classes.

*The average
programmer
writes an
average of six
lines of code
per day.*
Since code is so expensive to produce, the reuse of code should be promoted as much as possible. Avoiding the use of global variables makes it possible to increase code reuse and reduce coding time. We will see later, however, that code reuse is promoted by another concept, called inheritance.

In review, global variables are allowed by the language, but they are to be used sparingly. When in doubt, realize that programs can always be written without the use of static instance variables by simply passing more variables as parameters between methods.

4.7   Chapter Review

In this chapter, we have had our first opportunity to construct our own methods. Methods take on two informal forms: procedures (methods returning `void`) and functions (methods returning a type).

- Complex programs are written as one or more classes that contain several methods. Each method performs one logically complete task.

- Actual parameters are passed to the method by the user. Formal parameters are the internal variables that hold *copies* of the actual parameters.

- Primitive types passed as parameters cannot be modified. Objects may be modified indirectly through their references.

- Procedures perform actions based on their parameters. Since it is difficult for them to modify their parameters, they often have side effects on the screen or modify global variables.

- Functions compute values for use in expressions. They rarely perform input or output. The result value is ideally returned on the last line of the method.

- Static instance variables are often used to maintain the state of a program through many method calls. Within the class, these global variables are declared `static`. The drawing and console windows are good examples of useful static instance variables.

Problems

4.1★   Write a method to compute and return the maximum of two integers.

4.2   Why is it necessary that the answer to Problem 4.1 be a function?

4.3   Write a method that computes the distance between two points, in pixels. (Hint: It can return a double.)

4.4   Write a method that computes the *Manhattan distance* between two points. The Manhattan distance is the shortest distance that may be travelled if a mouse moves from one point to the other using only horizontal and vertical movements.

4.5   Write a method that takes two points p and q. It returns true if (and only if) p *dominates* q. A point dominates another if both of its coordinates are all at least as large as the corresponding coordinates of the other point.

4.6★   Write a function that takes a letter of the alphabet and returns the corresponding telephone digit. (Extra credit: Support phones that include all 26 letters of the alphabet.)

4.7   Describe the signature for functions or procedures associated with the following methods:

  a. A method that tests to see if two Rects overlap.

  b. A method that determines if an integer value is a palindrome; that is, it can be written the same forward and backward.

  c. A method that converts an alphabetic character to its alphabet code (e.g., 'a'=1, 'b'=2, etc.).

  d. A method that computes the greatest common divisor of two integers.

  e. A method that erases the drawing window.

  f. A method that draws the circle that intersects three nonlinear points.

  g. A method that draws n random points in a drawing window.

4.8   Describe the pre- and postconditions associated with each of the methods described in Problem 4.7.

4.9   Write a method that computes π by throwing n darts. Each dart is randomly thrown at a two hundred by two hundred pixel square. It is a hit if it is within 100 pixels of the center. An approximation of π is determined by dividing the number of hits by four times the number of darts.

4.10★   Write a method that prints the digits of a binary representation of an integer.

4.11   Write a method that prints the digits of a n-ary representation of an integer, where $2 <= n <= 16$.

4.12   Write a method that reads in a binary representation from a `ReadStream` and returns an integer.

4.13   Write a method that, using a loop, computes the greatest common divisor two numbers a and b. Euclid's algorithm works as follows: if a or b is zero, return the other. Otherwise, the problem is the same as finding the greatest common divisor of the smaller number and the larger number reduced by the smaller number.

4.14⋆   Write a method that times the length of a double-click (from mouse press to mouse press).

4.15   Write a method that waits for a double-click, where a double-click occurs within a tenth of a second.

4.16⋆   Write a method to draw an n-sided (n must be odd and greater than 2) smooth-rolling shape, with radius r, at center p. This method also accepts an angle that specifies the angle of a vertex from zero degrees. Each side is a portion of a circle whose center is the opposite vertex. Below, for example, we see a three-sided smooth-rolling shape.

Such shapes can be used as rollers, or for manhole covers, since they have a constant diameter.

4.17   Write a program that animates a smooth roller (see Problem 4.16) rolling. The `main` method should be short and contain at most a single loop.

4.18   Write a method that accepts fours points, and returns `true` if (and only if) the first point is contained within the triangle determined by the remaining three.

4.19   Write a method that prints itself out. It may not read any files or streams.

4.8   Laboratory: Writing a Library of Methods

Objective. Develop a collection of commonly used methods.

Discussion. In this lab we will be building up a library of methods that we may find useful at some later time. A little time spent now, carefully considering how these methods ought to be written, can save considerable amounts of time later when code reuse can be employed.

While we will not always know the context in which a method will be used, we can generally make a reasonable guess. Whenever possible, we should try to make the implementation of a method as general as possible. This includes:

- Careful thought about the appropriate information to be passed to each method.

- Consideration of the most general types that can be used as parameters and return values.

- Avoidance, if possible, of the use of static instance (global) variables.

- Appropriate documentation of pre- and postconditions.

Procedure. For each of the following functions and procedures, write the method and test it carefully before going on.

1. A method that picks a random number between low and high, inclusive.

2. A method that picks a random floating point number between low and high, inclusive (Hint: Read up on `Math.random` in Appendix D).

3. A method that draws a triangle in a drawing window.

4. A method that updates the position of three points to reflect three points clicked in the drawing window. A "rubber band" line should be drawn between the mouse and the last point (if any). When the point is placed, the rubber band line becomes solid.

5. A method to compute the distance between two points.

6. A method to compute the midpoint of two points.

7. A method to compute the center of mass (centroid) of three points.

8. A predicate to determine if two circles overlap.

9. A method that returns true if two `Rects` overlap.

10. A method that draws a `String` centered at point p, and returns a `Round-Rect` that was drawn about the `String` to form a button.

11. A method that waits for a both a click and a release within a provided rectangle.

12. A method that pauses for a `double` number of seconds.

Thought questions. Consider the following questions as you complete the lab:

1. How might you write a method that draws all the pixels within the triangular region defined by three points?

2. Is it possible to swap the value of two `ints` without the aid of a third?

Chapter 5

Strings

> *"Mrs. Brown caught a glimpse of the writing on the label.*
> *It said, simply,* PLEASE LOOK AFTER THIS BEAR.
> THANK YOU.*"*
> —Michael Bond

STRINGS PLAY AN OBVIOUS ROLE in supporting textual communication between the computers and people. Some programs even perform *computations* using `String` objects. The features of Java methods that manipulate `Strings` are thus important to programmers.

We have been using `Strings` from the very beginning. A `String` value is a series of characters delimited by double-quotation marks (`'"'`). As you will recall from Chapter 1, special characters such as newlines, tabs, and quotation marks are represented by escape sequences. Escape sequences may appear in variables of type `char`, but they are most frequently found embedded in `Strings`. You are encouraged to return to Chapter 1 to review these details; when you return we will consider basic methods of the `String` class.

5.1   Basic String Operations

Nearly every language provides certain basic functions for the manipulation of strings of characters, and Java is no exception. Java's approach is sometimes unnatural, so the reader is advised to read carefully.

Perhaps the most important operation on `String` variables is the joining of two `Strings` to form one, or *concatenation*. In Java concatenation is accomplished with the '+' operator:

Word warning: 'Catenation' means the same thing!

```
c.out.println("rest" + "rain"); // prints "restrain"
```

If we were to make this a little more complicated, it would be clear that neither of the constituent `Strings` is actually modified by the process of concatenation: the result `String` is an entirely new value. Thus

```
String first = "sure";
String second = "plea";
String combined = second+first;

c.out.print(first+" ");
c.out.print(second+":");
c.out.println(" "+combined);
```

StringOps

prints

```
sure plea: pleasure
```

This, of course, demonstrates one of the main uses of concatenation: to generate complex print statements from various Java values. Java actually has a means of converting *every* type into a `String`. For primitive types the `String` usually is human-readable representation of the internal value. For objects, Java calls the `toString` method (a feature of every object) that explicitly constructs a `String` from the object's current value. This may seem a rather mild feature of the language, until you realize that this allows every object to be printed, which can be quite useful for debugging. We can print out quite elaborate things:

```
DrawingWindow d = new DrawingWindow();
ConsoleWindow c = new ConsoleWindow();
Pt origin = new Pt(0,0);
Pt mouse = d.getMouse();
// generate a line (segment) from the origin to the mouse
Line segment = new Line(origin,mouse);
c.out.println(segment);
```

which prints:

```
<Line: (0,0) to (48,93)>
```

It is easy to imagine that the `toString` method for the `Line` object (called during the printing process) might concatenate the results of calls to the `toString` method for its constituent points!

You can use concatenation as a shorthand for converting arbitrary types to their `String` representation: you need only concatenate the type with the empty `String` (`""`). Whenever one of the operands to the '+' operator is a `String`, the result is a concatenation of `String` representations of both operands.

To determine the length of a string—the number of characters stored within the string—you can apply the `length` method. As an example of its use, the following method pads an existing `String` until it is at least n characters long:

```
public static String pad(String base, int n, char c)
// pre: n >= 0, base is not null
// post: result is base, padded out to length n with copies of c
{
    while (base.length() < n)
    {
        base = base + c;
    }
    return base;
}
```

The following call to pad prints a line of asterisks on the output:

```
c.out.println(pad("",80,'*'));
```

Salsa	J	u	m	p		U	p		a	n	d		K	i	s	s		M	e
	0	1	2	3	4	5	6	7	8	9	10	11	12	13	14	15	16	17	18

Figure 5.1   The indices associated with the various characters of a `String Salsa`.

As we will see in the next section, the `length` method is important to limiting loops that perform operations on each character found within a `String`. For example, when the length of a `String` is 0, we know the `String` is empty.

Exercise 5.1 *Modify the* `pad` *method so that the original string is padded on both sides. The original string is, essentially, centered in* n *characters.*

Exercise 5.2 *How is it possible that the result string of* `pad` *could have more than* n *characters?*

5.1.1   Indexing Strings

`Strings` are, of course, collections of characters. We have seen how we can build up a `String` from a series of characters. We now consider how we might break down a `String`. The main tool is the `charAt` method. This method allows the programmer to retrieve a single character from the `String`. For `charAt` to do its job, we must provide a position, or *index* (see Figure 5.1). The index of the first character in a `String` is 0 (zero), and the indices increase as we move toward the right.

   Suppose we are interested in generating a copy of a headline to a news story, but with spaces between each pair of adjacent characters of the headline. The following function returns such a string. The loop accumulates the characters of `text`, one character at a time. After each character, we append a single space:

StringOps

```
public static String headline(String text)
// pre: text is not a null String
// post: result is text, with a space between original characters
{
    String result = "";      // result might be empty (why?)
    int i;                   // index of character

    for (i = 0; i < text.length(); i++)
    {
        // collects characters of text, but followed by a space
        result = result + text.charAt(i) + ' ';
    }
    return result;
}
```

It is important to note that the space is printed as a `String` and not a character. If the space was concatenated as a character, the output would be a series of integers representing the sum of the ASCII codes of each character with the ASCII code of the space!

Exercise 5.3 *Why?*

We can now use this function to stretch out a flashy headline:

```
c.out.println(">"+headline("NEWS FLASH!")+"<");
```

The output generated looks like:

```
>N E W S   F L A S H ! <
```

Notice that there is a final space on the end of the result string. This is the result of adding the last character of the original text string.

Exercise 5.4 *Rewrite* `headline` *in a way that avoids generating the "extra" space at the end.*

Exercise 5.5 *What is the result of* `headline(headline("NEWS FLASH!"))`?

One of the most common uses of indexing of characters in `String`s is to scan across the characters using a loop and to conditionally do something based on the value of the character. In the following method, we determine if there is a space within a string:

Scans

```
public static boolean containsSpace(String s)
// pre: s is not null
// post: returns true if there is a space in s
{
    boolean found = false; // no spaces found...yet
    int i;

    for (i = 0; i < s.length() && !found; i++)
    {
        if (' ' == s.charAt(i)) found = true;   // found a space
    }
    return found;  // true if a space was found, else false
}
```

The flag `found` is pessimistic—it is set to assume that there are no spaces. When a space is encountered, `found` is set to `true`, and the loop stops on the next iteration (because `!found` is the `false` argument to `&&`). If no spaces are found, then the flag will never be `true`. This style loop is almost idiomatic: a flag signals some condition that is triggered by a *witness* to the condition. In order to compute something, we only need find a witness. Here, the witness is any location in the string that contains a space.

Exercise 5.6 *How would you modify the loop to count and return the number of spaces found within the* String*?*

Perhaps a more useful method is one that counts how many words there are within a String. For the purposes of this experiment, we will consider any sequence of nonspace characters between spaces to be a "word." As we begin to think about this problem, we consider the value of the function when applied to the following strings:

```
""                  // the empty string has 0 words
"   "               // a string with just spaces has 0 words
"my word!"          // this string has two words
"  word "           // this string has one word
```

The trick to solving this problem is to identify those parts of the string that are witnesses to the existence of a distinct word. For example, if there are two words in the string, we need two witnesses. Of course, if there are no words—that is if the string consists of zero or more spaces—there should be no witnesses. If we imagine the process of scanning across the string from left to right, the first indication that there is a word is the first nonspace character within the word. We will use this as the witness. To help us, we will keep track of two boolean values—wasSpace and isSpace: wasSpace is true if the last character was a space, and isSpace is true if the current character is a space. A word is signaled when the last character was a space and the current character is not.

```java
public static int wordCount(String s)
// pre: s is not null
// post: returns the number of space-delimited "words"
{
    int count = 0;
    boolean wasSpace, nowSpace;    // at beginning, not in a word
    int i;

    wasSpace = true;
    for (i = 0; i < s.length(); i++)
    {
        nowSpace = s.charAt(i) == ' ';

        if (wasSpace && !nowSpace)
        {
            count++;
        }
        wasSpace = nowSpace;
    }
    return count;
}
```

The tricky point here is the correct initialization of the variable wasSpace. At the beginning of the string, we must pretend that there was a space before the first character (it's fairly clear that adding a space to the front of the string wouldn't change the word count).

In the previous example, all the characters were scanned to generate one integer value, `count`. Another common loop is one that scans across a `String` and accumulates a result `String` whose characters are derived by transforming each of the characters of the source. The process of converting an uppercase `String` to an lowercase `String` is easily accomplished with a loop and the `toLower` method of Section 4.4.4:

Lowerize

```
public static String toLower(String s)
// pre: s is not null
// post: the uppercase letters of s are converted to lowercase
{
    String result = "";  // here, we'll accumulated the lower string
    char ch;
    int i;

    for (i = 0; i < s.length(); i++)
    {
        ch = s.charAt(i); // for speed, get character once, into ch
        if (isUpper(ch)) ch = toLower(ch); // make uppercase lower
        result += ch;      // append ch onto result
    }
    return result;       // same length as s
}
```

Notice, by the way, that the name of the method is `toLower`, the same as the method that converts uppercase characters to lowercase characters. The difference is in the type of the parameter. If a `String` is passed to `toLower`, the `String` version is called. Otherwise the character version is called. Thus the following method will convert all the input to lowercase, line by line:

```
public static void main(String args[])
{
    ConsoleWindow c = new ConsoleWindow();
    while (!c.input.eof())
    {
        c.out.println(toLower(c.input.readLine()));
    }
    System.exit(0);
}
```

This type of technique for accumulating results in a `String` is important since `Strings` themselves cannot be modified.

For our final application of string indexing, we write a function that converts alphabetic characters to the unique alphabetic character that falls 13 letters away in the alphabet. Nonalphabetic characters are left untouched. This is a primitive cipher technique—called "rot 13"—used by some mail systems. Again, we provide two methods—one that performs the translation of a single character and another that transforms an entire String. The character translation is the most difficult. We begin by computing the offset of the letter in the alphabet, and then determine the ciphered position by adding 13, modulo 26. (This has the effect of wrapping the positions of letters in the second half of the alphabet around to the first half.) Once computed, we convert it back to a character of the appropriate case:

```
public static char rot13(char c)
// post: ciphers c: maps alphabetic characters 13 away in alphabet
{
    int position;
    final int rotation = 13;
    if (('a' <= c) && (c <= 'z'))
    {
        position = c - 'a';
        position = (position + rotation)%26;
        c = (char)(position + 'a');
    }
    else if (('A' <= c) && (c <= 'Z'))
    {
        position = c - 'A';
        position = (position + rotation)%26;
        c = (char)(position + 'A');
    }
    return c;
}
```

For characters that are not letters, both of the if statements fail, and the character is not transformed.

Now, to encode the contents of a String, we need only accumulate the transformations of individual characters within the string. This method is very similar to the String version of the toLower method:

```
public static String rot13(String s)
// pre: s is not null
// post: the alphabetic characters of a string are rot13 encoded
{
    String result = "";
    int i;
    for (i = 0; i < s.length(); i++)
    {
        result += rot13(s.charAt(i));
    }
    return result;
}
```

The process of encoding the input from a keyboard is only a matter of reading in lines from the keyboard until the end-of file mark is encountered. As each line is read, the transformed line is written out:

```
public static void main(String args[])
// post: rot13 encode the console input; output on console
{
    ConsoleWindow c = new ConsoleWindow();
    while (!c.input.eof())
    {
        c.out.println(rot13(c.input.readLine()));
    }
    System.exit(0);
}
}
```

In each of the above `String` transformation methods, the characters are concatenated on the right end of the result `String`. If they are concatenated on the left, the output `String` would be reversed!

As our final example, then, we demonstrate a method for reversing a string. It makes use of our concatenation observation:

ReverseString

```
public static String reverse(String s)
// pre: s is not null
// post: the result is the reverse of the input
{
    String result = "";
    int i;

    for (i = 0; i < s.length(); i++)
    {
        result = s.charAt(i) + result;
    }
    return result;
}
```

Later we will see a *recursive* method to reverse `String`s that is (if it can be imagined) even simpler!

5.1.2 Substring Methods

Sometimes it is necessary to extract portions of `String`s. Suppose, for example, that a line of text is read with several words. To get access to each of the individual words as separate strings, we must be able to extract a *substring*. Java provides several substring methods called `substring`. The simplest form of the method takes an initial index (an integer) and returns the substring starting at the indicated index. Here are some examples:

Substring

```
ConsoleWindow c = new ConsoleWindow();
String s = "concatenate";

c.out.println(s.substring(3)); // prints "catenate"
c.out.println(s.substring(0)); // prints "concatenate"
c.out.println(s.substring(s.length())); // prints blank line
```

An alternative form takes two parameters: the index of the first character of the substring, and the index of the first position that *follows* the substring:

```
String s = "concatenate";

c.out.println(s.substring(3,s.length())); // prints "catenate"
c.out.println(s.substring(1,2));          // prints "o"
c.out.println(s.substring(2,2));          // prints ""
```

The value of the second parameter is selected so that the difference between the parameters is the length of the substring to be extracted.

Given the two forms of the `substring` method, we can develop methods to *omit* a substring. Here, for example, is a method called `omit` that omits the suffix of a `String`, starting at a particular index `i`:

```
public static String omit(String s, int start)
{
    return s.substring(0,start);
}
```

Since we wrote this method, it is not a part of the `String` class, and we must pass the `String` as a parameter. If we wish to omit a substring that lies within the middle of a `String`, we must work a little harder:

```
public static String omit(String s, int start, int finish)
{
    return s.substring(0,start)+s.substring(finish);
}
```

Exercise 5.7 *Rewrite the general (three parameter)* `omit` *procedure using a* `for` *loop and the* `charAt` *method, accumulating the results.*

It is unfortunate that Java does not have a procedure to omit substrings. Such a method would complement the other `String` methods and make the treatment of `Strings` a little more symmetric.

Principle 17 *Seek symmetry in design.*

Asymmetries in the interface of objects like `Strings` are often uncovered when we find ourselves writing methods like `omit`. Asymmetries make interfaces to objects difficult to predict and reduce the utility of a class.

5.1.3 Searching in Strings

Much of the manipulation of `Strings` involves some form of *parsing* or identifying the structure of a `String`'s content. For example, author names in a library information system might be formed as

⟨last-name⟩, ⟨first-name⟩ ⟨middle-name⟩

Identifying the author's last name involves finding the first comma within the `String`. Once found, the location of the comma can be used as the terminal position of a substring command to extract the name. Fortunately, Java `Strings` have several `indexOf` methods that search for characters and substrings. The character form takes a single character as a parameter and returns either the location of the first matching character in the `String`, or −1 if no match is found.

−1: the integer whose intrinsic value is least appreciated!

Exercise 5.8 *Using* `indexOf`, *write a method* `contains` *that returns a boolean value indicating whether or not its parameter (a character) is contained within a* `String`.

Armed with the `indexOf` method, we can sketch code to retrieve the various components of a name from a query `String`:

Library

```
String name, first, middle, last;
int pos;

while (true)
{
    name = c.input.readLine();   // read query & remove spaces
    name = name.trim();          // trim spaces (see Appendix D)
    pos = name.indexOf(',');
    if (pos < 0)                 // string contains last name only
    {
        last = name;
        name = "";
    } else {                     // extract last
        last = name.substring(0,pos);
        name = name.substring(pos+1).trim();
    }
    pos = name.indexOf(' ');     // locate first name
    if (pos < 0)
    {                            // first name only
        first = name;
        middle = "";
    } else {                     // first and middle
        first = name.substring(0,pos);
        middle = name.substring(pos).trim();
    }
    c.out.println("First = >"+first+"<");
    c.out.println("Middle = >"+middle+"<");
    c.out.println("Last = >"+last+"<");
}
```

One line is particularly interesting:

```
name = name.substring(pos+1).trim();
```

The `trim` method removes any leading or trailing spaces. Since the `substring` method returns a `String`, the programmer can "tack on" a `trim` method to immediately remove any unwanted spaces before the assignment.

Exercise 5.9 *Is it legal Java to write* `"  space jelly  ".trim()`*? If not, why? If so, what is the result?*

5.2 Comparison of Strings

With primitive types, operators such as '`==`', '`<`', and '`>`' are responsible for establishing an ordering between values. For `Strings`, we have seen (in Chapter 1) that the `equals` method is responsible for checking character-by-character equality. The ordering of `String` values can be verified with the `compareTo` method. `Strings` are compared letter by letter, from left to right. The first difference in ASCII character values determines the relationship between the `Strings`. For example,

```
"one".compareTo("once")
```

StringTest

would return a value that was greater than zero because the left `String` is "greater than" the right `String` when comparing the third character ('e' versus 'c'). The magnitude of a nonzero value returned by `compareTo` does not generally have a useful interpretation. When making a comparison like:

```
"park".compareTo("parkway")
```

the resulting value is less than zero. The end of a `String`, if encountered during the comparison, is less than any letter that might occur in the other. Some thought demonstrates that these rules are consistent with a *dictionary ordering*—an ordering similar to that of words in a common dictionary. The difficulty occurs when letters of different cases are compared: in the ASCII ordering, uppercase letters are less than lowercase letters.

Generally, if one is interested in testing if `String s` is less than `String t`, the test occurs as follows:

```
s.compareTo(t) < 0
```

while a "less than or equal to" ordering would be tested as

```
s.compareTo(t) <= 0
```

From these, the pattern is made obvious.

Exercise 5.10 *Suppose the* `equals` *method fails to work. How might you use* `compareTo` *to simulate the behavior of the* `equals` *method?*

Of course, one of the most common operations found in Java is the comparison of strings, so it is likely that a programmer will, at some point, attempt a string comparison using

```
s == t
```

It is almost always the case that the comparison is logically incorrect.[1] Such a test checks to see if s and t are *references to the same object* and not the *same value*. Since similarly valued Strings are generated by a variety of techniques, it is likely that the Strings are different objects, and the comparison would fail, even if their values were similar.

5.3   Example: Substitution Cipher Workbench

Suppose we are given a message that is the result of applying a *substitution cipher*:

```
MTVT: KP KPUDPZNKT!
```

Cryptogram

A substitution cipher replaces letters of a plaintext message with alternative letters in a unique way—identical letters in the ciphered message are identical in the plaintext, and *vice versa*. Our goal is to write a program that allows the user to discover, through experimentation, the encoding used to cipher the plaintext. These encoded messages are often called *cryptograms*. Here is an example of the output of the desired program:

```
cryptogram=MTVT: KP KPUDPZNKT!
    guess=    :               !
T A
T is substituted with A
cryptogram=MTVT: KP KPUDPZNKT!
    guess= A A:              A!
K I
K is substituted with I
cryptogram=MTVT: KP KPUDPZNKT!
    guess= A A: I  I      IA!
P N
P is substituted with N
cryptogram=MTVT: KP KPUDPZNKT!
    guess= A A: IN IN  N  IA!
QUIT
Better luck next time!
```

---

[1] An interesting approach to improving the performance of equality testing of Strings is the motivation of the **intern** method of the **String** class. Consistent use of the **intern** method allows the accurate use of s == t to perform **String** comparisons. More details of this technique can be found in the extended documentation of the **String** class online.

The program reads in guesses for the translation of letters in the cryptogram into letters of plaintext. This continues until the entire plaintext message is discovered, or until the user types the incantation QUIT.

We begin by imagining the data that maintain the state of the program. Clearly, several Strings are maintained in the program. First, plainText holds the to-be-discovered message hidden within the running program. It consists of uppercase letters, spaces, and punctuation characters. We choose to represent the cipher by a 26-character String encoder that indicates, for each letter, the corresponding cipher letter. These cipher letters are unique: each letter of the alphabet occurs within encoder exactly once. The plainText String is encoded using the encoder String to generate the cryptogram, or message. This message String is visible to the user. A guess at the plaintext message is also visible at all times. Initially, it is all blank, but over time the user makes guesses as to the encoding scheme. These guesses are maintained in a decoder that serves to rewrite the cryptogram to the plaintext message. As these guesses are applied, the plaintext message appears.

Several important utility methods must be developed. First, it is useful to be able to test for uppercase letters; we borrow the isUpper method previously discussed. Next, it is useful to be able to modify letters of a String. While this cannot be done with a fixed String, a new String can be generated with the required change incorporated. We call this method setCharAt:

```
public static String setCharAt(String s, int i, char c)
// pre: s is not null, 0 <= i < s.length()
// post: returns string s with char at i set to c
{
    String prefix = s.substring(0,i); // part of string before i
    String suffix = s.substring(i+1); // part of string after i
    return prefix + c + suffix;
}
```

Intuitively, the result String is the portion of the String up to the desired location, followed by the new character value, followed by those characters that followed the position in the old String. Note that the prefix or suffix of the String is empty when we set the value of the character at either end of the String.

To generate a random cipher, we can simply take all the letters between 'A' and 'Z' and shuffle them. The result is a String that indicates for each plaintext character (indicated by an index between 0 and 25) the cipher value for that character. Since the entire alphabet is mentioned in the String, each plaintext character is rewritten to a unique cipher value. We shuffle the characters of the String by swapping each character with another in a randomly selected location:

```
public static String shuffle(String source)
// pre: source is not null
// post: shuffles the characters of source
```

```
{
    int i;
    int dest;
    char sc, dc;

    // give every character a chance to move to a new destination
    for (i = 0; i < source.length(); i++)
    {
        dest = rand(0,source.length()-1); // pick destination
        sc = source.charAt(i);             // the ith character
        dc = source.charAt(dest);          // the destination char
        source = setCharAt(source,i,dc);   // swap two
        source = setCharAt(source,dest,sc); // locations
    }
    return source;
}
```

Since each character has a chance to be moved from its location, each character has an opportunity to become the cipher character for an alternative plaintext character, where each plaintext letter is consistently represented by a unique letter.

Exercise 5.11 *How would you test to see if a* String *is shuffled fairly by the* shuffle *procedure? (That is, how would you know if all outcomes are equally likely?)*

Our last utility is one that, given a plaintext String, generates a cryptogram using a particular encoding mechanism. We make use of the fact that the ASCII values of the uppercase characters appear contiguously and in order: by subtracting 'A' from the letter, we get an index into the 26-letter encoder string. At that location is the cipher character:

```
public static String apply(String encoder,String message)
// pre: encoder is not null shuffle of alphabet, message not null
// post: returns message encoded using cypher suggested by encoder
{
    int i;
    char c;
    int alphabetCode;
    String result = "";    // the ciphered string
    for (i = 0; i < message.length(); i++)
    {
        c = message.charAt(i);
        if (isUpper(c))     // other characters untouched
        {
            alphabetCode = c-'A';
            // look up c in the encoder string
            c = encoder.charAt(alphabetCode);
        }
```

```
        result = result + c;
    }
    return result;
}
```

We, of course, could have used the `setCharAt` method on the original message to generate our `result` string.

Given these utilities, we can now sketch out the remaining parts of the program that bring all of these facilities together. First, we have a number of static instance variables that are potentially accessed by several parts of the program:

```
static String encoder;       // the cipher
static String decoder;       // user's guess and encoder inverse
static String plainText;     // the secret message
static String message;       // the encrypted message
static String guess;         // user's guess at secret message
static Random gen;           // random number generator
```

A procedure, `initialize`, is responsible for initializing these variables. (We would show you, but that would show you our message!) The `initialize` procedure is called from `main`, a procedure with a loop that cycles once for each guess that the user makes in trying to decrypt the message.

```
public static void main(String args[])
{
    ConsoleWindow c = new ConsoleWindow();
    String firstWord;                        // first word on input
    char sourceCh, targetCh;                 // coded, uncoded letters

    initialize();                            // encode secret message
    c.out.println("cryptogram="+message);    // print message
    guess = apply(decoder,message);          // generates all spaces
    c.out.println("     guess="+guess);      // decrypted message

    do
    {
        firstWord = c.input.readString();    // read in word
        if (firstWord.equals("QUIT")) {      // to check for QUIT
            break;
        } else {
            sourceCh = firstWord.charAt(0); // get characters
            targetCh = c.input.readString().charAt(0);
            c.out.println(sourceCh+" is substituted with "+targetCh);
            // record user's mapping of characters
            decoder = setCharAt(decoder,sourceCh-'A',targetCh);
            // compute user's decoding of message
            guess = apply(decoder, message);
            c.out.println("cryptogram="+message);
            c.out.println("     guess="+guess);
```

```
            }
            // check to see if the message has been guessed
        } while (!guess.equals(plainText));

        // print appropriate finish message
        if (guess.equals(plainText)) {
            c.out.println("You figured it out!");
        } else {
            c.out.println("Better luck next time!");
        }
        System.exit(0);
    }
```

The `main` procedure simply develops a decoding that acts as an inverse to the encoding over the encrypted message. The user specifies (or respecifies) the individual decodings of letters and the program halts when the plaintext has been uncovered. If the word `QUIT` is typed, the program can be halted prematurely.

5.4   Chapter Review

In this chapter, we have investigated the manipulation of `Strings`. Strings are ordered sequences of characters often used to represent text within a program.

- `String` values are sequences of characters enclosed in double quotation marks (‘"’).

- `String` values cannot be modified. To get a modified version of the `String`, a new `String` must be constructed.

- Individual characters can be accessed using the `charAt` method.

- Substrings—portions of `String` values—can be extracted using two different forms of `substring`. In addition, the `trim` method removes leading and trailing spaces.

- `String`s can be searched using two different forms of the `indexOf` method.

Problems

5.1★ What is the simplest `String`? It is important to remember this, because it is often the simplest case that may be considered when writing methods.

5.2★ Does the `String` class have a `toString` method? How would you verify this?

5.3 Write a method that "adds one" to a single lowercase word stored within a `String`: starting at the rightmost character, the character is incremented (a becomes b, etc.). If the character is z, it is transformed to a, and a "carry" causes the next character to the left to be incremented. If it is necessary to "carry" past the leftmost character, the `String` is then prepended with an a. Check your work by writing a program to count, say, the number of four-letter `Strings`.

5.4 Write a method that sorts the characters of a `String` into ascending order. A simple technique is to make several passes at comparing each pair of characters in the string and exchanging those that are not in order (you may assume the availability of the `setCharAt` method). After pass i, the last i characters of the string are in order.

5.5★ In our method `pad`, what happens if the width n is negative?

5.6 Write a method that, given a `String` s and an integer w, returns a new `String` that, when printed, appears as the nonwhite content of s, centered. Be aware that s may already have leading or trailing whitespace. If the nonwhite portion of s is wider than w, it should be made flush-left.

5.7 The Soundex coding system is used to come up with phonetically consistent codes to represent words. These codes may then be used to index documents. Here's how it works: suppose you are given a word (usually a proper name). The first letter of the word is kept as the first letter of the Soundex key. The next characters of the key (up to three more) are numeric digits that are associated with the next consonants of the word:

coded digit	consonant
1	B P F V
2	C S G J K Q X Z
3	D T
4	L
5	M N
6	R

(Notice that similar consonants are coded similarly.) Thus the word `aardvark` has a Soundex value of `A631`. Write a method that converts a `String` to its Soundex equivalent.

5.8 Write a method that removes the unnecessary spaces from a `String`: leading spaces, trailing spaces, and any duplicate spaces between words.

5.9★ Write a method that, given a `String` potentially containing tabs, returns a tab-free `String` that, when printed, generates the same output. The method replaces each tab with the necessary number of spaces. You may assume that there are tab stops every 8 characters.

5.10   Write a method that, given a `String` containing the digits of a non-negative integer, returns the integer value.

5.11⋆   Write a method that, given a floating point value `d`, a string width `f`, and a number of decimal digits `d` returns a string representation of `d` that is right justified in a `String f` characters wide, and contains `d` decimal places to the right of the decimal point.

5.12⋆   Write a method that, given a `String` of (ASCII) characters, returns the bitwise exclusive-or of all the character values. This value is a primitive *checksum*: the value, when transmitted with the `String`, can detect the mistransmission of a single nonzero character. How?

5.13   Write a method that permutes the possibly (nonunique) characters of a string. Successive applications of this method suggest new permutations of the original `String` and will visit all permutations before the original `String` is revisited.

5.14   Thomas Jefferson, in preparing Lewis and Clark for their expedition, developed what is called the "artichoke" cipher. In this scheme, the letters of the original message are shifted by the alphabet position of each of the letters of *artichoke* turn, repeating the word as many times as necessary. For example, the word "Java" would become "Kspj". (Notice that ROT13 is simply an "m" cipher!) Write a method, `encode`, that takes two strings—a `message` and a `keyword`—and returns the encoding of `message` using the offsets of letters found in `keyword`. (Extra: How is decoding accomplished?)

5.5 Laboratory: The Unspeller

Objective. To gain experience with String manipulations.

Discussion. Because names can be spelled in a variety of ways (Bailey, Baily, Bailly Bailie, etc.), it is useful to come up with an organized approach to reducing a name to its constituent sounds. Once reduced, the distilled form of the word can be used as a key or locator, say in a census. If vowels and double letters are dropped, for example, each of the spellings of Bailey would be found under the entry "bl" (along with Bela and Boyle). The National Archives makes extensive use of the *Soundex* system. In this system, the first letter and the first three consonants form a four symbol key (the technique is described in the text).

Our approach, in this lab, is to write a method that reduces the word using the following process:

1. all double letters are reduced to one, then

2. if the first letter is a vowel, it is converted to an exclamation point ('!'), then

3. all remaining vowels are removed.

Thus `apple` becomes `!pl`; `bible`, `bubble`, and `babble` become `bbl`; `eye` and I become `!`; and `label` and `lable` become `lbl`. This last example demonstrates a potential use for the function: if a word is misspelled, alternatives can be derived from a dictionary by printing all correctly spelled words with similarly reduced forms.

In this lab, you are to write two functions: `isVowel` and `reduce`. `isVowel` is a method that takes a character and returns `true` if the character is a vowel. You may assume that the character is lowercase, and 'y' should be considered a vowel. The `reduce` method takes a word (represented as a lowercase `String`) and returns a `String` that has been fully reduced according to the rules above.

Procedure. Perform the following steps while completing this lab:

1. Write the method `isVowel` *as elegantly as possible*. (Hint: One technique uses the `indexOf` method of `Strings`.)

2. Test `isVowel` fully before going onward.

3. Write the method `reduce`. Be aware that if letters are removed from a `String`, it becomes shorter; this may confuse poorly designed loops. One approach might be to accumulate the result in a second `String`.

4. Test `reduce` fully before going onward. Does it work on cases discussed above? How about `llama` and `squill`?

5. If you are so inclined, you may download the `Undict` class from the book's web site. When included in the project along with a list of words in a text file called `dict` (any word list will do), the following code may be used to print out words in `dict` that sound similar to the `String s`:

```
ConsoleWindow c = new ConsoleWindow();
Undict d = new Undict();
String s;

do
{
    s = c.input.readString();
    c.out.println(d.like(s));
} while (!s.equals("quit"));
```

The program stops when the word `quit` is typed at the console. To verify the correctness of your `reduce` function further, correctly spelled words from the `dict` file should appear among the words found in `Undict` when typed at the keyboard. If they do not, there is a problem with your `reduce` method.

Thought questions. Consider the following questions as you complete the lab:

1. What words `reduce` to `!ck`?

2. Why is the leading vowel rule affective?

3. Outline three improvements to `reduce` that make use of various sound ambiguities in English. Provide examples of misspellings whose identification depends on your improvement.

Chapter 6

Recursion

"'It is good I have some one
To help me,' he said.
'Right here in my hat
On the top of my head!
It is good that I have him
Here with me today.
He helps me a lot.
This is Little Cat A.'"
—Dr. Seuss

THE SELF-REFERENCE FROM WITHIN THE ART FORM ITSELF is what makes this quote from Dr. Seuss and the verse of Figure 6.1 so interesting. It is a common practice among sonneteers to write lines that compare the timelessness of their love to the timelessness of the work itself. Here are the parting thoughts of Shakespeare's Sonnet CXVI:

Love alters not with his brief hours and weeks,
But bears it out even to the edge of doom.
If this be error and upon me proved,
I never writ, nor no man ever loved.

Obviously he has writ! It is this notion of *self-reference* that makes these works of art so interesting. Self-reference is a feature of many interesting works, including Shakespeare's plays within plays, Magritte's picture of a pipe (*Ceci n'est pas une pipe!*), and self-referential works of Escher and Rockwell.

Programming is an art as well and, as a result, it is possible to find self-reference within truly elegant programs. When self-reference is used in computer science, and in particular programming, we call it *recursion*. In this chapter, we apply the notion of recursion in its most common and beautiful way, in the writing of Java's methods. In Chapter 9, we will return to the notion of recursion in the construction of recursive structures for holding data.

Recursion: Chaos meets Order!

6.1 Self-Reference in the Method

When we discussed methods, we realized it was possible both to *call* a method and to *be called* as a method. Can a method call itself? Why not!

I will put Chaos into fourteen lines
And keep him there; and let him thence escape
If he be lucky; let him twist, and ape,
Flood, fire and demon—his adroit designs
Will strain to nothing in the strict confines
Of this sweet Order, where, in pious rape,
I hold his essence and amorphous shape,
Till he with Order mingles and combines.
Past are the hours, the years, of our duress,
His arrogance, our awful servitude:
I have him: his is nothing more or less
Than something simple not yet understood;
I shall not even force him to confess;
Or answer. I will only make him good.

—Edna St. Vincent Millay

Comerado, this is no book,
Who touches this touches a man,
(Is it night?
    are we now together alone?)
It is I you hold and who holds you,
I spring from the pages into your arms—
    decease calls me forth.
O how your fingers drouse me,
Your breath falls around me
    like dew, your pulse
    lulls the tympans of my ear,
I feel immerged from head to foot,
Delicious, enough.

—Walt Whitman, from *Song of Parting*

Figure 6.1   Self-referential verse of Millay and Whitman.

Here is a simple program that we encourage you to consider. It's a slippery program, so when you consider it, consider it carefully.

Wheee

```
public class Wheee
{
    public static void main(String[] args)      // line 0
    {
        System.out.println("Wheee!");           // line 1
        main(args);                             // line 2
    }
}
```

Noting that the authors left out the documentation, it is our job to figure out what this program does.

When the program starts (line 0), ($\star$) the `main` method is called with a collection of `String`s. These `String`s are unimportant to this demonstration, but they are required in every `main` method, so they come along for the ride.

Line 1 is responsible for printing out `Wheee!` on a line by itself.

Line 2 calls a method `main`, passing it `args`. Since `args` is a value of type `String[]` (see line 0), its use in this method call signals a call to *this very same method*, `main`. This is self-reference. *It's recursion.* When the call is initiated, we are precisely in the position of taking up the discussion at the $\star$, above.

"Wheee!": the sound of free-fall!

A full description of the program is too long to lay out here: it simply goes around and around, writing `Wheee!` an infinite number of times while calling more and more copies of `main`. It is, in a sense, an infinite loop:

```
Wheee!
Wheee!
Wheee!
Wheee!
Wheee!
Wheee!
    .
    .
    .
```

Exercise 6.1 *If you haven't run this program yet, we encourage you to do so. It will change the way you look at programming forever.*

This program is a beautiful but dangerous thing. On our computer, the program printed many lines and then—running out of memory keeping track of the many calls to `main`—it crashed.[1]

To control the level of recursion, we might consider the following new procedure. It's recursive as well.

---

[1] We accomplished 9228 calls on a FreeBSD system running JDK1.1.

LimitedWheee

```
public class LimitedWheee
{
    public static void main(String[] args)
    {
        loop(10);
    }

    public static void loop(int times)
    {
        if (times > 0)
        {
            System.out.println("Wheee!");
            loop(times-1);
        }
    }
}
```

It's not exactly the same as our infinite loop program. It passes a parameter called `times`. Our intention is that `times` tells us how many times we want to print `Wheee!` on the output. Let's see if it works for simple cases.

- If `times` is zero, then the condition in the `if` statement will fail, and the method will not print anything; that seems correct.

- If `times` is one, then the condition in the `if` statement will be successful, and the method prints `Wheee!` once. At this point, it (recursively) calls `loop` with a parameter of $1 - 1$, or zero. We've seen what happens in this case: nothing. After the recursive call, the method finishes, having printed exactly one `Wheee!`. It works! *We're on a roll!*

We're on such a roll, actually, that we can describe what happens whenever we pass a positive integer n to `loop`—it prints out `Wheee!` n times.

Exercise 6.2 *If you're not yet convinced, consider the following method:*

```
public static void loop(int times)
{
    System.out.print(times+": ");
    if (times > 0)
    {
        System.out.println("Wheee!");
        loop(times-1);
    }
}
```

Can you correctly predict the output?

An analysis of the `limitedWheee` program helps us with some general rules that apply to all recursive objects. (We use the term *object* here because these rules are true of recursive methods as well as other recursive structures. A

seasoned computer scientist or programmer revisits these notions frequently.)
The rules are

- Recursion must *test a condition*.

- Recursion must have one or more *base cases*.

- Recursion must make *progress* toward the base case.

For methods, these rules are so important we state these characteristics in a
basic programming principle:

Principle 18 *Recursive methods perform tests to identify one or more simple
base cases. In other cases, progress is made toward the solution using recursion
to solve a simpler problem.*

Let's consider these rules as we write up a program to sum up the first **n**
natural numbers:

```
import element.*;

public class RecSum
{
    public static void main(String args[])
    {
        ConsoleWindow c = new ConsoleWindow();
        c.out.println(sum(10));
    }

    public static int sum(int n)
    // pre: n >= 0
    // post: returns 1+2+...+n
    {
        if (n <= 0) return 0;
        else return sum(n-1)+n;
    }
}
```

RecSum

Here, we see that **sum** makes a decision, based on the value of **n**. The simplest
case of this problem is when **n** is 0. Another potential base case might have been
when **n** was 1, but handling zero is more complete and, frankly, more *elegant*.
The base case is so simple we simply return zero.

In the recursive branch of the **if** statement, we do a little work (subtracting
1 from **n**) to make a recursive call whose parameters bring the computation
closer to the base case: computing the sum of 0 natural numbers. Once the
recursive call is computed, we have the sum of the first **n-1** integers, and we
need only add in **n** to finish the computation.

We might visualize the recursive call to a routine as making calls to new
copies of the **sum** procedure (see Figure 6.2). As the computation progresses,

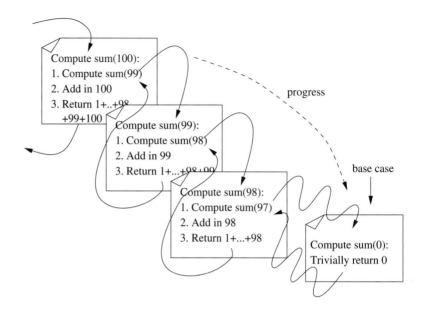

Figure 6.2   The unrolling of the recursion in the recursive **sum** routine.

more and more copies of the method are created, and the computation moves toward the base case. When the base case is encountered, each method performs a portion of the work of constructing the final answer.

We are happy with this solution of the sum program. It involves many features that make the method elegant: it is compact, it is self-referential, and it demonstrates our artistic talent!

Exercise 6.3 *Write a program that computes the* factorial *of n, that is, the* product *of the first n numbers. (Hint: Mathematicians agree that 0! is 1.)*

Of course, recursive methods can be more active. This method converts a **String** to lowercase (the **toLower** method is found on page 117):

Recursion

```
public static String lowerString(String s)
// pre: s is not null
// post: s is converted to lowercase
{
    char c;
    String rest;
    if (s.equals(""))
    {
        return s;
    } else {
        // break the problem apart
```

```
            c = s.charAt(0);
            rest = s.substring(1);
            // solve and glue back together
            return toLower(c)+lowerString(rest);
        }
    }
```

Let's consider this method. Its base case is the simplest String that might have to be converted to lower case: the empty String. (A common mistake is to consider the String that has just a single character, but it is nearly always the case that the empty String is the appropriate example.) In this base case, the empty String has no characters and so can be returned immediately as the answer. In all other cases, we imagine that converting the String happens by first converting the first character and then converting the rest of the String. The process of converting a single character requires only calling toLower (recall that toLower does nothing to characters that are *already* in lower case.) The remainder of the String—which has one fewer characters—is closer to the base case and can be considered a simpler problem that may be solved recursively. Once the rest of the String has been converted to lowercase, we concatenate both the converted character and the converted remainder of the String. The result is a String that is a lowercase version of the original.

The key to solving this last problem was to realize that the resulting string could be composed of two solutions to simpler transformations on the original String. The key to operation is the use of toLower on a single character.

Sometimes, however, the recursive case involves a solution that requires a little more subtle manipulation. Suppose, for example, that we're interested in writing a function that reverses the order of the characters that make up the String. We begin by establishing a relationship between the original String and the reversed String. Notice, for example, that if we reverse a slightly shorter *suffix* of the String, it forms the *prefix* of the reversal of the entire String. It seems reasonable, then, that the splitting of the string into a character and a suffix is a step toward concatenating a reversed suffix and the initial character. Here's the solution:

```
    public static String reverse(String s)
    // pre: s is not null
    // post: returns the reverse of s
    {
        char c;
        String rest;
        if (!s.equals(""))
        {
            c = s.charAt(0); // must be at least one character
            rest = s.substring(1);
            s = reverse(rest)+c;
        }
        return s;
    }
```

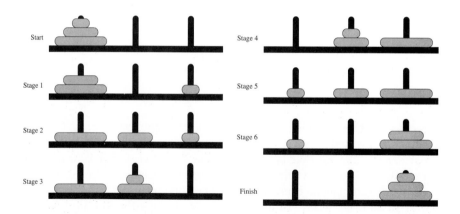

Figure 6.3   The progression of the three-disk Towers of Hanoi puzzle.

Notice that the base case is not explicitly handled here—it is the result of *failing* the test for the complex case. Thus, in the base case, the string is empty, and the **reverse** method does nothing. It is instructive to compare this solution to the solution to the previous problem: the reversal stems from reversing the order of the concatenation. No other work is involved.

Exercise 6.4 *Write the iterative solution—the solution that uses loops—to the* **reverse** *method. Which is more complex? Which seems more elegant? Which requires more local variables?*

6.2   A Classic Example: Towers of Hanoi

One can easily convert each of the previous recursively solved problems into iterative equivalents. For this reason, one might be tempted to argue that the decision to use recursion over a loop-based solution was only a matter of style. It is true, for example, that for efficiency reasons many compilers will convert *tail recursive* problems (problems whose recursive statement appears near the bottom or *tail* of the method) to **while** loops. Some problems, however, are, for various reasons more easily solved using recursion. Consider the following interesting puzzle: the Towers of Hanoi. n disks of radii 1 through n are placed in a pile of decreasing size on one of three pegs (see Figure 6.3 for $n = 3$). The goal is to move the pile, one disk at a time, from one peg to another. The only constraints are that only a top disk may be moved, and that a disk may not be placed upon a disk with a smaller diameter.

The trick is to try a few simple cases. When $n = 1$, the process consists of moving the single disk from the "source" peg to the "destination" peg. When $n = 2$, we must use all three pegs: we move the top (smaller) disk from the

source peg to the "extra" peg, then move the larger disk from the source peg
to the "destination" peg, and then finally move the smaller disk from the extra
peg to the destination. It is fairly easy to see that these three moves are the
most direct route to the solution.

When n is two or more, we decompose the problem into three steps:

1. Move the top $n-1$ disks from the "source" peg to the "extra" peg, possibly
   using the "destination" peg as a help.

2. Move the largest disk from the "source" peg to the "destination."

3. Move the $n-1$ disks from the "extra" peg to the "destination," possibly
   using the "source" peg as an aid.

No rules can be broken by this solution technique. It also turns out that this
recursive technique generates the most direct solution. Steps 1 and 3 involve
the solution of problems that are of size $n-1$, a case that is simpler, and makes
progress to the base case of moving a single disk.

We can now present a solution using the recursive method, hanoi.

Hanoi

```java
import element.*;

public class Hanoi
{
    static ConsoleWindow c;
    public static void main(String[] args)
    // post: solve the n disk tower of hanoi problem
    {
        c = new ConsoleWindow();
        int n = c.input.readInt();
        hanoi(n,"left","right","middle");
    }

    public static void hanoi(int n,
              String source, String destination, String extra)
    // pre: n > 0, source, destination, and extra are distinct
    // post: n disks are moved from source to destination
    {
        if (n == 1)
        {
            c.out.println("Move disk from "+source+
                            " to "+destination);
        } else {
            hanoi(n-1,source,extra,destination);
            hanoi(1,source,destination,extra);
            hanoi(n-1,extra,destination,source);
        }
    }
}
```

Here is the output, when $n = 3$:

```
Move disk from left to right
Move disk from left to middle
Move disk from right to middle
Move disk from left to right
Move disk from middle to left
Move disk from middle to right
Move disk from left to right
```

Notice that this solution uses more than a single recursive call: it uses three-way recursion (it can be reduced to two-way recursion by changing the middle case to a `println` statement, but we believe our solution is more elegant). Solutions that are cast in this manner are not easily converted to a single loop.

6.3   Example: Drawing Lines Using Points

Recursion

Get the point?

Our final problem is to draw a line segment in the drawing window by drawing only single pixels. The difficulty is finding the pixels that most closely approximate the line. If, of course, the endpoints of the line segment are within a pixel of each other, we can draw the endpoints. In fact, line drawing methods routinely draw just one of the endpoints, say, the destination point. Otherwise, a point very close to being on the line is the midpoint—the average of the two endpoints. We need only draw the line segment from the starting point to the midpoint, and then the segment from the midpoint to endpoint.

```
public static void drawLine(int x0, int y0, int x1, int y1)
// pre: drawing window d is not null
// post: a line is drawn on d from (x0,y0) to (x1,y1)
{
    int mx = (x0+x1)/2;             // midpoint
    int my = (y0+y1)/2;
    int dx = Math.abs(x1-x0);       // span in x and y direction
    int dy = Math.abs(y1-y0);
    if (dx <= 1 && dy <= 1)  // very close endpoints
    {
        d.draw(new Pt(x1,y1));      // draw destination
    } else if (dx > 1 || dy > 1)
    {
        drawLine(x0,y0,mx,my);      // draw first half
        drawLine(mx,my,x1,y1);      //     and second half
    }
}
```

Before any pixels are drawn, the computer develops intermediate destination points (first the midpoint, then the point a quarter of the way from (x_0, y_0) to (x_1, y_1), then the point an eighth of the way, and so on) until the destination is next to the start point. The drawing then begins and continues from the source to the destination. Reordering the statements of the `else` part causes the points of the line to be drawn in a different order. Reordering the parameters of the `drawLine` statement also reorders the points drawn.

Exercise 6.5 *Consider how you might write the* `drawLine` *method without using recursion. Which approach seems most elegant? Which draws the straightest line?*

6.4 Challenge: The Self-Reproducing Program

One feature of any reasonably powerful programming language is that there is a program in that language that prints itself out (without directly reading the source file!). Examples of this kind of program are simple to find—computer viruses are, for example, self-reproducing programs.

"Reasonably powerful" is a formal concept.

To see how difficult this is, you might try writing the first few lines of the program that accomplishes this in Java. Our attempt is guided by the philosophy that shorter programs are simpler, so our program begins with a minimal amount of overhead:

```
public class a
{
  public static void main(String[] args)
  {
    System.out.println("public class a");
    System.out.println("{");
    System.out.println("  public static void main(String[] args)");
    System.out.println("  {");
    System.out.println("    System.out.println(\"public class a\");");
```

CloneAttempt

Notice that each print statement prints a line that is four lines before it. It does not (yet) seem to make any progress toward finishing off the program. Perhaps it would help to try to finish off the program. It should end up something like this:

```
    System.out.println("    System.out.println(\"}\");");
    System.out.println("  }");
    System.out.println("}");
  }
}
```

Here, the print statements appear before the statements they print! Sometime between top and the bottom of the program, this relationship has switched. This does not seem possible with straight print statements. Still, theoreticians tell us that *every* language—including Java—has at least one such program.

Clone

Exercise 6.6 *Write a program that is self-reproducing. (You may find arrays useful, but they're not necessary.)*

6.5   Chapter Review

Recursion is an important tool for developing solutions to both simple and complex problems. While it is often used for specifying complex algorithms compactly, its comparison with iterative solutions often proves its elegance.

- Recursion is self-reference in methods: a method that eventually calls itself.

- All recursive programs have three features: a test, a base case, and progress toward a recursive call.

- Progress occurs most often through the reduction of a complex problem to one or more simpler problems. This reduction requires some work. The solution for the complex problem is constructed from the solutions to smaller problems.

- The state of the recursion is usually passed through parameters.

- Recursive procedures depend heavily on local variables and formal parameters. An unusual recursive procedure makes use of global variables.

- Self-reference also occurs in self-reproducing programs. All languages have self-reproducing programs.

We will return to self-reference in Chapter 9, when we discuss self-reference in data structures.

Problems

6.1⋆   Write a recursive method to perform addition of two nonnegative integers. You may only use the increment operator '++', and not addition itself.

6.2   In Problem 6.1, the number of recursive calls might be dependent on the *order* of the parameters provided. For example, `add(0,500)` might run significantly faster (or slower) than `add(500,0)`. Either indicate why this is not the case, or improve your solution to Problem 6.1 to make your method run as fast as possible.

6.3   Write a recursive method to remove double letters from a word (represented by a `String`).

6.4⋆   Write a method `syrLength(n)` that returns the length of the Syracuse sequence starting at value $n > 0$. (Recall that the Syracuse function is $syr(x) = 3x + 1$ if x is odd, and $syr(x) = x/2$ if x is even. The Syracuse sequence starting at n is the sequence $\{n, syr(n), syr(syr(n)), syr^3(n), \ldots, syr^l(n) = 1\}$ for which l is minimum. This sequence is not known to be infinite for any positive n.)

6.5⋆   Write a recursive method to construct a `String` that is the binary representation of an integer.

6.6   Using recursion, write a method to print all the letters of a `String` out in random order.

6.7⋆   Given a loop of the form

```
// i and n are ints
for (i = initial; i < n; i = f(i)) s();
```

write an equivalent recursive method to accomplish this same task.

6.8   Given a recursive method:

```
public static void recur(int n)
{
    if (C(n)) {
        X();
        recur(f(n));
    }
}
```

rewrite the method using an appropriate loop.

6.9   Write a recursive method to perform rot13 encoding of the alphabetic characters of a `String`: map each letter to the unique letter that is 13 away in the alphabet. (See page 132.)

6.10   Write a recursive method to compute the remainder of $n >= 0$ divided by $m > 0$, only using subtraction (no division or modular arithmetic is allowed).

6.11⋆   Euclid's algorithm to compute the *greatest common divisor* of values a and b works as follows: if a or b is zero, return the other. Otherwise, return the greatest common divisor of the smaller number and the larger number reduced by the smaller number.

6.12   Write a recursive procedure to compute x^i, $i >= 0$ and an integer, using the least number of multiplications (and only multiplications may be performed).

6.13   Write a program to print out the lines of the console input stream in reverse order.

6.14   Write a program to print out the characters of the input in reverse order.

6.15   The following method is used to print out the lines of the input but in random order:

```
public static void randomize(ReadStream r)
// pre: r is a valid read stream
// post: the output is the input, with lines randomly shuffled
{
    String l = r.readLine();
    if (random number < .5)
    {
        Randomize(r);
```

```
            c.out.println(1);
        } else {
            c.out.println(1);
            Randomize(r);
        }
    }
```

Do you believe the postcondition? If you do, explain why. If you do not, suggest why the output is not randomly shuffled.

6.16★   Write a program to draw the following treelike shape:

Each of the three branches of the tree is itself a tree-like shape.

6.17   In the `drawLine` procedure, describe what happens if the two recursive calls are interchanged.

6.18   In the `drawLine` procedure, describe what happens if the first of the two recursive calls is replaced with `drawLine(mx,my,x0,y0)`.

6.6   Laboratory: Recursive Doodlings

Objective. To experiment with recursion using graphics.

Discussion. We are all used to drawing silly "doodles" on napkins and scraps of paper. The purpose of this assignment is to construct computerized doodles in the drawing window. We will focus on triangle-shaped doodles that are constructed in a variety of ways.

Our first technique is to draw a triangle and then connect one "top" vertex to the midpoint on the opposite side. The result is two triangles that can be further subdivided. When each of these triangles is halved, the newest vertex (the one that was once a midpoint) is considered the top of each. The doodling continues, recursively, until the distance from the top to the midpoint becomes shorter than, say, 10 pixels. Here is the progression of the figures drawn with this technique:

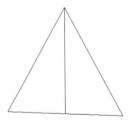 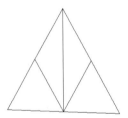 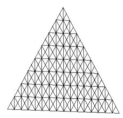

The second technique divides the triangle into three subtriangles by connecting the midpoint of each side to the *centroid* (a point that is the coordinate-wise average of the three vertices). If the centroid is far from each of the vertices, each of the three triangles is further subdivided. Here is the progression of the figures drawn with this technique:

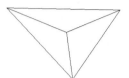 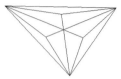 

Our final technique divides the triangle into four subtriangles by connecting each of the three midpoints. The three corner triangles are further subdivided if each of their sides is sufficiently large. This pretty doodle has the following progression:

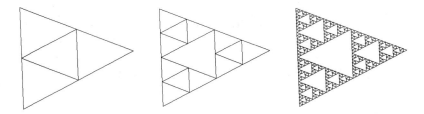

Procedure. Follow these steps to complete at least two of the three doodle methods:

1. Download the file `lab/doodle.java` from the book's web site. Peruse this file. It contains working code for determining the distance between two points, the point halfway between two others, and a utility method for reading three vertices from the drawing window. Computing the centroid of three points is similar to computing the midpoint of two.

2. Pick one of the three doodle techniques, and write a recursive method `doodle` that accepts three points and draws a doodle within that triangle. It is useful to declare a constant for the minimum length side that may be easily changed.

   Make sure that your recursive method has all the features we might expect: a base case, self reference, and progress.

3. Test your program with triangles of various sizes.

4. Complete another program that implements one of the other doodle forms.

Thought questions. Consider the following questions as you complete the lab:

1. What is "progress" in these recursive methods?

2. Suppose you change the color of the pen before each recursive call within one of your doodles. Can you predict the color pattern?

3. What happens if you change the order of the actual parameters in the recursive calls? Which of the black-and-white doodles would be different?

Chapter 7

Arrays and Vectors

> *"She took down a jar from one of the shelves as she*
> *passed; it was labeled 'ORANGE MARMALADE', but to*
> *her great disappointment it was empty..., so managed to*
> *put it into one of the cupboards as she fell past it."*
>
> —Lewis Carroll

SO FAR, LIFE AS A JAVA PROGRAMMER SEEMS SIMPLE. In fact, some may argue that our programs have been *too* simple. In Chapter 3 we learned that we can design programs that run for an arbitrary length of time (even forever), but we have yet to be able to manage large quantities of data at one time. Our first step toward understanding how to manipulate more than a handful of variables is an investigation of two important Java constructs—the *array* and the *vector*.

The array provides an efficient method for storing lots of data together in a single location. The `Vector` is a Java class that acts much like an array, but provides some basic extensions that are commonly required by programs using arrays. As we will see, the extensions hide the details of basic array manipulations, but are provided at a cost of sometimes unnecessary abstraction.

7.1 Arrays

The array is a *data structure* that is common to nearly all programming languages. When working with variables, a useful bookkeeping technique is to draw a box near the variable name: the box holds the current value of the variable as we simulate the program by hand. Array variables, on the other hand, potentially have more than one value associated with the variable. Our box analogy would be extended to a series or an *array* of boxes. These values, of course, are often referred to individually, so we associate a number or an *index* with each location. These indices are used with the variable name to identify the value to be used in a computation.

Let's look at a computation that might make use of an array. We'll discuss the details shortly:

```
import element.*;
public class MonthTable
{
    public static void main(String args[])
    {
        ConsoleWindow c = new ConsoleWindow();
```

MonthTable

```
            int daysInMonth[] = { 31, 28, 31, 30, 31, 30, 31,
                                  31, 30, 31, 30, 31 };
            String monthName[] = { "January","February","March","April",
                                  "May","June","July","August","September",
                                  "October", "November", "December" };
            int i, shortest;

            c.out.println("Long months:");
            for (i = 0; i < 12; i++)
            {
                if (daysInMonth[i] == 31) c.out.println(monthName[i]);
            }
            c.out.print("A shortest month is ");
            shortest = 0;
            for (i = 1; i < 12; i++)
            {
                if (daysInMonth[i] < daysInMonth[shortest])
                    shortest = i;
            }
            c.out.println(monthName[shortest]+".");
        }
    }
```

This program simply generates the output

```
Long months:
January
March
May
July
August
October
December
A shortest month is February.
```

At the top of this program, we see declarations for two different arrays—days-
InMonth and monthName. The square brackets ('[]') indicate to Java that the
variable is an array, not a single-valued or *scalar* variable. We'll see these square
brackets are used later to specify an index, but here they just signal that the
variable is an array. The value of an array variable is a *reference* to a series of
values of the specified type. Thus daysInMonth is an array of int variables.

As with object references, initially the reference does not refer to anything
useful. The initialization we see here is from an array constructed from a list of
values enclosed between curly braces ('{}'). It is important to remember that
each of the elements must be of the desired type; there is no mixing of types
(we'll see how to do that later). The variable monthName is similar, but the type
of each element is a String. It is important that the order of the month names
is the same as the order of month lengths. (We have actually seen another
array declared—main's parameter, args—which we may now understand to be
an array of Strings that are passed to every Java application.)

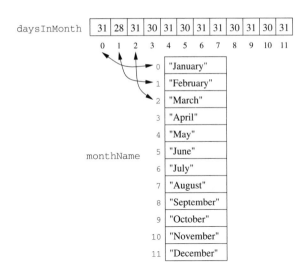

Figure 7.1 The arrays declared in the MonthTable program. One array keeps track of month lengths; the other, month names. It is important that corresponding data values appear in equivalent positions within the two arrays.

The elements of the array are stored in the order suggested. And that order determines the association of array indices with values. The first element is stored at location 0 (zero), the second at location 1, and so on. Thus, if there are 12 elements in an array, they are indexed by integers 0 through 11. Again, this indexing scheme may seem strange at first, but soon it will become natural. We, of course, have seen a similar indexing mechanism for the characters of a String. It is often useful to think of the index as a *distance from the first element* of the array (see Figure 7.1).

The first task of this program is to print out all of the long months—months with 31 days. Because we know that there will be a fixed number of months to consider, we use a for loop to consider each element of the daysInMonth array, selectively printing the names of months with exactly 31 days. The form of the for loop is to start at zero (0), and to loop while the index (i) is *less than* the length of the array (12). Again, this may seem strange, but it is an idiom of Java programming; other loop forms may make your code somewhat less readable to an experienced Java programmer. (While this may not be important to you now, effective collaboration with other programmers is a skill to be learned.)

As with a String, an array is *random access*, meaning that the elements of the array may be accessed in any order. In our second loop, for example, we identify the shortest month of the year by keeping track of the index of the month that is "shortest so far" (see Figure 7.2). This shortest month is initially assumed to be January, at index 0. The program then loops over the remaining

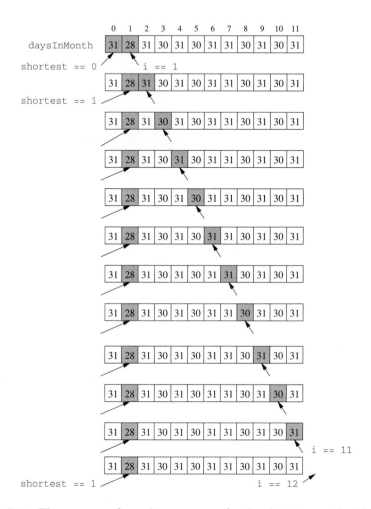

Figure 7.2   The progress of searching an array for the shortest month. The index of the smallest value (so far) is kept and compared with values to the right (two gray values). After a complete pass through the array of months, `shortest` must be the index to the smallest value.

months comparing the length of month i with that of month `shortest`. If month i is shorter, as it is with February when i is 1, then the `shortest` index is updated to "point" to that month. When the loop is finished, `shortest` is the index of the month with the fewest number of days.

This program can be improved in a variety of ways. For example, we use the value 12 as a constant to represent the number of months. We can ask the array directly what its length is and use that value instead. Here's how the `for` loop is written:

```
for (i = 0; i < monthName.length; i++)
```

(Notice that there are no parentheses after `length`.) In this way, if we changed our program to include more months, we need only change the initialization of the array. The `for` loop is automatically updated to loop across the longer array. We, of course, must be careful to lengthen both arrays at the same time!

MonthTable2

Our second modification is to provide an alternative initialization of the array of `int`s.

```
int daysInMonth[] = new int[12]; // (or use int[monthName.length])

// first, set all month lengths to 31
for (i = 0; i < daysInMonth.length; i++)
{
    daysInMonth[i] = 31;
}
// then set the shorter month lengths
daysInMonth[3] = daysInMonth[5] =
    daysInMonth[8] = daysInMonth[10] = 30;
daysInMonth[1] = 28;
```

Here, `daysInMonth` is initialized to refer to a new array of 12 integers, each of which takes on a default value (for `int`s, the default is zero). At this point, we can initialize the elements of the array as a series of assignments. While it is not obviously an improvement over the bulk initialization technique, it is desirable in some circumstances when only a few elements of the array are different.

7.1.1   Example: The Sieve of Eratosthenes

Sometimes we think of the *index* to the array as the data. As an example, we compute a list of prime numbers (positive numbers n with exactly two factors— 1 and n) by implementing the Sieve of Eratosthenes. This technique is best tested on a piece of paper. Write down all the integers, in order, from 2 to n (for some large n). We now consider each value in order, from lowest to highest (see Figure 7.3):

"Exactly two factors": 1 isn't prime

- If the number is crossed out, it is not prime (it's *composite*). In fact, since the number has been crossed out by one of its factors, all of its multiples have been crossed out as well.

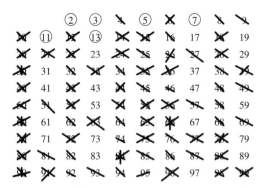

Figure 7.3   The sieve of Eratosthenes after having crossed out multiples of (circled) values up to 13. (Since $13^2 > 99$ the uncrossed values are, in fact, all prime.)

- If the number is not crossed out so far, it is prime. Circle it. We then cross out each of the nontrivial multiples of the newly discovered prime: each of these values is, after all, divisible by a number (the prime) other than one and the value itself.

After we have crossed out the multiples of every uncrossed-out number, what remains is a list of circled primes.

Exercise 7.1 *How many times does a composite number get crossed out?*

Our implementation uses an array of boolean values, called `prime`. We interpret `prime[n]` as the answer to the question: *Is n potentially a prime number?* To consider primes less than or equal to `max`, we create an array of `max+1` booleans. We will consistently ignore the entries in locations 0 and 1, since they're not potential primes. Here is an overview of our program, the `main` method:

Sieve

```
public static void main(String args[])
// post: compute the primes between 2 and max, inclusive
{
    ConsoleWindow c = new ConsoleWindow();
    final int max = 100;
    boolean prime[] = new boolean[max+1];
    int n;

    // assume all values are potentially prime
    initialize(prime);

    // cross out multiples of uncrossed numbers
    for (n = 2; n <= max; n++)
```

```
    {
        if (prime[n]) // needn't cross out multiples of composites
        {
            crossOut(n,prime);
        }
    }

    // print out indices of entries that remain "prime"
    print(c,prime);
}
```

If a number is potentially prime, it has not been crossed out. Since the sieve starts with all the numbers *not* crossed out, the `initialize` method sets all of the boolean values in the array to `true`; every number is prime until we find a witness to the fact that it is composite:

```
public static void initialize(boolean prime[])
// pre: prime is an array of booleans
// post: all entries in prime are optimistically set to true
{
    int n;
    // initialize the array (entries 0,1 unused)
    for (n = 2; n < prime.length; n++)
    {
        prime[n] = true;
    }
}
```

Every time a prime is found in the `main` loop, we cross out the nontrivial multiples (m) of n. The `if` statement in `main` is a simple check to see if a call to `crossOut` is even necessary—if n is not prime, then it is a composite number, that is, a multiple of a smaller value. This smaller value has already crossed out all the multiples of n, and we needn't duplicate that effort. Still, the `if` can be avoided, without changing the result.

```
public static void crossOut(int n, boolean prime[])
// pre: n < prime.length
// post: all nontrivial multiples (m) of n are marked composite
{
    int m;

    for (m = 2*n; m < prime.length; m += n)
    {
        prime[m] = false;
    }
}
```

Notice that the loop in `crossOut` is a little unusual. It is responsible for making sure that m takes on all the nontrivial multiples of n. Java's `for` loops provide for a great flexibility, but they can be confusing to read if you're not careful.

By the time we get to calling `print`, the `prime` array has a `true` at every location whose index is prime. At all other locations, the number has been crossed out once for each factor encountered. Thus, `print` simply prints out the indices of all the elements of the `prime` array that are `true`:

```
public static void print(ConsoleWindow c, boolean prime[])
// pre: c is not null, prime is a computed sieve
// post: the indices of the true entries of prime are printed on c
{
    int n;
    // print out primes: uncrossed numbers
    for (n = 2; n < prime.length; n++)
    {
        if (prime[n]) {
            c.out.print(n+" ");
        }
    }
    c.out.println();
}
```

When put together, the entire program will print out primes between 2 and `max`. The value of `max`, of course, may be changed to generate longer lists of primes.

Exercise 7.2 *A perfect number is equal to the sum of its factors other than itself. Examples include 6 and 28. Modify the sieve program to print a list of perfect numbers less than 10000.*

Notice that this example, essentially, has treated an array of booleans as a set of integers between 0 and `max`. While Java does not directly support the manipulation of sets of numbers, this representation of a set can be useful (see Problem 7.8).

7.1.2 Variable Length Arrays

In our next example, we read in several lines of a poem and print the lines out in random order. We'll put an upper limit on the number of lines of poetry that we can handle—say, `max`. Initially, we allocate an array that potentially holds `max Strings`. We also maintain an integer `count` that reminds us of how many of the array elements actually are being used, that is, how many lines of poetry are stored within the array.

Poetry

```
String poem[] = new String[max];
int count;
```

If, for example, `count` is 6, we know that locations 0 through 5 hold valid `Strings`, but entries 6 through `max-1` are not to be considered. Since the entries at `count` and above are possibly undefined, it is important that the program never read a value from the array at that point or beyond. We will use the convention that we will read until we encounter the end of the file. Each line is placed in location `count`. Once the line has been stored, the `count` is increased.

```
count = 0;
while (!c.input.eof())
{
    poem[count] = c.input.readLine();
    count++;
}
```

One flaw in our approach is that we will not have enough room in the array if we try to read in more than max lines of poetry. To avoid trying to store values beyond the end of the array, we can modify our loop so as to stop reading when the array reaches its limit:

```
count = 0;
while ((count < max) && (!c.input.eof()))
{
    poem[count] = c.input.readLine();
    count++;
}
```

Later we will see this limitation is easily removed if we use Vectors. At this point, the poem is stored, line-by-line, within the array. Printing the poem is simply a matter of printing each of the strings in the poem array:

```
int i;
for (i = 0; i < count; i++)
{
    c.out.println(poem[i]);  // print line i
}
```

Writing out the poem in random order takes a little more care. We'll use a two-step process (see Figure 7.4). First, pick one of the lines entries and print it out. Then, logically remove the line from further consideration by copying the last line (which has not been printed) to this location. We can then safely decrement the lines variable, indicating that there is one fewer remaining line to be printed. The loop looks like the following:

```
int lines = count;
int selected;
while (lines > 0)
{
    // pick a line number from 0 to lines-1
    selected = Math.abs(g.nextInt())%lines;
    // print the selected line
    c.out.println(poem[selected]);
    // overwrite selected line with last line
    poem[selected] = poem[lines-1];
    // decrement logical # of lines remaining
    lines--;
}
```

At the end of the loop, lines is zero: all the lines have been printed.

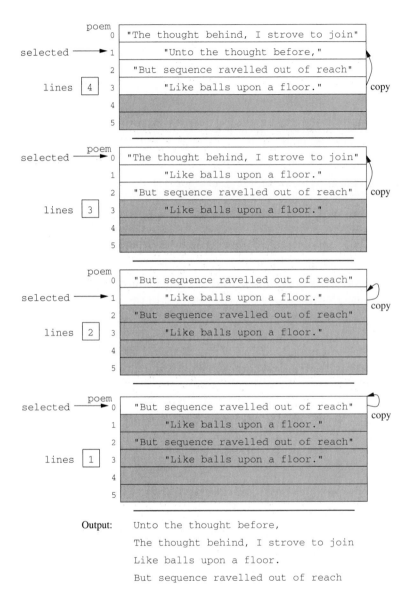

Output: Unto the thought before,
          The thought behind, I strove to join
          Like balls upon a floor.
          But sequence ravelled out of reach

Figure 7.4   The printing of lines from a poem by Emily Dickinson, in random order. At each step, a line is selected, printed, and overwritten by the last remaining line. After **lines** steps, the random poetry is complete.

all
fits
news
print
that
the
stop

Figure 7.5   The display of the **news** program.

7.1.3   Example: Printing Ransom Notes

We now consider a program to print a number of buttons, each of which has an associated label (see Figure 7.5). After the buttons are drawn, pressing the buttons causes the corresponding label to be printed on the output. The program stops when the button marked **stop** is pressed.

Ideal for generating ransom notes!

To begin with, we keep two arrays of the same length: one is an array of labels and the other is an array of the corresponding rounded rectangles.

```
String labels[] = { "all", "fits", "news", "print",
                    "that", "the", "stop" };
RoundRect buttons[] = new RoundRect[labels.length];
```

News

The array of rounded rectangle references is declared to be exactly the same length as the array of labels. These references will eventually refer to rounded rectangles that describe the outlines of pressable buttons. Our first task is to display the buttons on the screen. We use a technique that is similar to the painting of crosswalks by your local highway department: a *template* is built and used once for each item drawn. Here, we use a variable **template**. It is constructed to be in the correct location for the first button. Our loop then constructs a new button using the template and paints it on the screen along with the label. Once used, the template moves on.

"The moving finger writes; and having writ, moves on...."
—Omar Khayyám

```
public static void drawButtons(RoundRect buttons[], String labels[])
// pre: the labels are valid
// post: labels (and associated buttons) are drawn on the screen
{
    final int width = 30, height = 10;
    final int spacing = 5;
    int n = labels.length;
    int i;

    // the template
    RoundRect template = new RoundRect(10, 10, width, height);

    for (i = 0; i < n; i++)
```

```
        {
            // copy template
            buttons[i] = new RoundRect(template);
            d.draw(buttons[i]);
            d.draw(new Text(labels[i],
                            buttons[i].right()+spacing,
                            buttons[i].bottom()));
            // move template downward
            template.move(0, height+spacing);
        }
    }
```

Once we have drawn the buttons, we must be able to accept a mouse press and return the `String` associated with the selected button. This is accomplished by keeping a "virtual finger" on the last button that contains the mouse press. This technique is like the selection of the shortest month: we keep track of the last button that contained the mouse *so far*.

```
    public static int selectButton(RoundRect buttons[])
    // pre: buttons are valid, and drawn on screen
    // post: the index of the button pressed is returned
    {
        int i;
        Pt pressPoint;
        int which = -1;

        pressPoint = d.awaitMousePress();
        d.awaitMouseRelease();
        for (i = 0; i < buttons.length; i++)
        {
            if (buttons[i].contains(pressPoint)) which = i;
        }
        if (which == -1) which = selectButton(buttons);
        return which;
    }
```

As the loop progresses, the index of any `RoundRect` that contains the point of press will be remembered. If a valid button is not pressed, we try again (recursively!); otherwise the indicated `String` is returned.

Exercise 7.3 *What type of loop would you use to replace the recursion in the* `selectButton` *procedure?*

Finally, our `main` method simply draws the buttons on the screen and prints the labels as they are selected. The method halts when the "stop" button is pressed.

```
    public static void main(String args[])
    {
        d = new DrawingWindow();
```

```
c = new ConsoleWindow();
String labels[] = { "all", "fits", "news", "print",
                    "that", "the", "stop" };
RoundRect buttons[] = new RoundRect[labels.length];
int index;

drawButtons(buttons,labels);
while (true)
{
    index = selectButton(buttons);
    // stop on the press of button "stop"
    if (labels[index].equals("stop")) break;
    c.out.print(labels[index]+" ");
    c.out.flush();  // make word show up immediately in console
}
c.out.println();
}
```

Our sample output is based on an old printer's witticism about the *New York Times*:

```
print all the news that fits the print
```

Exercise 7.4 *What changes are necessary to add a new button labeled, say, "money"?*

Exercise 7.5 *Modify the* News *program so that the message is stored in an array of* String *values. This will allow you to add a new "delete" button that forgets the last word added to the message (if any). When the "stop" button is pressed, the array of words is printed in order.*

7.2   Multidimensional Arrays

The elements of an array can be anything—including other arrays. In Java we are provided a shorthand for declaring and allocating arrays of two or more dimensions: we simply tack on the additional dimensions in both the declaration and **new** constructs. For example, here is a declaration for a multiplication table with 10 rows and 20 columns:

```
int table[][] = new int[10][20];
```

Mult

After such a declaration, you should imagine **table** to be an array of 10 elements, each of which is itself an array of 20 integers (see Figure 7.6). Traditionally, we consider the first dimension to be the number of rows, while the second dimension is the number of columns. (Frankly, it doesn't matter, as long as you are consistent in your use of the array.) What makes this a shorthand is that the rows are automatically allocated for you. Any time that you can get a

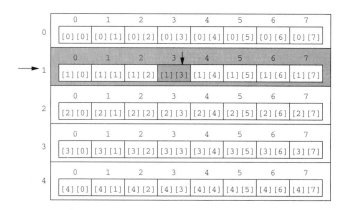

Figure 7.6   The logical layout of a 5×8 array. Element `[1][3]` (highlighted) is the fourth element of the second row array.

programming language to automatically do something for you as a programmer, you should take advantage of the situation!

In case you're inclined to avoid multidimensional shorthand, the previous declaration would be equivalent to the somewhat messier:

Astronomers: this is not a Messier object!

```
// table is an array of arrays of ints
int[] table[] = new int[10] [];
int i;

// now, allocate each of the 20 element rows
for (i = 0; i < table.length; i++)
{
    table[i] = new int[20];
}
```

This last bit of code is painful to read, so divert your eyes! If, however, you're interested in developing multidimensional arrays that have unusual shapes (for example, if you're fond of triangular arrays), this latter technique is necessary.

Now, once a multidimensional array is declared, it may be accessed as we might expect: simply tack on the indices associated with the added dimensions. We might fill out our multiplication table with a pair of nested loops:

```
int row, column;
for (row = 0; row < 10; row++)
{
    for (column = 0; column < 20; column++)
    {
        table[row][column] = row * column;
    }
}
```

Java provides some flexibility not found in other languages. For example, as we stated above, `mult` is simply an array of arrays. Thus

```
c.out.println("table has "+table.length+" rows");
```

tells us the number of rows, while

```
c.out.println("table has "+table[0].length+" columns");
```

tells us the number of items in the first row. We can now make our nested loop work on an array of any shape, by directly asking the array the pertinent questions:

```
for (row = 0; row < table.length; row++)
{
    for (column = 0; column < table[row].length; column++)
    {
        //...
```

7.2.1   Example: The Life Simulation

As an example of the use of multidimensional arrays, we write a population simulation program, called `Life`. Its inventor is John Conway. The simulation follows the progress of a colony of individuals that reside within a square array (see Figure 7.7). We'll only be interested in whether or not an individual is alive or dead, so it's common to represent the individuals by boolean values— `OCCUPIED` (`true`) indicates the presence of an organism in the particular cell; `VACANT` (`false`) indicates a vacancy.

Three carefully crafted rules govern life and death in the array. All are based on the eight potential neighbors of a cell:

Birth. An empty cell surrounded by three neighbors produces a new individual.

Life. Any individual surrounded by 2 or 3 neighbors lives on.

Death. Any individual surrounded by fewer than 2 or greater than 3 neighbors dies from loneliness or overcrowding, respectively.

For ease in applying rules, we will assume the left side of the array is neighbors with the right side, and that the individuals along the top are neighbors with those along the bottom. (This "petri dish" is a *torus*.) The simulation imposes these rules on all cells of the array simultaneously. One application of the rules across the array we will call a *generation*.

We will provide a graphical version of the simulation, with the petri dish extending across the entire drawing window. When our program begins, the user clicks on the screen to place (or remove) an individual from the array. This process continues until the user drags the mouse from one cell to another. (We realize this is not an ideal method for ending the editing session, but we have to leave *some* room for improvement!) In this case, no individuals are modified

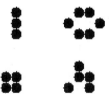

Figure 7.7 A `Life` population consisting of several groups of individuals. Which will live on, and which will die off?

and simulation begins. The simulation stops and returns to editing mode when the user clicks the mouse.

Here's our `main` method. It is typically short and declares a square array that fits within a square drawing window:

Life

```
static DrawingWindow d;
final static int SIZE = 10;          // edge size of petri dish
final static boolean OCCUPIED = true; // named constant for life
final static boolean VACANT = false;  // named constant for vacancy

public static void main(String args[])
{
    d = new DrawingWindow(400,400);
    int n = d.bounds().width()/SIZE;
    boolean dish[][] = new boolean[n][n];

    initialize(dish);                // clear dish
    while (true)
    {
        edit(dish);                  // make changes
        while (!d.mousePressed())    // life goes on...
        {
            simulate(dish);
        }
        d.awaitMouseRelease();       // until click
    }
}
```

Our array is carefully sized to fit within the drawing window, with each cell having a width and height of 10. Notice that if we change the dimensions of the drawing window, or the cell size, the array is automatically sized appropriately.

(The authors made very large and stable populations after this writing! Can you?) An outer loop executes once for each time we simulate an edited population. The inner loop simulates the dish as long as the mouse is not pressed. Note that SIZE, OCCUPIED, and VACANT are declared as final instance variables for easy access by other methods.

The initialize method simply sets all the locations to VACANT and paints the (empty) dish on the screen.

```
public static void initialize(boolean dish[][])
// pre: the dish has been allocated
// post: the population is cleared from the dish
{
    // we use a square dish, so n is the width and height
    int n = dish.length;
    int r,c;
    for (r = 0; r < n; r++)        // all rows
    {
        for (c = 0; c < n; c++)  // all entries within a row
        {
            dish[r][c] = VACANT; // are vacant
        }
    }
    paint(dish);                   // update the screen
}
```

Here, as we write the program, we're not sure how paint will do its job, but we can be sure that paint will need the contents of the dish. Notice that the size of the dish is determined from the array itself. We could have made n of main a global variable as well.

The paint method has a very similar structure, but draws the individuals on the screen as small disks. Notice that we use hold and release to paint the entire colony as a single unit. This approach can also speed up graphics that would otherwise have to be synchronized with Java's painting system, which can be slow:

```
public static void paint(boolean dish[][])
// pre: dish is allocated with valid contents
// post: dish is represented by dots on the screen
{
    int n = dish.length;
    int r,c;
    d.hold();      // we'll delay the update of the display
    d.clear(d.bounds());              // erase screen
    for (r = 0; r < n; r++)           // every row
    {
        for (c = 0; c < n; c++)       // and every cell within row
        {
            if (dish[r][c] == OCCUPIED) // is painted if occupied
            {
```

```
                    d.fill(new Oval(c*SIZE,r*SIZE,SIZE,SIZE));
                }
            }
        }
        d.release(); // update the display
    }
```

Now we consider the process of editing the population. We realize that if the entire dish takes up the drawing window, then we can number the rows and columns from the upper left of the screen. Each cell occupies size pixels along each dimension. If a mouse is pressed in the window, then the "array coordinates" (the row and column) can be computed from the mouse coordinates. The row number is simply the mouse's y coordinate divided by size with the remainder thrown away. Similarly, the column number can be gleaned from the x coordinate. Both the mouse press and release positions are kept to determine if any nontrivial dragging of the mouse has occurred. In that case, we break from what would otherwise be an infinite loop:

A wonderful reason to index arrays from 0

```
public static void edit(boolean dish[][])
// pre: the dish is allocated
// post: individual cells in the dish have been toggled;
//       mouse was dragged to stop editing
{
    int n = dish.length;
    paint(dish);
    while (true)
    {
        // read the mouse press and release points
        Pt press = d.awaitMousePress();
        Pt release = d.awaitMouseRelease();

        // convert to row and column numbers
        int pr = press.y()/SIZE;
        int pc = press.x()/SIZE;
        int rr = release.y()/SIZE;
        int rc = release.x()/SIZE;

        if (pr != rr || pc != rc)
        {
            break; // dragging? stop this loop!
        }
        // not a click, so change OCCUPIED<->VACANT
        dish[pr][pc] = !dish[pr][pc];
        // update screen
        paint(dish);
    }
}
```

Since the individuals are stored as boolean values, the logical negation ('!') operation can be used to toggle between life and death. Finally, painting the screen after each edit gives immediate feedback about the state of the population.

We might take a breath here and look back at the simplicity of the previous procedure. Essentially, we've provided the user with n^2 buttons that allow us fine, interactive control over the contents of our population—a pretty piece of Java.

Exercise 7.6 *Improve this code by having it paint only the cell that changes.*

Our final two methods do all of the computational work. The first method counts the number of neighbors by scanning over all of the nine cells in the local neighborhood about a particular cell. The r and c here are offsets that describe *relative* indices. So, for example, when r==-1, we're counting neighbors above a particular location.

```
public static int neighbors(boolean dish[][], int row, int col)
// pre: 0 <= row, col < dish.length
// post: returns the number of OCCUPIED cells surrounding (row,col)
//       on torus
{
    int n = dish.length;
    int r, c;
    int pop = 0;
    for (r = -1; r <= 1; r++)        // for rows about row
    {
        for (c = -1; c <= 1; c++)    // and columns about col
        {
            if (r != 0 || c != 0)    // if not (row,col)
            {                        // count any occupied cells
                if (dish[(row+n+r)%n][(col+n+c)%n]==OCCUPIED) pop++;
            }
        }
    }
    return pop;
}
```

Because we wish to have the left and right side of the array be adjacent (and the same with the top and bottom), it is convenient to use modular arithmetic. Thus, if we're looking to the right of column col, we add 1, modulo n. This ensures that the ultimate value of the column index is a value between 0 and n-1, the legal range of indices within each row. Note that adding any multiple of n to an expression modulo n will not change the value of the result. This trick can be used to make row-1, which may be negative, become positive. Thus, when we look up, or to the left, we must add in n to ensure that the modular arithmetic will generate n-1 along the left and top edges of the array.

We encourage you to experiment with Life on a torus, but if you wish to simulate Life in a square dish with sides, you can use the following alternative version of **neighbors**. As is usually the case, when there are boundary conditions, they appear in code as increased complexity.

```
public static int neighbors(boolean dish[][], int row, int col)
// pre: 0 <= row, col < dish.length
// post: returns the number of OCCUPIED cells surrounding (row,col)
//       in square dish with sides
{
    int n = dish.length;
    int pop = 0;
    if (row > 0     && col > 0     && dish[row-1][col-1]) pop++;
    if (row > 0                    && dish[row-1][col  ]) pop++;
    if (row > 0     && col < (n-1) && dish[row-1][col+1]) pop++;
    if (             col > 0       && dish[row  ][col-1]) pop++;
    if (             col < (n-1)   && dish[row  ][col+1]) pop++;
    if (row < (n-1) && col > 0     && dish[row+1][col-1]) pop++;
    if (row < (n-1)                && dish[row+1][col  ]) pop++;
    if (row < (n-1) && col < (n-1) && dish[row+1][col+1]) pop++;
    return pop;
}
```

Exercise 7.7 *Simplify the tests in this later version of* neighbors.

Finally, we have all the tools necessary for the simulation. The important concept here is that the next generation must be copied into a new dish. If we didn't, then newly hatched individuals might alter the count of neighborhoods about them. This wouldn't, then, be a valid concurrent simulation of each of the cells of the array. The array, work, is used to store the results, and these are copied back to the petri dish after the entire computation is finished.

```
public static void simulate(boolean dish[][])
// pre: dish is allocated with valid contents
// post: one generation of the dish is simulated and painted
{
    int n = dish.length;
    boolean work[][] = new boolean[n][n];
    int r,c;
    int pop;
    for (r = 0; r < n; r++)        // every row
    {
        for (c = 0; c < n; c++)        // and every cell within row
        {
            pop = neighbors(dish,r,c);  // count neighbors
            if (pop == 3 && !dish[r][c])
            {
                work[r][c] = OCCUPIED;
            } else if (dish[r][c] && (pop <= 1 || pop >= 4))
            {
                work[r][c] = VACANT;
            } else {
                work[r][c] = dish[r][c];
            }
        }
    }
```

```
    }

    // copy over the work array to the dish
    for (r = 0; r < n; r++)
    {
        for (c = 0; c < n; c++)
        {
            dish[r][c] = work[r][c];
        }
    }

    // update the screen
    paint(dish);
}
```

Notice that we do not paint the dish until the very end, because this helps to give the impression of simultaneous simulation across the screen.

We encourage you to play with the life simulation. The petri dish is itself a form of computer: the configuration of initial populations is the process of programming, and the simulation is the computation. Many interesting programs have been developed for Conway's life simulation; you'll find the latest by searching the web!

7.3   Vectors

In each of the previous examples, the programmer committed to an absolute upper bound on the number of elements that could be stored within the array. Even in cases where the *logical* length of the array varies, the *allocated* length of the array must be determined when the array is initially constructed with the **new** statement.

Imagine the task of writing a general purpose program to keep track of the inventory of a store. At some points within the program, it would be useful to have the entire inventory available. For example, when planning product exposures, several competing items must be considered. When calculating the worth of the inventory, it's useful to know about all the items stored on shelves. Such a program could be written with arrays, but what would be a reasonable upper bound on the number of items? Hot Tomatoes, a pizza building establishment, might get by with a small array, but DulMart, a fanatically large chain store, would need a large array. Undersized arrays can't be used in large stores, while oversized arrays can chew up precious memory in small stores. What can be done?

Java provides a class, **Vector**, that solves many of the allocation difficulties of arrays. To make use of **Vectors**, we must import the **Vector** class from the **java.util** package:

```
import java.util.Vector;
```

VectorDemo

A `Vector` is like a variable length array that can grow arbitrarily large. Initially, a `Vector` is constructed with no cells. Here we begin a list of names for people from Michigan:[1]

```
// names is a vector of polite names for people from Michigan
Vector names = new Vector();
```

As we wish to add objects to the `Vector`, we can append them to the end with `addElement`, making the `Vector` one cell longer. The first three statements below append three `String`s onto (an initially empty) `Vector`, in order:

```
names.addElement("Michiganer");
names.addElement("Michigander");
names.addElement("Michiganian");
c.out.println(names);
```

The final statement prints out the contents of the `Vector` yielding:

```
[Michiganer, Michigander, Michiganian]
```

Each of the elements of the `Vector` has an *index*, much like the index of the array. Like arrays, `Vector`s are indexed beginning at 0. To fetch a value from the array we can use the `elementAt` method. It takes, as a parameter, an index and returns the desired object. Here, we print the last element:

```
c.out.println("Officially, a person from Michigan is a "+
              names.elementAt(2));  // a "Michiganian"
```

Actually, things are a little more subtle. Since *any* nonprimitive Java value may be stored within a `Vector`, Java will not commit to the specific type of the object returned by `elementAt`. If, for example, we are interested in assigning the result to a `String`, the assignment

```
String official;
official = names.elementAt(2);
```

generates the unfortunate compiler error:

```
Explicit cast needed to convert java.lang.Object to java.lang.String.
```

Java is telling us that we must explicitly *cast* the result of `elementAt` to type `String` if we are interested in assigning the result *to* a `String`:

```
String official;
official = (String)names.elementAt(2);
```

---

[1] For more on this topic, see the text of Merriam Webster's wonderful radio program, *Word for the Wise*, January 28, 1999, at `http://www.m-w.com/wftw/wftw.htm`.

In general, when using object-returning `Vector` methods, we must explicitly cast the result to the expected type. If, in fact, the item turns out not to be the expected type (indicated by the cast), a similar error is produced, but when the program *runs*.

As with the `length` field arrays, it is possible to get the size of the `Vector`. The `size` method returns the number of elements that are logically part of the `Vector`. So, to print the values of the `Vector` in an application-specific format, we might use the following Java:

```java
int i;
char item;
for (i = 0; i < names.size(); i++)
{
    item = (char)('A'+i);
    c.out.println(item+". "+(String)names.elementAt(i));
}
```

Here, we've generated lettering for multiple choice questions. The output appears as:

```
A. Michiganer
B. Michigander
C. Michiganian
```

Finally, we demonstrate `removeElementAt` and `insertElementAt`. Suppose we are interested in reordering the current list of elements so that the names are in alphabetical order. It is necessary, then, to remove the second element from `names` and reinsert it in the first slot. Remembering that elements are numbered from zero, and printing out intermediate results, we end up with the following code:

```java
String temp;
temp = (String)names.elementAt(1);
c.out.println(names);
names.removeElementAt(1);
c.out.println(names);
names.insertElementAt(temp,0);
c.out.println(names);
```

Here is the output:

```
[Michiganer, Michigander, Michiganian]
[Michiganer, Michiganian]
[Michigander, Michiganer, Michiganian]
```

Clearly, the `elementAt` method does not change the state of the `Vector`. Removing a value, however, causes all following values to be moved toward the front of the `Vector`. The name `Michiganian`, for example, has moved from element 2 to element 1. When the `temp` value (`Michigander`) is reinserted into the `Vector`, we provide its desired index, and the following elements move one higher.

7.3.1 Example: Sorting

In the previous example, we sorted the three strings by hand. We actually can get the computer to do this sorting for us. Sorting is, in fact, a major portion of what keeps computers busy in a modern world.

Before going into sorting in detail, we write a method that swaps two elements of a `Vector`. The method must have the `Vector` as well as the location of the two elements. We extract the two values from the `Vector` and then reinsert them in the opposite order:

Insertion

```
public static void swap(Vector list, int index1, int index2)
// pre: index1, index2 < list.size()
// post: values at locations index1 and index2 are swapped in list
{
    String value1 = (String)list.elementAt(index1);
    String value2 = (String)list.elementAt(index2);
    list.setElementAt(value2,index1);
    list.setElementAt(value1,index2);
}
```

Now the sorting technique we will investigate is *insertion sort*. This technique is similar to the technique used by card players to insert new cards into a sorted hand. Given a `Vector` of values, we start with no cards sorted and then, one by one, insert the cards we have in their appropriate positions. Our approach will be to write a method that sorts the first few `Strings` found in a `Vector`. The precise number is passed as a parameter:

```
public static void Sort(Vector list, int number)
// pre: number <= list.size()
// post: elements 0..number-1 of the Vector are sorted
{
    String one, other, small, big;
    int location;
    if (number > 1) {
        Sort(list,number-1);  // sort most of the list, recursively
        // now we must only insert list.elementAt(number-1)
        // in among the first number-1 elements, which are sorted
        location = number-1;
        while (location > 0) {
            big = (String)list.elementAt(location);
            small = (String)list.elementAt(location-1);
            if (big.compareTo(small) < 0) { // they're out of order
                swap(list,location-1,location);
                location--;
            } else {
                break;
            }
        }
    }
}
```

If there are fewer than two values to be sorted, we've trivially finished—the
`Vector` is already in sorted order! On the other hand, if we have more than one
value, we can call `Sort` recursively to sort all but the last value. We then start
at the high end of the vector and swap any pairs of values that are out of order.
In effect, this moves the last value into its proper location. When the value is
in the correct place, it will be in the correct order with respect to its neighbors.

Exercise 7.8 *Rewrite the* `Sort` *method to avoid swapping values. Instead, pull
out the value to be inserted and move larger values to the right. After the correct
location for the insertion is found, reinsert the new value.*

Of course, we are usually interested in sorting *all* of the elements of a `Vector`.
To make this easier, we write a version of `Sort` that accepts one parameter—the
`Vector`—and calls the two-parameter version with the appropriate length:

```
public static void Sort(Vector list)
// pre: list is not null vector of strings
// post: elements of list are sorted into increasing order
{
    Sort(list,list.size());
}
```

The following `main` method reads the entire input into a `Vector`, calls `Sort`,
and prints the lines in increasing ASCII order:

```
public static void main(String args[])
{
    ConsoleWindow c = new ConsoleWindow();
    int i;
    Vector data = new Vector();

    while (!c.input.eof()) // while we haven't hit end of input
    {
        data.addElement(c.input.readLine()); // add lines to list
    }
    Sort(data);          // sort them
    c.out.println(data); // print them
}
```

Insertion sort, as it turns out, is fairly efficient for a small number of values, especially if the values are nearly sorted already. When the `Vector` gets
quite long, however, more complex sorting techniques can be used to sort the
`Vector` efficiently. It is interesting to note that while humans practice a form
of insertion sort when they sort cards, very efficient sorting techniques are not
often practiced by humans since the thresholds for efficiency involve very large
collections of data. We will spend considerable time on sorting in the next text,
Java Structures.

7.3.2   Example: Poetry, Revisited

VectorPoetry

Armed with the `Vector` class, we can now modify our array-based **poetry** program from page 170. Recall that this program reads the entire input and echos the lines on the output, but in random order. In our previous attempt, we explicitly kept a count of lines stored within the array. In this version, that information is maintained by the `Vector` object. Here is our modified version of the **poetry** program:

```java
import element.*;
import java.util.Vector;
import java.util.Random;

public class VectorPoetry
{
    public static void main(String args[])
    {
        ConsoleWindow c = new ConsoleWindow();
        Random g = new Random();
        final int max = 100;
        Vector poem = new Vector();
        String line;
        int i;

        while (!c.input.eof())
        {
            poem.addElement(c.input.readLine());
        }
        while (poem.size() > 0)
        {
            i = Math.abs(g.nextInt()) % poem.size();
            c.out.println(poem.elementAt(i));
            poem.removeElementAt(i);
        }
    }
}
```

Subbookkeeper: someone proficient with duplication

Comparison between the array and `Vector` versions of the **poetry** programs suggests that the `Vector`-based bookkeeping is simpler. The greatest feature of the `Vector` version, however, is that input of arbitrary size can be manipulated easily. To test this, we fed the program all of Shakespeare's sonnets. We leave you now to reflect on the first 14 lines of output (Java must be blamed for the rhyming scheme!):

```
Then do thy office, Muse; I teach thee how
With my extern the outward honouring,
These poor rude lines of thy deceased lover,
Look in your glass, and there appears a face
But as the marigold at the sun's eye,
Steal from his figure and no pace perceived;
```

```
That 'gainst thyself thou stick'st not to conspire.
Crooked elipses 'gainst his glory fight,
   So will I pray that thou mayst have thy 'Will,'
So thou be good, slander doth but approve
When I shall see thee frown on my defects,
Is lust in action; and till action, lust
Thy edge should blunter be than appetite,
Thy pyramids built up with newer might
```

7.4 Chapter Review

Arrays and Vectors are random access structures that store zero or more values
in a particular order.

- Arrays are allocated with a specific number of elements. Vectors are
  allocated and then extended as needed.

- Arrays use a traditional bracket-based syntax for indexing. Vectors use
  the elementAt and setElementAt methods to access and modify values.

- The length of an array is available through a length field. The length of
  a Vector is retrieved using the size() method.

- Arrays and Vectors must be accessed within particular bounds. Addressing beyond these bounds generates errors when the program runs.

- Random access structures allow the programmer to access elements in any
  order.

- Variable length arrays can be supported using an additional integer variable that keeps track of the number of logical elements within the array.
  The programmer should not read from beyond the logical end of the array.

- Two-dimensional arrays are equivalent to an "array of arrays." Java provides a shorthand for declaring and allocating multidimensional arrays.
  Life would be more difficult without multidimensional arrays.

Problems

7.1★   Is it possible to allocate an array with zero elements?

7.2   Is it possible to allocate a `Vector` with zero elements?

7.3★   Suppose we wished to remove an element from a variable length array of `String`s (as in the `poetry` program), but without disturbing the *order* of the remaining elements. Describe how this might be done.

7.4   In the `news` program, what is necessary to add another button labeled, say, `money`?

7.5★   In the `news` program, buttons do not currently overlap. Suppose the buttons were allowed to overlap and the mouse was pressed in the overlapping area. What would `selectButton` do? Rewrite the loop to support a different behavior, and carefully describe its behavior.

7.6   Write a method that reverses the order of the elements in an array of `int`s.

7.7★   Describe how one might implement a two-dimensional structure using only `Vector`s.

7.8   Write a method that takes two sets—represented by arrays of `boolean` values—and returns a new set that is the union of the elements found in either of the original sets.

7.9   Write a program that uses a variable length array of `int`s to keep a sorted list of values read from the console. Initially, it should be logically empty. At all times, the array maintains a list of nondecreasing values. When a value is read in, it should be inserted in the correct location (much like you do when you pick up cards individually to build a card hand). It is easiest if you start by trying to insert the new value at the high end of the array.

7.10   Write a program that keeps a sorted list of values (as discussed in Problem 7.9) in a `Vector`.

7.11   What are the advantages of the solution of Problem 7.10 when compared to the solution of Problem 7.9. What are the disadvantages? (Hint: Consider, among other things, running time.)

7.12★   Write a loop to print out the so-far-largest values found in an array `String`s. The `String` at location `i` is printed only if it is larger than *every* value at locations less than `i`. True or false: Your loop prints out the longest sequence of increasing values found in the array? If true, think again. Optional and hard: if false, describe a method for printing the longest sequence of increasing values.

7.13   Write a method, `swap`, that takes an array of `int`s and two indices, `i` and `j`. The method should swap the two values indexed in the array. (Note that, if your method works, you have demonstrated that the array is passed as a value parameter, but is a *reference* to its elements.)

7.14   Write a method, `swap`, that takes an array of objects and two indices, `i` and `j`. The method should swap the two objects indexed in the array. (Unlike the version we provide in the text, you may assume (the truth:) that the values returned from the Vector methods are of type Object.) Demonstrate that your program works with Vectors that contain Strings.

7.15 ⋆ First, write a method, trial, that selects 23 random integers between 1 and 365. The method should return true if (and only if) a pair of selected integers are the same. Then, write a program that performs 10000 calls to trial and prints the percentage of trials that are true. (It should be near 50.72%.)

7.16   Write a program that computes and prints the first n lines of Pascal's triangle. The first line consists of a single 1. The nth line consists of a 1, followed by the sums of pairs of numbers found in the $(n-1)^{\text{st}}$ line (you may assume a zero appears at the end of the previous line). Here are the first five lines:

```
1
1 1
1 2 1
1 3 3 1
1 4 6 4 1
```

7.17 ⋆ Write a program to shuffle the contents of an array into another. For an array to be shuffled, it must be the case that every possible shuffling of the values is equally likely. Make an argument that your shuffling technique indeed shuffles the array.

7.18   Write a program to shuffle the contents of an array *in place*. As with Problem 7.17, make an argument that the array is actually shuffled.

7.5 Laboratory: Packing Bins

Objective. To implement a game with unbounded memory, using arrays or vectors.

Discussion. We frequently write programs that have to remember an increasing amount of data. In this lab, we will write a program that challenges you to stuff as many disks into a rectangular box as possible. The program appears as follows while running:

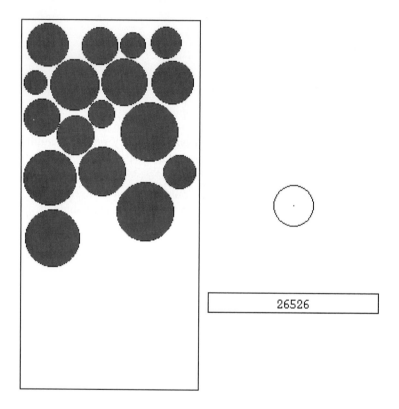

On the right side of the screen, disks of random diameter appear, one at a time. When pressed, the mouse is able to drag the disk into the rectangular bin, on the left. Releasing the button drops the disk at that location. If the disk overlaps an existing disk, it returns to the start location. If, when dropped, the disk laps outside the bin, the game ends. Otherwise, the disk is permanently placed in the indicated location. Each placed disk increases the score by the approximate number of pixels covered.

The program, of course, must remember where all the previously placed disks are located. For this reason, you will need either an array or a **Vector** to store the disks.

Once constructed, the program has the interesting feature that there is no obvious winning strategy to placing the disks in a manner that maximizes the number of pixels covered.

Procedure. Before you approach this program, you should consider whether you wish to use arrays or `Vectors` to store the disks. If you use an array, you should be careful to select a bound on the number of disks that is not so large as to be wasteful of memory, and not so small as to potentially cause problems if large numbers of small disks are to be placed. You should then follow these steps:

1. On graph paper, lay out the drawing window. This will help you in determining the size of the score box and the potential size of the disks you are to place.

2. Write (or reuse) a function that computes the distance between two points. Why is this necessary?

3. Write a program that draws the screen and score box (with a score of zero).

4. Extend this program to pick a random circle and place it within the bin. The program should stop after this one placement.

5. Extend this program to include the storage of previously placed disks. Add the disks to the array, but don't worry about checking for overlap. Stop when a disk falls outside the bin.

6. Finally, add the check for overlapping disks.

Thought questions. Consider the following questions as you complete the lab:

1. Suppose you were placing `Rect` objects. How would you check for overlap of two `Rects`?

2. Suppose you wanted to help the user place the disks correctly. How would you draw all the target pixels where the center of the disk could be located within the bin?

3. It is possible to construct a `Random` with a starting random number, called a *seed*. The seed determines the entire sequence of random values selected from that point on. Why might we want to have the user specify a starting seed when the program is run?

4. (Hard.) What percentage of the area would you expect to be able to cover with disks?

Chapter 8

Classes

*"The widder wouldn't let me smoke; she wouldn't let me yell,
she wouldn't let me gape, nor stretch, nor scratch, before folks...
And dad fetch it, she prayed all the time!
I never see such a woman! I HAD to shove, Tom—I just had to.
And besides, that school's going to open,
and I'd a had to go to it—well, I wouldn't stand THAT!"*
—Mark Twain

WE NOW CONSIDER THE DEVELOPMENT OF CLASSES. We have, of course, seen classes heavily used as the glue that holds our program's static methods together. Here, however, we consider the main use of classes: to describe new objects within Java. In their simplest form, classes are used to hold together data that serve a common purpose. In more elaborate programs, classes are used to extend the functionality of an existing package or system.

There are, of course, many features to be considered in a full discussion of classes. Our approach, however, will be to present a large number of examples, from which we can learn about many issues associated with type design, extension, and implementation.

8.1 First Things

A new class with name, say, `number` is usually defined and implemented in a single file `number.java`. Many Java environments will enforce this by refusing to compile a class that comes from the wrong file. As we learn to define new classes, it is important to take the time to be organized. While a few environments will allow the definition of several classes in a single file, it is best to define them separately. Since files usually reside in folders or directories, and since many environments allow the construction of projects that contain several files, keeping one class in each file is a natural organizational technique.

There is another good reason: you may wish to reuse your code. A modern programming language such as Java rewards the programmer that thinks ahead and defines projects and classes as generally as possible. If, for example, you find yourself rewriting code that you wrote last week for a different project: STOP! Search for the old code and include it in the current project. If it doesn't exactly meet your needs, ask yourself if its design is improved by being made general enough for your current use. If it is, you spend your time honing your code, not rewriting it from scratch. Usually, this is time well spent. Thus, the

Goal: Write Mom, not code!

concept of one class per file is important not only for organizational purposes, but also for building libraries of solid code.

We will see many examples in this chapter. Each has its place and describes an important feature of the language. Some examples will turn out to have clear flaws. Discovering these flaws is part of the learning process. If at all possible, you are encouraged to download our examples and modify them: remove and add methods, change representations, play with the protections. Trying to push the envelope in the wrong direction usually serves to demonstrate limits. The more you know about the limits of Java, the more you learn about avoiding limits and improving your programming skills.

Early languages had no records.

We are now ready to turn to our first example of class design, which, in its simplest form, serves the role of a *record* or *structure* in other programming languages you may know.

8.2 Encapsulation

The single most important feature of classes is that they provide a mechanism for associating related pieces of data. In most cases, these data represent a single logical *object*. We emphasize the word "object" here because we are using it in its most formal form. Java is an *object-oriented* language because much of the programmer's time is spent writing code to support objects. In Java, the supporting code is placed in a class. Classes don't take any space in a running program, but their *instances* or *objects* do. We might think of a class as a cookie cutter and the objects we use as cookies. The process of writing code for objects shapes the cookie cutter. The `new` operator provides a mechanism for allocating memory and shaping it for use as a new object.

8.2.1 Example: A Number Holder

Perhaps the simplest class we can construct has the following definition:

Number

```
public class Number
{
    int value; // an integer storage location
}
```

Word warning: 'Instance' and 'instantiate' mean the same thing.

That's it! As we can see, this is a `public` class. Objects of a public class may be referenced and used by any code you write.[1] Our `Number` class has a declaration for a non-`static` *instance variable*, `value`. This instance variable is responsible for representing the state of a `Number`. Each instance of a `Number` created by the `new` operator has its own instance variable that maintains its own distinct state. If this variable was declared `static`, it would be shared among *all* objects constructed or *instantiated* from the `Number` class. When creating objects, we

---

[1] Classes that are not declared `public` are not as widely accessible. The constraints on classes are unimportant here, so we will assume all classes are declared `public`.

Figure 8.1 On the left, a conceptual view of primitive `int` named `count`. On the right, a `Number` object referred to by `myFavoriteInteger`. The `int` instance variable `value` is accessed through `myFavoriteInteger.value`.

will (almost) always represent our state using instance variables. When writing "program classes," we nearly always use static methods and variables.

This class sits in its own file. When we compile it, our environment creates a *class file*, which may be loaded by programs. The `Number` class is not a program itself, because there is no `main` procedure. In fact, if we try to run the `Number` class, we get the cryptic remark:

```
In class Number: void main(String argv[]) is not defined
```

Obviously, the Java environment is disappointed!

What we have created is a new type of object, and we've tried to run it as a program. To make use of the `Number` class, we must write *another* class—a program—that makes use of the `Number`. Here, for example, we have a program that allows us to store an `int` value in a `new Number` (see Figure 8.1):

```
import element.*;
public class FavorInt
{
    public static void main(String args[])
    {
        ConsoleWindow c = new ConsoleWindow();
        Number myFavoriteInteger = new Number();
        myFavoriteInteger.value = 2;
        c.out.println("My favorite integer is "+
                    myFavoriteInteger.value);
    }
}
```

FavorInt

The second line of the method declares and creates a new `Number`; failing to construct a new `Number` makes it impossible for us to store an integer since there are no other `int`s declared within the program. We then have a new object (referred to by `myFavoriteInteger`) that contains a single `int`, whose name is `value`. We can refer to that `int` as `myFavoriteInteger.value`, and may be used as an `int`. We choose simply to store an integer in `value` and then use it in a `println` statement. The output is what we might expect:

```
My favorite integer is 2
```

So what is the use of such an object? On page 107, we made the comment that it was impossible to write a procedure that modifies integer values. An attempt at such a method might be one that swaps the values of two int variables:

Swapper

```
public static void swap(int a, int b)
// post: fails to swap a and b
{
    int temp;
    temp = a;
    a = b;
    b = temp;
}
```

Unfortunately, this method will not swap the values a and b because the formal parameters are *copies* of the actual parameters. No amount of coaxing will fix this problem. We will have some success with an equivalent method, written with Number objects:

```
public static void swap(Number a, Number b)
// pre: a and b are not null references to Numbers
// post: the values of a and b are exchanged
{
    int temp;
    temp = a.value;
    a.value = b.value;
    b.value = temp;
}
```

What is different here is that while the two parameters—references to Number objects—cannot be changed, *the values they reference* can be changed. To wit:

```
public static void main(String args[])
{
    ConsoleWindow c = new ConsoleWindow();
    Number big = new Number();
    Number small = new Number();

    big.value = -10;
    small.value = 10;

    swap(small,big);

    c.out.println("small="+small.value+", big="+big.value);
}
```

prints

```
small=-10, big=10
```

This asymmetry between the treatment of primitive values and objects is a sign that Java is a language that heavily favors the use of objects. Our focus in this chapter is to familiarize you with the basics of object design.

8.2.2   Example: A Button Class

We have seen in Chapter 7 that a simple graphical button can be constructed from a rectangular "active area" on the screen and a `String` that serves a button label. Unfortunately, in our program that displayed several buttons on the screen (`News`), we were required to pass two arrays of data—an array of rectangles and an array of `Strings`—to each routine that manipulated buttons. By developing a class, `Button`, that describes all the features of a single button, we are able to store our buttons in a single array structure. Not only does this simplify our program, but it helps to reduce errors that often occur when maintaining consistency of "parallel" array structures. The general approach to wrapping all the features of a logical object in a single class is called *encapsulation*. Here, then, is our first attempt at writing a `Button` class that makes use of encapsulation. The two instance variables `activeArea` and `label` represent the data values that were previously stored in the two arrays.

```
import element.*;

public class Button
{
    DrawingWindow targetWindow; // the window containing the button
    Rect activeArea;            // the area we can press w/mouse
    Text label;                 // the label on the area

    public Button(DrawingWindow d, Rect r, String l)
    // pre: d,r,l not null; l.width <= r.width
    // post: button with text l is created (though not displayed)
    {
        targetWindow = d;
        activeArea = new Rect(r);
        label = new Text(l);
        label.center(r.center());
        targetWindow.draw(activeArea);
        targetWindow.draw(label);
    }

    public boolean contains(Pt p)
    // post: returns true iff p within the button
    {
        return activeArea.contains(p);
    }
}
```

ButtonAlpha

Already, the first method, `Button`, appears a little unusual. Since it is named after the class, we know it is a *constructor*. A constructor is called when a `Button` object is first created with the **new** operator. It is responsible for initializing the instance variables to reasonable values. Any parameters required in the constructor are provided as parameters to the class name in the **new** statement. In this case, the constructor takes three parameters; these are sufficient

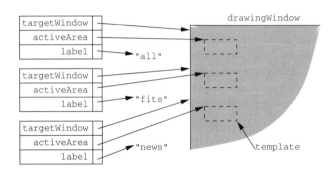

Figure 8.2 Dedicated buttons require their own `Rect` objects. If they share a reference to an external `Rect` (e.g., `template`, above), modifications to the external `Rect` may unexpectedly modify the state of the internal `Rect`.

for constructing a labeled button within a drawing window. If no constructor is provided (as was the case with the `Number` class), instance variables are set to zero for primitive types or `null` for references.

Another identifying characteristic of the constructor is that *it does not return a value*. If you should declare a constructor to return a value, it will not be considered a constructor and will not be called when you construct an object. This mistake is the source of many nasty programming errors!

As with instance variables, the constructor is not declared `static`. It is an example of an *instance method*. Instance methods may only be called in the context of a particular object. Put another way, it is not possible to call an instance method if you do not have an instance of the class. This was clearly not the case with the `static` methods we have written to this point: we can call our `main` method any time we wish, even if no objects have been created.

Let us look at the innards of this constructor with a bit more care. First, even though the instance variables (e.g., `targetWindow`) and the formal parameters (e.g., `d`) are used to hold references to similar things, they are named differently. Within the context of any method, the instance variables are accessible if they are not masked by local variables or parameters with similar names. In general, given several identifiers with the same name, the one closest to the point of reference will be the one seen; the others will be *hidden*. Since instance methods often make use of instance variables, it is important that we pick appropriate names for parameters so that they do not hide the instance variables. In cases where there might be confusion, the instance variables of an object can be referred to by prefixing the name of the instance variable with `this`, which refers to the object at hand. Thus, within the method, while `label` might refer to a local variable or formal parameter, `this.label` identifies the instance variable.

Next, we note that `activeArea` is initialized to a new `Rect`. If a reference were kept to the external `Rect` passed in, external and unexpected changes could be made to the `Rect` without the `Button`'s knowledge (see Figure 8.2). Making a copy of the `Rect` allows `Button` to limit changes to the active area.

Finally, we note that the label of the `Button` is stored as a `Text` object rather than a `String`. This allows `label` to maintain its location at the center of the `Button`. We might have saved it as a `String`, but then the placement of the `String` would have to be recomputed every time the button had to be repainted. We avoid this in favor of a little more complexity in our representation.

Predicting our `Button` might need to be pressed, we also provide a predicate, `contains`, that returns `true` when a point is within the `Button`'s active area. Since the `contains` method is part of the definition of the `Button` class, we can make changes to this common test in one location. Such a change might be necessary if we decide to change the shape of the button at some future time.

To demonstrate how we might use our new `Button` class, we consider an updated form of our `News` program from Chapter 7. Let's peek at it quickly.

NewsAlpha

```java
import element.*;
import java.util.Vector;

public class News
{
    static DrawingWindow d;
    static ConsoleWindow c;

    public static void drawButtons(Vector buttons)
    // pre: buttons is not null
    // post: labels (and associated buttons) are drawn on the screen
    {
        final int width = 40, height = 15;      // button dimensions
        final int spacing = 5;
        Rect template = new Rect(10, 10, width, height); // template
        Button b;

        // call 3 parameter constructor, once for each button:
        b = new Button(d,template,"all");
        buttons.addElement(b);
        template.move(0, height+spacing);
        b = new Button(d,template,"fits");
        buttons.addElement(b);
        template.move(0, height+spacing);
            . . .
    }

    public static String selectButton(Vector buttons)
    // pre: buttons drawn on screen
    // post: the label of the first button pressed is returned
    {
        int i;
        Pt p;
```

```
        p = d.awaitMousePress();
        d.awaitMouseRelease();
        for (i = 0; i < buttons.size(); i++)
        {
            Button b = (Button)buttons.elementAt(i);
            if (b.contains(p)) return b.label.string();
        }
        return selectButton(buttons);
    }

    public static void main(String args[])
    {
        d = new DrawingWindow();
        c = new ConsoleWindow();
        Vector buttons = new Vector();
        String s;

        drawButtons(buttons);
        while (true)
        {
            s = selectButton(buttons);
            if (s.equals("stop")) break;
            c.out.print(s+" "); c.out.flush();
        }
        c.out.println();
    }
}
```

This version of News is different from the original in a number of ways. First, our program now consists of two files—Button.java, which contains the definition of the Button class, and News.java, which contains our program. When compiling the program, make sure both files are located in the correct place for your environment. Next, we have chosen to use a single Vector of Buttons. Another alternative, of course, would be to keep our Buttons in a variable length array, but that would necessitate careful manipulation of the length, and the passing of multiple parameters to procedures like drawButtons. Finally, our initialization of the Button objects has been changed from a loop to an "unrolled" sequence of Button constructions (we have not shown all of these initializations, but the remainder are easily constructed). This unrolling was necessitated by our use of a template to define the location of each button.

The use of Buttons has simplified our approach: we have reduced the number of parameters that must be passed to methods, and we have also made the program slightly more readable. Notice that when we construct a Button object in the drawButtons, we must always pass it three parameters—the drawing window, the active area of the screen where the button is pressable, and the label associated with the button. Since we have provided only one constructor, we have little choice but to construct Buttons in this way.

Exercise 8.1 *What is necessary to add another button to our latest* `News` *program?*

One serious side effect of our `Button` design is that we, as the user of the `Button` class, must know something about how `Buttons` are implemented: in `selectButton`, the `String` of the associated `Button` must be gleaned from `label`, the `Text` instance variable.

```
if (b.contains(p)) return b.label.string();
```

This can be unnatural, since the *user* of a `Button` might not be its *implementor*. Ideally, implementation decisions would be hidden from the user by controlled access through an *interface*—a collection of methods that provide the expected functionality of a `Button`. This notion is central to the concept of an *abstract data type*. In our next section, we discuss this form of abstraction that, like procedural abstraction, simplifies the construction of programs by hiding unsightly details.

8.3 Abstract Data Types

When you last purchased a calculator, it was unlikely that the type of processor or memory used within the calculator was of much concern to you. These are details that are unimportant to owners of calculators. Calculators live up to a simple contract: they should support a basic set of math operators and a little memory for storage of intermediate results. The details about *how* these features are actually implemented are unimportant. It is clear that the concept of a calculator is an *abstract* concept. As long as a machine provides us the features we expect in a calculator, we are satisfied. Manufacturers enjoy this abstraction: if less expensive processors become available, the manufacturer can redesign the inside of the device. As long as the external features are the same, users are none-the-wiser. Users enjoy this abstraction: learning how to program one calculator is similar to learning how to program the next.

An *abstract data type* is an object that hides its representation within, and allows the user to manipulate the object solely through the use of a collection of methods that we loosely describe as the object's *interface*. The use of abstract data types allows us to more effectively write classes that can be used and reused. Once an abstract data type is implemented, it can be re-implemented without fear, as long as the interface does not change.

We now consider examples of abstract data types. They are crafted in a manner that makes heavy use of instance methods. These methods, in turn, make use of instance variables. At all times, however, the particular representation of the state is hidden from the user.

8.3.1 Example: The Button Revisited

A good design for an object like our `Button` class involves identifying all of the *operations* that must be performed on `Buttons`. For example, we saw that once

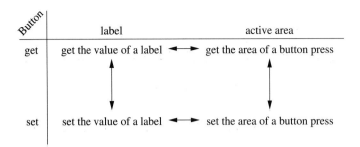

Figure 8.3 The symmetries of the proposed `Button` interface.

`Button`s are constructed, they may be tested to see if they contain a point. We've also found out that labels of `Button`s are used for the `selectButton` method. We could improve our design by including a *method* that provides us access to this information.

An even stronger design would also provide features that might be useful even though we know of no current application that can make use of them. For example, if we can retrieve the label of a `Button`, we should consider providing a similar method for retrieving the active area. The basis for this reasoning is a desire for *symmetry*. A symmetric interface for an object is more predictable, and a predictable interface is more effectively used.

Carrying our symmetry argument further, we imagine methods that allow the user to *set* the label and active area of a `Button` (see Figure 8.3). These methods are similarly named procedures that take the new value as the sole parameter. This decision is fairly dramatic since a change in the area requires redrawing the button on the associated drawing window. By similar reasoning we can see, also, that a label-setting method must also paint our `Button`. Perhaps it is useful, then, to have methods `draw` and `clear` that isolate the `Button` painting code. We've declared these *methods* `private` as well. The purpose is similar to declaring instance variables `private`: a `private` method is inaccessible and cannot be called by the user. If we had allowed the user to call these methods, then the mutator methods would have to check to see if the screen needed to be updated. Our implementation avoids this complexity.

Here, then, is an implementation of a `Button` as an abstract data type:

ButtonBeta

```
import element.*;

public class Button
{
    private DrawingWindow targetWindow; // the window
    private Rect activeArea;     // the area we can press w/mouse
    private Text label;          // the label on the area
```

```
public Button(DrawingWindow d, Rect r, String l)
// pre: d,r,l not null; l.width <= r.width
// post: button with text l displayed on window d
{
    targetWindow = d;
    activeArea = new Rect(r);
    label = new Text(l);
    label.center(r.center());
    draw();
}

private void draw()
// pre: button not showing
// post: paints button
{
    targetWindow.draw(activeArea);
    targetWindow.draw(label);
}

private void clear()
// pre: button showing
// post: erases button
{
    targetWindow.clear(activeArea);
}

public String label()
// post: return the label of the button
{
    return label.string();
}

public void label(String l)
// pre: l.width < activeArea.width
// post: changes the label and repaints the button
{
    clear();
    label = new Text(l);
    label.center(activeArea.center());
    draw();
}

public Rect area()
// post: returns the active area of the button
{
    return new Rect(activeArea);
}

public void area(Rect r)
// pre: r.width >= label.width
```

```
// post: sets button active area to r, updates button on screen
{
    clear();
    activeArea = new Rect(r);
    label.center(activeArea.center());
    draw();
}

public boolean contains(Pt p)
// post: returns true iff p within the button
{
    return activeArea.contains(p);
}
}
```

Since there are methods for consistently accessing the instance variables, we can protect the instance variables with the `private` keyword. This makes it impossible for code outside the `Button` class to access these fields directly, helping to secure the implementation-hiding characteristic of the abstract data type.

Principle 19 *Declare instance variables of classes* `private`.

Once private, we can be assured that modification of the instance variables only occurs through methods. Any changes in the internal representation of the object are now hidden from view, and users are not directly affected by changes in the implementation.

Our hiding of the representation has forced a small change in our coding of the `News` program: it must now get the label of a `Button` through the parameterless `label` method. Our (now error-free) line in the previous version of the `News` program becomes:

```
if (b.contains(p)) return b.label();
```

Exercise 8.2 *We've spent some time considering the symmetry of our design. How is our design currently not symmetric?*

NewsBeta

8.3.2   Example: An Abstract Die

As we have seen, designing an abstract data type involves the following steps:

1. Identify and declare the data that are necessary to represent the state of the object. These declarations make up the instance variables of the class.

2. Write appropriate constructors. Consider the data necessary to initialize the instance variables of the object and make sure your constructors get the necessary information through parameters.

3. Identify and write the `public` methods. These include state accessing methods (accessors), as well as those that modify state (mutators). As a rule, each method would leave the object in a consistent and valid state.

4. Implement any "helper methods" that are needed (e.g., the `draw` method of the `Button` class) and declare them `private`.

5. Test your code. Make sure that methods are tested in a variety of situations.

Suppose we are interested in developing an object that models a single general die with n faces.[2] For a single die, two quantities are necessary to model the state of the die: the number of faces and the number that appears on the face that shows:

```
private int faces;       // shape of die
private int faceValue;   // current value of die
```

Die1

We, of course, have declared these instance variables `private` to protect them from inappropriate access. We will access these values through methods.

Next, we argue for declaring two different constructors:

```
public Die(int n)
// pre: n >= 1
// post: construct a randomly oriented die with n faces
{
    faces = n;
    roll();
}

public Die()
// post: construct a randomly oriented die with 6 faces
{
    this(6);
}
```

The single parameter constructor would be called if we were trying to construct a die with a nonstandard number of faces:

```
Die icosahedron = new Die(20);
```

When the die is constructed, we `roll` it immediately to get a random value. We're not sure how `roll` is to be implemented, but we'll get to that shortly. The second constructor is parameterless. We have chosen to use this constructor to construct a standard six-sided die with random initial value. The different number of parameters—the different *signature* of the method—helps to distinguish between the two different types of initialization. So, for example, the statement

Die1

```
this(6);
```

---

[2] Those who have not played with dice are encouraged to drop this book and fetch a pair.

constructs the desired `Die`. In this case, we can come up with a good use for the parameterless constructor. If we should fail to declare any constructors, Java will provide us a parameterless constructor automatically; this *default constructor* does nothing, essentially leaving all the instance variables initialized to zero.

Next, we consider two `public` methods necessary to support the use of our new `Die`. One is the promised `roll` method. It constructs a new random number generator, and then has it give us a random value. The other is the `value` method. It returns the current face value of the die:

```
public void roll()
// post: reselect the upward-pointing face
{
    Random rand = new Random();
    faceValue = 1+(Math.abs(rand.nextInt())%faces);
}

public int value()
// post: return the current value of the die
{
    return faceValue;
}
```

As we have observed, methods applied to other objects are invoked by writing the name of the object, followed by the name of the method and its parameters. For example, the following constructs a coin (a two-sided `Die`) and then possibly flips the coin again (perhaps we're cheating!):

DieTest

```
Die coin = new Die(2); // 1 or 2
if (Die.value() == 1)
{
    coin.roll();  // try again!
}
```

Exercise 8.3 *What are the chances that the final state of* coin *is 0.*

Die1

The other way that a method is called is within the object itself. For example, the parameterless constructor for the object indirectly could have set the value by calling the `roll` method on itself:

```
this.roll();
```

DieTest

As with instance variables, the prefix `this` indicates that the `roll` method is being applied to the object being constructed. In most cases—in cases where there is no ambiguity—the word `this` may be dropped. We, in fact, used the short form of the method call in our code.

We can now write a program that demonstrates the use of these structures to determine the percentage of the time that two cube-shaped dice can be rolled to have the same value. We expect the results to be about 17%.

```
import element.*;
public class DieTest
{
    public static void main(String[] args)
    {
        ConsoleWindow c = new ConsoleWindow();
        Die d1 = new Die();
        Die d2 = new Die();
        int rolls;
        int pairs = 0;

        for (rolls = 0; rolls < 100; rolls++)
        {
            d1.roll();
            d2.roll();
            if (d1.value() == d2.value()) pairs++;
            c.out.println("Dice have values "+
                            d1.value()+" "+d2.value());
        }
        c.out.println("Of "+rolls+" rolls, "+pairs+" were pairs.");
    }
}
```

Notice that nowhere do we see the gritty details of selecting random numbers. They are hidden within the `roll` method of the `Die` class. Notice, also, that we never mention `faceValue`, which is an instance variable in the hidden implementation. In fact, because `faceValue` is declared `private`, it's impossible.

Exercise 8.4 *What happens if the instance variables are used instead of the* `value` *method calls in the above program?*

8.3.3   Example: Refined Randomness

If you play with these `Die` objects much, you'll find that rolling a `Die` many times in a row will generate sequences of equal values. The reason is that each time we roll a `Die`, we are constructing a new, dedicated generator that gives us a new face value. The *seed*, or initial value of this random number generator, is based on the system's wall-clock, which changes, if we're lucky, once a millisecond. Two or more calls to `roll` in a single time interval generate similar `Random` number generators that, in turn, produce the same initial random value. We could test our hypothesis by checking to see if we were more likely to roll pairs with a single die than two.

Exercise 8.5 *Check to see if it's more likely to roll a pair with a single die using our last implementation. What do your results tell you about the speed of Java?*

One improvement would be to have each `Die` maintain a single generator that is sampled many times over its life. Since the generator is now part of the state of the Die, we must "promote" it to an instance variable that is initialized when the Die is constructed. The rolling of a Die only involves fetching a newly generated integer:

Die2

```java
import java.util.Random;
import element.*;
public class Die
{
    private int faces;        // shape of die
    private int faceValue;    // current value of die
    private Random rand;      // per-die random generator

    public Die(int n)
    // pre: n >= 1
    // post: construct a randomly oriented die with n faces
    {
        rand = new Random();
        faces = n;
        roll();
    }

    public Die()
    // post: construct a randomly oriented die with 6 faces
    {
        this(6);
    }

    public void roll()
    // post: reselect the upward-pointing face
    {
        faceValue = 1+(Math.abs(rand.nextInt())%faces);
    }

    public int value()
    // post: return the current value of the die
    {
        return faceValue;
    }
}
```

Now when two dice are constructed, two generators are constructed, but only once (see Figure 8.4).

We still have one problem, though: two *different* dice that are constructed close together in time will tend to generate the same face values. (In fact, we had to run our testing program 10 times to get independent dice!) The solution is to use a **static** generator. Recall that **static** instance variables are available for shared use among all objects, and are available whether or not actual instances of Die objects exist. When the first Die is constructed, it will construct a new **Random** generator. This is accomplished by testing to see if the only instance

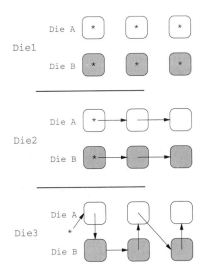

Figure 8.4 In the `Die` object defined in `Die1.java`, a new random number generator ($\star$) is constructed for each roll. In `Die2`, a single generator generates a sequence (follow arrows) of random values. In `Die3`, a shared `static` generator determines the sequence for all instances of the `Die` class.

variable, `rand`, is `null`. If it is, a new generator is constructed. Otherwise, the existing generator is used. Here is the code for our best version of the `Die` class:

Die3

```java
import java.util.Random;
import element.*;
public class Die
{
    private int faces;          // shape of die
    private int faceValue;      // current value of die
    private static Random rand = null; // shared generator

    public Die(int n)
    // pre: n >= 1
    // post: construct a randomly oriented die with n faces
    {
        if (rand == null)
        {
            rand = new Random();
        }
        faces = n;
        roll();
    }
}
```

```
    public Die()
    // post: construct a randomly oriented die with 6 faces
    {
        this(6);
    }

    public void roll()
    // post: reselect the upward-pointing face
    {
        faceValue = 1+(Math.abs(rand.nextInt())%faces);
    }

    public int value()
    // post: return the current value of the die
    {
        return faceValue;
    }
}
```

The results of running the program with this version of the Die class yielded 16 pairs, or about 1 in 6, for a standard six-sided die.

Looking back at these implementations, we note that the integrity of the internal state of the object is maintained because the only way to modify the state is through one of the methods. It is not possible, for example, to have the user of the dice explicitly set the face value of the Die between rolls. In this way, the language helps preserve the integrity of objects.

We have also seen that the details of the implementation are, effectively, hidden from the user of the class. When we determined that there was a better way to implement the Die, we were able to modify the internal representations. As long as the external view—the *interface* or list of method signatures—was maintained, we were secure. This feature allows mistakes to be fixed in code without users having to recompile their programs.

8.3.4   Example: A Stopwatch

As we have seen a number of times, it is useful to be able to time events in a computer with reasonable accuracy. We consider, here, the implementation of a virtual stopwatch that is able to accumulate several intervals of time. The watch should meet the following requirements:

   ⋆ The watch should keep accurate time.

   ⋆ Starting the watch causes it to start accumulating time.

   ⋆ Stopping the watch causes it to stop accumulating time.

   ⋆ Resetting the watch clears the accumulated time.

   ⋆ Reading the watch returns the currently accumulated time in seconds.

We will begin by thinking about the external view of the stopwatch. It seems reasonable to have a simple constructor and methods start, stop, reset, and read to support the logical operations of the watch. With this information, we sketch out the following headers for the methods of our class:

```
public class Watch
{
    public Watch()
    // post: returns a stopped watch

    public void start()
    // pre: watch is stopped
    // post: starts watch, begins accumulating time

    public void stop()
    // pre: watch is running
    // post: stops watch, and accumulates time

    public double read()
    // post: returns the accumulated time on the watch

    public void reset()
    // post: stops running watch and clears the accumulated time.
}
```

Watch

Notice that the read method returns elapsed seconds even though internally it is likely that we'll be keeping track of them as an integral number of milliseconds. Again, the feature of abstraction is that the interface insulates us from the details of the internal representation.

We now consider the instance variables necessary to keep track of the watch state. Clearly, the watch should have some method for storing the current total elapsed time and should know whether the watch is running or not. We need to be able to construct these pieces of information, based on the instance variables of the watch. In this implementation, keep three pieces of information: the time accumulated before the last time the watch was started, the time of the last start, and a flag indicating whether or not the watch is currently running. Here are the private fields of the watch:

```
private boolean running; // is the watch keeping track of time?
private long strt;       // starting millisecond count
private long accum;      // total milliseconds
```

We now work on completing the methods. When the watch is constructed, it should be off, and the accumulated time should be zero:

```
public Watch()
// post: returns a stopped watch
{
    running = false;
```

```
        strt = 0;
        accum = 0;
}
```

When the watch is started, we set the running flag to true and record the current wall-clock time. This will help us recover the time elapsed since the last start. Notice that it would be bad to start a watch multiple times without intervening calls to reset or stop:

```
public void start()
// pre: watch is stopped
// post: starts watch, begins accumulating time
{
    running = true;
    strt = System.currentTimeMillis();
}
```

Exercise 8.6 *What minor change is necessary to protect the* Watch *from the problems of multiple starts? (The same fix will work with* stop.*)*

Stopping the watch clears this flag and accumulates the recently elapsed time into the total:

```
public void stop()
// pre: watch is running
// post: stops watch, and accumulates time
{
    running = false;
    accum += (System.currentTimeMillis()-strt);
}
```

Exercise 8.7 *A reader pointed out that the above statements were in the wrong order. How much longer will this extend the accumulated time?*

Since internally we store the accumulated time in milliseconds, we read the watch by computing (if necessary) the accumulated time and divide it by 1000. Care must be taken to ensure that we use double division values to avoid losing the fractional part of the seconds.

```
public double read()
// post: returns the accumulated time on the watch
{
    if (running)
    {
        return (double)(accum+
                        (System.currentTimeMillis()-strt))/1000.0;
    } else {
        return (double)accum/1000.0;
    }
}
```

The process of clearing the watch simply involves turning it off and clearing the accumulated value:

```
public void reset()
// post: stops running watch and clears the accumulated time.
{
    running = false;
    accum = 0;
}
```

Exercise 8.8 *How long does it take for your computer to roll 7 equivalent dice? 8? 9?*

Exercise 8.9 *How would you measure how long it takes to read the watch? (Hint: Use multiple trials for accuracy.)*

8.3.5   Example: A Word List

Our next example considers the construction of a class to help keep track of the frequencies of words on the input. Similar programs have been used to "fingerprint" the authors of texts. The structure we will design maintains a list of entries, each of which is an object containing a word-frequency pair. We start at the most abstract level, the design of the list itself.

The operations we wish to support are add, which inserts a word reference (new or old) into the list, and the toString method, which generates a String representation of the structure. The state of this list is supported by an array of Word entries and an integer that keeps track of the number of entries in the array that are logically "active." Here is the outline of what we have so far:

WordList

```
public class WordList
{
    private Word[] words;      // words is an array of word objects
    private int entries;       // a count of the number of entries

    public WordList()
    // post: construct a new word list

    public void add(String w)
    // pre: w is not null, room for a word in list
    // post: w has been added to the list

    public String toString()
    // post: return a string representation of word list
}
```

Logically, the array consists of a vocabulary of unique words. The variable entries tells us exactly how many of the array's Words are actually used. The constructor, then, is responsible for setting the number of entries to zero and allocating a reasonably sized array of, say, 1000 words.

```
public WordList()
// post: construct a new word list
{
    words = new Word[1000];
    entries = 0;
}
```

Next we implement a useful method, toString, which is responsible for constructing a String representation of the WordList. We will use this to print out the list when the analysis is complete. The concept is straightforward: loop down the list appending each entry to the result string:

```
public String toString()
// post: return a string representation of word list
{
    String s;
    int i;
    s = "Word list has "+entries+" entries: \n";
    for (i = 0; i < entries; i++)
    {
        s = s + words[i] + "\n";
    }
    return s;
}
```

At this point, we don't exactly know what the Word structure will be, but we depend on its ability to print itself out (using its own toString method).

Now, we must face the task of adding a Word to the WordList. We begin by writing a method that searches for a String in the word list. It returns the index of the word in the list, if it is found, or the first available index, if it must be inserted; we make careful use of the final value of i after the loop is finished:

```
private int locate(String s)
// pre: s is not null
// post: return location of word s in array, or empty slot
{
    int i;
    for (i = 0; i < entries; i++)
    {
        if (words[i].equals(s)) return i;
    }
    return i;
}
```

We have had to depend on the equals method for Words; we must remember this when we are designing the Word class. Since our locate method is only for internal use, we declare it private. Now we consider the add method. We begin by finding the correct location in the list (using locate). If this location is less than the number of entries in the list, it must be a word we have encountered previously. We need only indicate now that we've encountered another occurrence. If it is a new word, it is inserted at the indicated spot:

```
public void add(String w)
// pre: w is not null, room for a word in list
// post: w has been added to the list
{
    int location = locate(w);
    if (location >= entries)
    {
        // add word to array
        words[location] = new Word(w);
        entries = location+1;
    } else {
        words[location].encounter();
    }
}
```

We must be careful to remember that the newly constructed words have a frequency of one.

That's it for the WordList. We now move on to design the Word class. Each entry has a String and its associated frequency. The constructor simply initializes the frequency to one and sets the String to the suggested value (it will never change):

Word

```
private String theWord;      // the word to be tallied
private int theCount;        // its frequency

public Word(String w)
// post: construct a word entry from the string w
{
    theWord = new String(w);
    theCount = 1;  // saw it at least once!
}
```

By now we have three methods that must be implemented because of our design of the WordList class: encounter, which increments the frequency; equals, which compares words to Strings; and toString, which develops a string representation of the word. They are each fairly straightforward:

```
public void encounter()
// post: the frequency of the word is incremented
{
    theCount++;
}

public boolean equals(String s)
// pre: s is not null
// post: returns true iff the word within is equal to s
```

```
    {
        return theWord.equals(s);
    }

    public String toString()
    // post: return a string representation of a word entry
    {
        return "<Word: "+theWord+" frequency: "+theCount+">";
    }
```

Since the data fields are private, they are tightly controlled. The `equals` method is interesting since it compares `Word`s and `String`s, but the reverse is not possible. The value of the word never changes, and the frequency only increases.

Life gets more complex!

In the process of designing a `WordList`, we actually had to design another class, `Word`. When writing a program that makes use of a word list, we must include both of these class definitions in the project. We can use the following simple test program, which tallies the frequency of words appearing at the console:

WordListTest

```
    public static void main(String args[])
    {
        ConsoleWindow c = new ConsoleWindow();
        String w;
        WordList wl = new WordList();

        for (c.input.skipWhite();
             !c.input.eof();
             c.input.skipWhite())
        {
            w = c.input.readString();
            wl.add(w);
        }
        c.out.println(wl);
    }
```

When given a famous tongue twister, the following output was generated:

```
Word list has 8 entries:
<Word: how frequency: 1>
<Word: much frequency: 1>
<Word: wood frequency: 2>
<Word: could frequency: 2>
<Word: a frequency: 2>
<Word: woodchuck frequency: 2>
<Word: chuck frequency: 2>
<Word: if frequency: 1>
```

Exercise 8.10 *What feature of the* add *method makes it fairly easy to determine the tongue twister from the output? What other techniques could be used?*

8.4   Inheritance and Subclasses

When designing solutions to problems, we often encounter the need to refine a definition of a type. A calculator watch is a refined watch, a record for a patient of an HMO is a specific type of medical record, and an integer is a less general concept than a number. Each of these refinements is an instance of *subtyping*: wherever the more general type of object is required, the more refined object is suitable. Thus, if you needed a watch, a calendar watch would be a suitable alternative. The opposite, by the way, is not always true: if you need the calendar feature of a calendar watch, an arbitrary watch will probably not suffice.

In Java, subtypes can be declared by having a new class *extend* an existing class. The newly defined class is called the *subclass*, while the more general object is called the *superclass*. The subclass definition automatically borrows or *reuses* or *inherits* all of the nonconstructor instance variables and methods associated with the superclass. Because of this inheritance of characteristics from a superclass to a subclass, this subclassing can also be thought of as generating a new *subtype*. The subclass must always provide its own constructors, and may optionally choose to define additional instance variables and methods. Where methods have the same signature as their counterparts in the superclass, the subclass methods are always preferred over those of the superclass and are said to *override* the superclass methods.

8.4.1   Example: A Graphical Die

As an example, suppose we are interested in constructing a graphical class, called a CubeDie, a standard six-sided die. In addition to the functions of a Die, the CubeDie knows how to paint its image on a DrawingWindow (see Figure 8.5). Here is what the entire definition looks like:

```java
import java.util.Random;
import element.*;

public class CubeDie extends Die
{
    private Pt center;  // center of die, when drawn in window

    public CubeDie(Pt center)
    // post: construct a randomly oriented die with 6 faces;
    //       drawn about center
    {
        super(6);
        this.center = new Pt(center);
    }

    public CubeDie()
    // post: construct a randomly oriented die with 6 faces
    //       drawn about origin
```

CubeDie

```
    {
        this(new Pt(0,0));
    }

    public void moveTo(Pt c)
    // post: centers the die at the location c
    {
        center = new Pt(c);
    }

    public void drawOn(DrawingWindow d)
    // post: draw the die on the drawing window about center
    {
        Circle pip = new Circle(center.x()-15,center.y()-15,4);
        RoundRect r =
            new RoundRect(center.x() - 22, center.y()-22,34,34,5,5);

        d.draw(r);
        if (value() != 1) d.fill(pip); // northwest
        pip.move(20,0);
        if (value() > 3) d.fill(pip);  // northeast
        pip.move(-20,10);
        if (value() == 6) d.fill(pip); // west
        pip.move(10,0);
        if (value()%2 == 1) d.fill(pip); // center
        pip.move(10,0);
        if (value() == 6) d.fill(pip); // east
        pip.move(-20,10);
        if (value() > 3) d.fill(pip);  // southwest
        pip.move(20,0);
        if (value() > 1) d.fill(pip);  // southeast
    }

    public String toString()
    // post: return a string representation of the CubeDie
    {
        return "<CubeDie: "+value()+">";
    }
}
```

We have made use of *inheritance*, as is indicated by the line:

```
public class CubeDie extends Die
```

The CubeDie inherits each of the nonconstructor features of the superclass Die.
With that in mind, we investigate the rest of the class definition.

The one-parameter constructor for a CubeDie calls the superclass constructor
(using the keyword super) with a single parameter. Like this, super is a
reference that allows us to refer to parts of the subclass that are attributable
to the superclass definition. The call to super initializes the Die characteristics

Figure 8.5   A pair of `CubeDie` objects, drawn in a drawing window, showing boxcars.

of the `CubeDie`. Recall that the single parameter constructor in the `Die` class causes a die with n faces to be constructed. Here, n is 6, so we have a `Die` shaped like a cube, with six sides. The constructor also initializes the `center` point of the `CubeDie`—the location where the picture of the die will be located on the screen. The default constructor is useful to us: we simply have it construct a `CubeDie` whose center is at the origin. Centering it at the origin is probably not directly useful, but it can be changed later with the next method, `moveTo`. Since there are no other constructors, and constructors are not inherited from the superclass, the only type of die that can be constructed with this class has six sides.

Our `drawOn` method accepts a `DrawingWindow` and paints the exposed face on the window at the desired center point. We make extensive use of the `value` method—since all nonconstructor methods of the `Die` class are inherited, it acts like a `Die` in this regard. For example, it is possible to get the `value` of the `CubeDie`, or to `roll` the `CubeDie` again.

The last method, `toString`, describes how to represent the `CubeDie` as a `String`. Because all objects extend `java.lang.Object` implicitly, and since the inherited `toString` method of the `java.lang.Object` class returns a (nearly useless) representation of the object, it is useful to have the `toString` method in the subclass override the `Object` method. Thus we see that we have been writing class extensions to `java.lang.Object` for some time. Good design involves writing the `toString` method for each new class.

8.4.2   Example: The Square Class

Sometimes, it is useful to use class extension to *constrain* an object. For example, we might find it useful to develop a new class, called a `Square`, that is a `Rect` with equal length sides (see Figure 8.6). We will use inheritance to borrow some of the features of a `Rect` and constrain others. Our definition starts, then, with

```
import element.*;

public class Square extends Rect
```

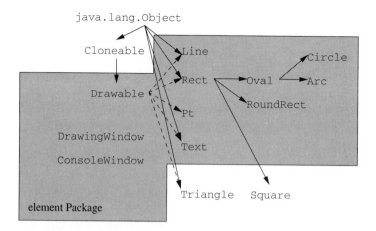

Figure 8.6 The hierarchy of graphical classes and interfaces. Solid lines indicate extensions; dashed lines indicate implementation. Only those classes and interfaces in the gray area are classes of the `element` package.

Now, it is important to realize that we need not add any instance variables to the existing `Rect` class to constrain its behavior (the `Rect` class is fully documented in Appendix E). Instead, we need to constrain the parameters of the constructors. Since the constructors of the `Rect` class are not inherited as constructors for the `Square`, we can perform much of the modification of the behavior of a `Rect` through new constructors:

Square

```
private Square()
// post: constructs a trivial square
{
    this(0,0,0);
}

public Square(Square other)
// pre: other is not null
// post: construct a square, based on another drawable object
{
    this(other.left(),other.top(),other.width());
}

public Square(int left, int top, int d)
// pre: d >= 0
// post: constructs a diameter d square with (left,top) corner
{
    super(left,top,d,d);
}
```

The last constructor does most of our work. It is responsible for constructing a rectangle whose width and height are the same. The first constructor constructs a trivial square at the origin, whose size and position can be changed with other methods. The middle constructor is a *copy constructor* that creates a new Square from one that already exists. Each of these constructors is quite simple because they pass the buck and have some other constructor do the work. In the end, the Square constructors depend on the super (for Rect objects) to initialize all the fields appropriately. If more fields must be initialized, those computations must appear after the super constructor call.

Once a Square is constructed, we must think about how one might change its shape. Rect objects can change shape with the width and height methods, as well as the extend method. In the case of width and height, we make sure that both methods change both dimensions of the underlying rectangle. The width method calls both superclass methods, while the height method calls the width. This arrangement makes it possible to localize problems if we make a mistake.

```
public void width(int w)
// pre: w >= 0
// post: sets width and height of square;
//       center and height remain unchanged
{
    super.width(w);
    super.height(w);
}

public void height(int h)
// pre: h >= 0
// post: sets the height of the square;
//       center and width remain unchanged
{
    width(h);
}
```

The extend method has a slightly different precondition than is found in the Rect case. It simply assumes that both parameters are the same and uses the first to determine the extent of the extension:

```
public void extend(int dx, int dy)
// pre: dx == dy
// post: extends sides of square out by dx (== dy)
{
    super.extend(dx,dx);
}
```

An even better improvement would be to provide a new extend method (as opposed to one that overrides the Rect method) that takes a single parameter—the amount by which the Square is grown in each dimension.

Finally, we complete our extension of the `Rect` by overriding the `toString` method to describe a `Square` object:

```
public String toString()
// post: returns a string representation of this square
{
    return "<Square: left="+left+" top="+top+" diameter="+width+">";
}
```

All together, these methods form a new class `Square` that is an extension of the `Rect` class in the `element` package. The fact that it is a subclass of the `Rect` class means that we can use it anywhere a `Rect` can be used. To demonstrate this, we present a simple game: a random `Square` is presented on the screen every second; those pressed by the mouse have their area added to the player's score. We call it "beat the squares":

Beat-
TheSquares

```
import element.*;
import java.util.Random;

public class BeatTheSquares
{
    public static void main(String args[])
    {
        final int gameTime = 60 * 1000; // one minute game
        final int winSize = 300;        // 300x300 window
        final int targetTime = 1000;    // 1000 msec (1 sec) targets
        final int minDiam = 5;          // smallest target
        final int maxDiam = 50;         // largest target
        final int diamRange = maxDiam-minDiam;
        DrawingWindow d = new DrawingWindow(winSize,winSize);
        long endTime;                   // time game ends
        Random rand = new Random();
        int score = 0;

        d.invertMode();                 // animation painting
        endTime = System.currentTimeMillis()+gameTime;

        while (endTime > System.currentTimeMillis())
        {
            // pick random square, keep on screen for short time
            long targetEndTime =
                    System.currentTimeMillis()+targetTime;
            int dia = (Math.abs(rand.nextInt()))%diamRange + minDiam;
            int x = (Math.abs(rand.nextInt()))%(winSize-dia);
            int y = (Math.abs(rand.nextInt()))%(winSize-dia);
            Square target = new Square(x,y,dia);
            boolean hit = false; // turns true if mouse hits square

            d.draw(target);     // draw target
            while (targetEndTime > System.currentTimeMillis()
```

```
                && !hit)
        {
            // constantly check for mouse down in square
            if (d.mousePressed()
                && target.contains(d.getMouse()))
            {
                score += target.width()*target.width();
                hit = true;
                d.awaitMouseRelease();
            }
        }
        d.draw(target);       // erase (invert) target
    }
    d.draw(new Text("Your score: "+score,50,150));
}
}
```

As you can tell, the `Square` objects have inherited all the features of `Rects` that we have not overridden: the `contains` method, the `width` function, and others. In fact, since the `Square` is a subclass of the `Rect` class, it is possible to change the type of the `target` variable to be a `Rect` (leaving the `new` statement as it is), and the game will function just as well! Even though we have not had to write very technical graphics code, our `Squares` have become integrated with the existing `element` package quite easily.

8.5 Interfaces

Occasionally, it is useful to generate an outline of what we expect of a certain type of class. In Java, we can describe the methods we expect to find in class definitions using an *interface*. The declaration of an interface is similar to the declaration of a class, except that there can be no instance *variables* (there can be constants), and there is no code associated with any of the methods. Here, for example, is a description of an interface for objects (like dice) that may be rolled:

```
public interface Rollable
{
    public void roll();
    // post: reselect the upward-pointing face of the object

    public int value();
    // post: return the current value of the object
}
```

Rollable

Instead of providing a code body, each method's declaration is terminated with a semicolon. This interface says, essentially, that there must be `roll` and `value` methods for something to be called `Rollable`.

Recalling our definitions of various `Die` classes, it is easy to verify that they all meet the specification of a `Rollable` object. We then can update our `Die` class one last time to reflect that it supports the interface or "contract" of being a `Rollable` object. We say that the `Die` **implements** the `Rollable` interface:

Die4

```
public class Die implements Rollable  // can be "rolled"
{
    private int faces;          // shape of die
    private int faceValue;      // current value of die
    private static Random rand; // global random number generator
        ...
```

With this little change, the `Die` class becomes a subtype (but not a subclass) of the `Rollable` type: we are able to write a program that makes use of `Die` objects anywhere `Rollable` objects are required. (Incidentally, the `CubeDie` class, which extends the `Die` class, becomes a `Rollable` as well.) As an example of this subtyping, the following program simply checks to see how many pairs of people we might meet on the street before we find two with the same birthday:

RollableTest

```
public static void main(String args[])
{
    ConsoleWindow c = new ConsoleWindow();
    Rollable birthdayChooser1 = new Die(365);
    Rollable birthdayChooser2 = new Die(365);
    int trials = 0;
    do // pick pairs of birthdays until a pair matches
    {
        birthdayChooser1.roll();
        birthdayChooser2.roll();
        trials++;
    } while (birthdayChooser1.value() != birthdayChooser2.value());
    c.out.println("Stopped after "+trials+" pairs were chosen.");
}
```

By the way, we cannot change the type of the **new** statement to `Rollable` since `Rollable` is the name of an **interface**. Among other things, interfaces do not have constructors, so it is impossible to construct one directly.[3] An analogy is to say some pets are "black pets" if they have black fur. Black Labrador Retrievers meet this criterion, so they support the "black pet" interface. You can say things like *Your black pet will get hot in the summer sun!* even if you don't know what kind of pet it is; it's simply a black pet. It could be a dog or a snake or even a cow. Now, if you wanted to create a "black pet," that is not *A* "pro-creation" *argument!* directly possible since the process of constructing a pet requires, at least, the specification of a species of animal.

Exercise 8.11 *Is it legal to change one of the* `Die` *objects in the above program to a* `CubeDie`*? Try it!*

_____

[3] Well, almost impossible. Java's *inner class* system provides the necessary loophole.

8.5.1 Example: Clonable Objects

Sometimes we can use an interface to describe a feature or a function of a class, even if it does not make any constraints on the outward appearance of a class. In Java, we say that an object is "clonable"[4] if calling the `clone` method returns a carbon copy of the object in hand. The interface, however, is very simple:

```
public interface Cloneable
{
}
```

Cloneable

Since there are no methods demanded, any class, if it chooses, can decide to implement the `Cloneable` interface. The key here is the phrase *if it chooses*. As it turns out, every class is a subclass of the class `java.lang.Object`, which includes a `clone` method. Thus, every object can have its `clone` method invoked, but only those that *choose* to override the default method should signal that they are clonable by implementing the `Cloneable` interface.

Thus the `Cloneable` interface serves as a signal that the `clone` method will create a new copy. A piece of code can test to see if the `clone` method works by using the `instanceof` operator. The `instanceof` operator has the syntax

⟨variable⟩ `instanceof` ⟨type⟩

The result of the operator is a boolean value: `true` if the ⟨variable⟩ is either type ⟨type⟩ or a subtype of ⟨type⟩. Now, code that potentially clones an object can check to see if this cloning is possible by doing a check of support for the `Cloneable` class:

```
public static void main(String args[])
{
    DrawingWindow d = new DrawingWindow();
    ConsoleWindow c = new ConsoleWindow();

    c.out.print("DrawingWindows ");
    if (d instanceof Cloneable)
    {
        c.out.println("are clonable");
    } else {
        c.out.println("are not clonable");
    }
}
```

ClonableTest

The output is:

```
DrawingWindows are not clonable.
```

Thus, interfaces can be used to signal functionality that is not directly observable in a class's method signatures.

---

[4] Unfortunately, the word clonable is misspelled consistently throughout the Java libraries as "cloneable."

8.5.2   Example: The `Drawable` Interface

In the `element` package, we have provided a number of graphical objects, including points, lines, and rectangles. These objects implement each of the methods of a `Drawable` object:

Drawable

```
public interface Drawable extends Cloneable
{
    public int height();
    // post: returns the height of the drawable object

    public int width();
    // post: returns the width of the drawable object

    public int left();
    // post: returns the left-most coordinate of the bounding
    //       box containing the drawable object

    public int right();
    // post: returns the right-most coordinate of the bounding
    //       box containing the drawable object

    public int bottom();
    // post: returns the bottom-most coordinate of the bounding
    //       box containing the drawable object

    public int top();
    // post: returns the top-most coordinate of the bounding
    //       box containing the drawable object

    public void center(Pt p);
    // post: sets the center of the bounding box of drawable to p;
    //       the dimensions remain the same

    public Pt center();
    // post: returns the center of the bounding box of
    //       the drawable object

    public void drawOn(DrawingWindow d);
    // post: draws outline of this object on window d;
    //       same as d.draw(this)

    public void fillOn(DrawingWindow d);
    // post: draws the interior of this object on window d;
    //       same as d.fill(this)

    public void clearOn(DrawingWindow d);
    // post: erases this object from window d;
    //       same as d.clear(this)
}
```

Clearly, they can all be drawn and erased from the screen, they all know where
their left and right sides are, and so on. To extend our collection to include
another object, we must implement the `Drawable` interface; the drawing window
uses this interface to identify types of objects that support drawing.

Now, suppose we want to provide support for drawing triangles in the drawing window. Clearly, the triangle does not look very much like any of the objects
we have seen in the `element` package, so we are not able to extend an existing
`Drawable` subtype. Instead, we must implement the interface afresh. The minimum requirements are the implementation of all the methods outlined in the
`Drawable` interface.

We begin our implementation by deciding that we will keep an array of three
points as our instance variable. This should be enough to describe any triangle,
and all the `Drawable` methods can be accomplished using only these data. This
also allows us to refer to the three points using a small loop that considers each
of the three points in turn. Finally, if we want to consider implementation of
general polygons, this will provide us a good start.

As is usual, we identify the information that must be conveyed to instance
variables during construction and carefully consider the form of our constructors. There aren't many choices, so we provide three versions—the default
constructor, the copy constructor (it makes a triangle from another triangle),
and a three-point constructor. Others may be added later, if we feel the need.

Triangle

```
private final int n = 3;    // n is number of vertices
private Pt v[];             // vertices of the triangle

public Triangle()
// post: generate an equilateral triangle with side 200;
//       "base" along top
{
    this(new Pt(0,0), new Pt(200,0), new Pt(100,173));
}


public Triangle(Triangle other)
// pre: other is not a null triangle
// post: this becomes a copy of the triangle
{
    this(other.v[0], other.v[1], other.v[2]);
}


public Triangle(Pt p, Pt q, Pt r)
// pre: p, q, r are not null
// post: new triangle with vertices pqr
{
    v = new Pt[n];
    v[0] = new Pt(p);
    v[1] = new Pt(q);
    v[2] = new Pt(r);
}
```

We have used n as a constant that describes the number of vertices in the object. Notice that we are very careful to ensure that the vertices are stored within the array constructed anew for this object. If we use the points passed in from the user, it is possible that they may change during the life of the `Triangle`, and that is potentially undesirable.

The drawing window makes significant use of the bounding box associated with a drawable object. We must be careful, therefore, to compute this correctly. As an example, we show the computation of the `left` side the bounding box of the `Triangle`:

```
public int left()
// post: returns the left-most coordinate of the bounding
//       box containing the triangle
{
    int i;
    int result = v[0].x();
    for (i = 1; i < n; i++)
    {
        result = Math.min(result,v[i].x());
    }
    return result;
}
```

As we can see, the choice of an array is paying off, and the loop is easily generalized to arbitrary polygons. The computation of `right`, `top`, and `bottom` follow this pattern. The computation of the `height` of the `Triangle` can now be written:

```
public int height()
// post: returns the height of the triangle
{
    return bottom()-top();
}
```

The `width` method is similar.

The computation of the "center" of the triangle uses the center of the bounding box. This point is simply the point whose x and y coordinates are the average of the left and right, and top and bottom, respectively. (Another alternative might be the *center of mass* of the triangle, which would be the average x and y coordinate of the vertices.) To set the `center` of the `Triangle`, we compute the center and move each of the vertices the distance necessary to make the new center and the desired center correspond:

```
public Pt center()
// post: returns the center of the bounding box of the triangle
{
    return new Pt((left()+right())/2,(top()+bottom())/2);
}
```

```
public void center(Pt p)
// post: sets the center of the bounding box of triangle to p;
//       the dimensions remain the same.
{
    int i;
    Pt old = center();
    int dx = p.x()-old.x();
    int dy = p.y()-old.y();
    for (i = 0; i < n; i++)
    {
        v[i].move(dx,dy);
    }
}
```

We can see that the computation of the center point involves considerable computational effort. This might be reduced if we had computed the bounding rectangle once and saved it in an instance variable. We will stick with our implementation, with the security of knowing that if we don't like the performance, we can change the implementation without changing applications that make use of the Triangle. We are beginning to see significant advantages to using abstract data types!

The last three methods of Triangle are responsible for drawing, filling, and clearing a Triangle on a DrawingWindow. Once these are implemented, a DrawingWindow can use these methods when the draw, fill, and clear methods are invoked on our drawable Triangle.

```
public void drawOn(DrawingWindow d)
// post: draws outline of this triangle on window d;
//       same as d.draw(this)
{
    int i;
    for (i = 0; i < n; i++)
    {
        d.draw(new Line(v[i],v[(i+1)%n]));
    }
}

public void fillOn(DrawingWindow d)
// post: draws the interior of this triangle on window d;
//       same as d.fill(this)
{
    drawOn(d);
}

public void clearOn(DrawingWindow d)
// post: erases this triangle from window d;
//       same as d.clear(this)
{
    int i;
```

```
    for (i = 0; i < n; i++)
    {
        d.clear(new Line(v[i],v[(i+1)%n]));
    }
}
```

Casting drawing commands in terms of other `Drawable` objects (here, `Lines`) ensures that features such as painting and inverting are supported consistently. We have fudged the `fillOn` method, calling `drawOn` instead, because the implementation is unnecessarily complex for our purposes here.

Exercise 8.12 *How would you* `fillOn` *and* `clearOn` *a triangle by, say, drawing lines? (Remember, it's important that* `fillOn` *draw every pixel exactly once so that inverting mode works.)*

At this point, we have completed the support of the `Drawable` interface. As a result, our `Triangle` objects are already quite usable. Here is a simple test application for drawing a `Triangle` on the screen. After the vertices have been indicated by three mouse clicks, we are able to drag the `Triangle` and its bounding box around the screen. The program finishes when the mouse is released the fourth time (see Figure 8.7):

TriangleTest

```
public static void main(String args[])
{
    DrawingWindow d = new DrawingWindow();
    Pt p,q,r;
    // read a triangle, using three mouse clicks
    p = d.awaitMouseClick();
    q = d.awaitMouseClick();
    r = d.awaitMouseClick();
    Drawable t = new Triangle(p,q,r);
    // construct bounding rectangle
    Drawable k = new Rect(t);

    d.invertMode();
    // draw both on screen
    d.draw(t); d.draw(k);
    d.awaitMousePress();
    while (d.mousePressed()) // drag both centered about mouse
    {
        d.draw(t); d.draw(k);
        k.center(p=d.getMouse());
        t.center(p);
        d.draw(t); d.draw(k);
    }
}
```

This program demonstrates a couple of interesting features. First, the type `Triangle` is mentioned only in the **new** command. Because the `Triangle` implements the `Drawable` interface, it is possible to assign it to a `Drawable` reference.

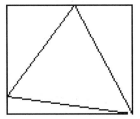

Figure 8.7 The display of a program to test the `Triangle Drawable`. The bounding box is constructed from information gleaned from the `left`, `top`, `width`, and `height` methods.

To play with `Circles` instead, we need only change the call to the `Triangle` constructor to an appropriate call to the `Circle` constructor! Next, to construct a bounding `Rect` for the `Circle`, we simply call the `Rect` constructor, passing the `Drawable` as a parameter. Since every `Drawable` object has enough information to generate a `Rect`, this does the trick. In fact, this constructor serves as the copy constructor for `Rect` objects.

8.6   Chapter Review

We have seen that classes serve as the templates for constructing objects in Java. Most object classes maintain *state information* that is stored in *instance variables*. These variables are usually declared `private`, and their access is controlled by *instance methods*. Variables and methods declared `static`, on the other hand, exist regardless of the number of instances of a class.

- Class extension is used to relate superclasses to subclasses. It also defines a new subtype. A subtype may be used in any situation where a superclass can be used, but the opposite is not true. The assignment of superclass references to subclass variables is only valid if the reference is in actuality a reference to a subclass value. This must be verified by a cast.

- Subclasses inherit all the instance variables and instance methods from their superclass. Constructors are not inherited, but may be referred to using the `super` method call. The `super` prefix can force the call to an overridden superclass method or refer to a superclass variable.

- An interface is used as a means of checking the structure of public methods in classes that implement the interface. Interfaces do not have class variables, and their methods are never directly coded.

Problems

8.1★   What is code reuse, and why is it important to modern programmers?

8.2   What is an "abstract data type," and why is it considered an improvement over systems that don't support data abstraction?

8.3★   Implement a `counter`. Such a class returns an increasing sequence of integer values, through a single method `value`. Such an object would be useful in situations like the corner deli, where tickets are handed out to keep customers in order.

8.4   Modify the `Die` class to support arbitrary ranges of random integers. This would allow for coins with sides 0 and 1, as well as dice with 1 to 6 pips.

8.5   Design a `Name` class that keeps track of the first, middle, and last names of an individual. It should have at least two constructors—one that takes a `String` describing the entire name and another that accepts three parameters describing the individual parts of the name. Make sure your class allows retrieval of any of the three names but does not allow them to be modified.

8.6★   For the `Name` class of Problem 8.5, how should the default (parameterless) constructor be declared?

8.7★   A `clone` method is inherited automatically from the `java.lang.Object` class. If invoked for an object that implements the `Cloneable` interface, it returns a distinct copy of the object. Since the `Drawable` interface extends the `Cloneable` interface, we were remiss in not writing the `clone` method for `Triangles`. Write the `clone` method for `Triangles`.

8.8   Develop a `WeightedCoin` class. It should implement the `Rollable` interface for a two-sided die. One of its constructors should take a `double` that indicates the percentage of time the `WeightedCoin` returns a 0. Write a test to verify the weighting of your coin.

8.9★   Having an upper bound of 1000 words in our `WordList` class has its disadvantages. What are they, and how might they be resolved with the use of a `Vector`? Why are these (dramatic) changes in implementation of little concern to the users of the `WordList` class?

8.10★   Java implements a point class, called `Point`. It consists of two public instance variables, `x` and `y`. The `element` package implements points with `Pt`, where these values are hidden. Discuss the advantages and disadvantages of these decisions.

8.11   Construct an `Ngon` class that implements a `Drawable` polygon of `n` vertices. (Hint: Start with the `Triangle` class.) You needn't fully implement the `fillOn` or `clearOn` methods.

8.12★   We have all heard of the "Y2K" problem: programs depending on the storage of dates using only two digits within the year may break when the year reaches 2000. Fixing such a problem can be difficult. How would object-orientation and code reuse have facilitated the fixing of logical problems such as Y2K?

8.13   Supposing the `Ngon` class of Problem 8.11 has been implemented. Decide whether the `Triangle` class should extend the `Ngon` class, or *vice versa*. Indicate the necessary modifications to each of the classes.

8.7 Laboratory: Implementing a Curve Class

Objective. To consider the various issues associated with developing a new class.

Discussion. The `element` package, as distributed, does not have any objects that support the drawing of smooth curves, or *splines*. In this lab we will develop a new class, called a `Curve`, that implements Bézier curves. We will accomplish this in two steps. First, we will construct a bare-bones class with only a few methods. We will then provide all the methods required by the `Drawable` interface and develop a full-fledged `Drawable` object that could be included as an extension to the `element` graphic package. This process is similar to the incremental construction of most objects in Java.

Procedure. Initially, you are to build a small class, `Curve`, that has three constructors, drawing methods called `drawOn`, `fillOn`, and `clearOn`, as well as a `toString` method that would be called if a `Curve` was printed to an output stream.

1. Recall that the code supporting the drawing of Bézier curves is described in the text. A natural method for representing these curves is a group of four points:

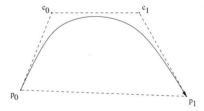

2. Once you determine how you will support your `Curve` with instance variables, you may start development of your class by filling out the details of the following class definition (you may implement `fillOn` by calling `drawOn`):

```
public class Curve
{
    private Pt p0,c0,c1,p1;

    public Curve(Curve c)
    // post: constructs curve with the same control points as c

    public void drawOn(DrawingWindow d)
    // post: draws the curve on window d

    public void fillOn(DrawingWindow d)
    // post: draws (like draw) curve on window d
```

```
        public void clearOn(DrawingWindow d)
        // post: erases curve from window d

        private Pt bez(Pt p0, Pt c0, Pt c1, Pt p1, double t)
        // pre: p0, p1 are endpoints; c0, c1 are control points
        //      0 <= t <= 1
        // post: returns the point along Bezier curve determined
        //       by p0, c0, c1, p1, and t

        public String toString()
        // post: constructs a string representation of curve
    }
```

3. Write a program that tests the functionality of the Curve class. You should be able to draw a Curve in the DrawingWindow with the Curve's drawOn method, but it should be impossible to use the DrawingWindow's draw method, which takes a Drawable object.

4. Once you have verified that your Curve is drawing correctly, implement the remaining features of the Drawable interface:

```
    public Object clone()
    // post: returns a carbon copy of this curve

    public int height()
    // post: returns the height of the curve

    public int width()
    // post: returns the width of the curve

    public int left()
    // post: returns the left coordinate of the bounding box

    public int right()
    // post: returns the right coordinate of the bounding box

    public int top()
    // post: returns the top coordinate of the bounding box

    public int bottom()
    // post: returns the bottom coordinate of the bounding box

    public Pt center()
    // post: returns the center of the bounding box

    public void center(Pt c)
    // post: re-center the curve at point c
```

5. Demonstrate that your class is, indeed, a drawable class by indicating that it implements the `Drawable` interface. Test your code by drawing a curve in the `DrawingWindow` with the `DrawingWindow`'s `draw` method.

Thought questions. Consider the following questions as you complete the lab:

1. What changes in the interface would be necessary to allow the adjustment of the various control points of a `Curve`?

2. Suppose you could fill in a triangle. How would you fill in a `Curve`?

3. The drawing of a `Curve` takes considerably longer than drawing a `Line`. How would you measure the time needed?

4. Suppose you wished to make a new `MultiCurve` object, which is a series of `Curves` spliced together with *smooth* joins. What constraints would be put on the individual curves?

Chapter 9

Recursive Structures

IN THE SAME WAY that recursion can be used to express compact and elegant designs for methods, self-reference can be used to express the relation between the classes we use to structure data. We investigate, in this chapter, a single implementation of a structure that is compactly presented, yet exposes much of the beauty of the ways that modern languages can structure data. The focus of this chapter is a recursively structured `List` class.

9.1   The Concept

We may think of the state of the program as being represented by the values of each of the variables. If, for example, a single integer variable is used, we may encode the state of the program using one integer; the program is essentially only capable of "remembering" one thing. If we are to remember a million items, a million values must be stored, potentially in a million variables.

We have seen a number of ways of relaxing this relationship. Arrays and vectors, for example, are capable of storing seemingly unbounded amounts of information, but the data must be stored contiguously. The expansion of an array is best done by doubling the size of the array. A similar technique is used to grow the length of a `Vector`, though, of course, these details are usually hidden within the structure.

One way to smooth out the overhead of allocating memory is to allocate the storage in small chunks: each chunk of the structure maintains a reference to a data value *and* a reference to the rest of such a structure. When the object references are made to other objects in the same class, the entire structure—rolled out to its full extent—is called a *self-referential* or *recursive* structure.

The simplest form occurs when the self-references are used to form a linear structure that we call a *list*. Here, we see the simplest outlines of the structure. Each element maintains a reference to an `Object`, and a reference to all the

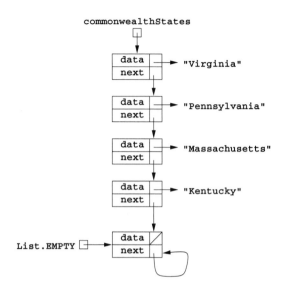

Figure 9.1   The structure of a four element list.

List objects that follow this element in the List. One can think about the List as a train: each car forms the first car in the remainder of the train (see Figure 9.1).

List

```
public class List
{
    private Object data;        // the value stored within list
    private List next;          // the remaining values of the list
}
```

The difficulty with this technique is that we must come to some agreement about the representation of the end of the List. We adopt the following strategy. We construct a single **final static** List called the **Empty List**. From outside the List class, this object is referred to as List.EMPTY. This one object is used as the value of the element that follows the last element of every List. The result is that an empty List is a List upon which List methods may be applied.

Principle 20   *The base case of a recursive class should, itself, be an instance of the class.*

The difficulty with this statement is that a cursory investigation of a recursive design may serve to convince the programmer that some other representation of the trivial case may be desirable. Usually, however, as methods are implemented they become difficult to support, with many special cases. Furthermore, the *user* of the class—probably not the programmer—must be constantly aware of how methods are to be applied.

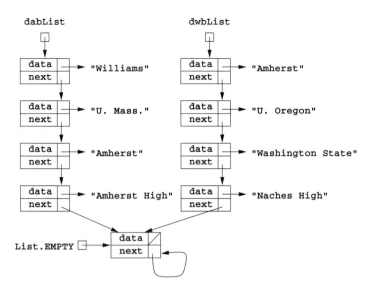

Figure 9.2 Two different `List`s. Each element of each `List` refers to a value and the `List` of values that logically follow. The end of each `List` is a special `List`, `List.EMPTY`.

9.2   Basic Implementation Details

We now consider the implementation of basic methods of the class. First, we provide three constructors. The first constructor takes no parameters and is declared `private`. Its only purpose is to construct the empty `List` element and is called once to initialize the static constant, `EMPTY` in the `List` class. Any reference to an empty `List` will be a reference to this unique element. In particular, if the user is interested in making an empty `List`, the reference must be initialized to `List.EMPTY`.

```
public final static List EMPTY = new List(); // the empty list
private List()
// post: construct nil list.  Called once only.
{
    this.data = null;
    this.next = this;
}
```

We declare this method `private` because it is not for general use by the clients of this class; it is only to be used in the initialization of `List.EMPTY`. As we can see from Figure 9.2, the last element of every `List` is a reference to the unique element `List.EMPTY`.

The one- and two-parameter constructors are used to construct `List` elements that actually contain data. The two-parameter constructor allows the programmer to specify initial values for both references. The one parameter constructor simply constructs a `List` with one element: the `next` field is a reference to the empty `List`, `List.EMPTY`. Both of these methods are declared `public` because we expect the user to make calls to these constructors.

```
public List(Object head, List rest)
// pre: construct a "cons" head, followed by rest.
{
    this.data = head;
    this.next = rest;
}

public List(Object head)
// pre: head is not null
// post: construct a list with one element, d.
{
    this(head,List.EMPTY);
}
```

Here is a typical use of these constructors. We construct a `List` with one element for every commonwealth within the United States:

```
public static void main(String[] args)
{
    List commonwealths = List.EMPTY;

    commonwealths = new List("Kentucky",commonwealths);
    commonwealths = new List("Massachusetts",commonwealths);
    commonwealths = new List("Pennsylvania",commonwealths);
    commonwealths = new List("Virginia",commonwealths);
}
```

The value of `commonwealths`, here, is assigned because the `List commonwealths` always references the `head` of the `List`. As we add elements to the `head` of the `List`, it grows longer, and we expect the value that `commonwealths` references to change over time. The end result is a `List` whose elements appear in the order opposite of the constructor calls.

Not surprisingly, one of the most useful methods we can apply to `Lists` is the method that checks for an empty `List`, `isEmpty`. An empty `List` can be identified either by checking for a `next` reference to `this` object (accomplished with `next == this`) or by checking to see if `this` object is the unique `List.EMPTY`. We choose the latter technique, but either would be fine.

```
public boolean isEmpty()
// post: return true if this list is empty
{
    return this == List.EMPTY;
}
```

Exercise 9.1 *Is it legal to compute* `List.EMPTY.isEmpty()`*? If so, what is the value?*

Frequently, we are interested in getting access to either the first element of the `List` or the remainder of the `List`, after the first element has been removed. These two parts of the `List` can be used, of course, to reconstruct the `List` from the two-parameter constructor. Thus, the `List`s `l` and `m` have the same *logical* structure:

```
List l = ...;

// assume, here, that l is nonempty
List m = new List(l.head(), l.rest());
```

The two methods `head` and `rest` are implemented in the following straightforward manner:

```
public Object head()
// pre: this list is not empty
// post: return the first element of list
{
    if (isEmpty()) return null;
    else return data;
}

public List rest()
// post: return part of list following head
{
    // note that EMPTY has EMPTY as rest
    return next;
}
```

As with the `String` class, we will not provide any methods that will allow you to *modify* `List`s. Instead, you must construct a new `List` whose modifications are incorporated within the structure. We will see more on this momentarily.

9.3 The Recursive Methods

A number of methods that provide information about the `List` structure are easily written as recursive method calls. Suppose we are interested in determining how many elements are in the `List` `l` (see Figure 9.3). As with all recursive methods, we can identify base cases and care for them individually. The simplest case is if the `List` is empty. If so, then `l` is a reference to `List.EMPTY` and we should return zero. On the other hand, if the `List` is longer than zero elements, we can recursively determine the length of the `rest` of the `List`, and add one to the result:

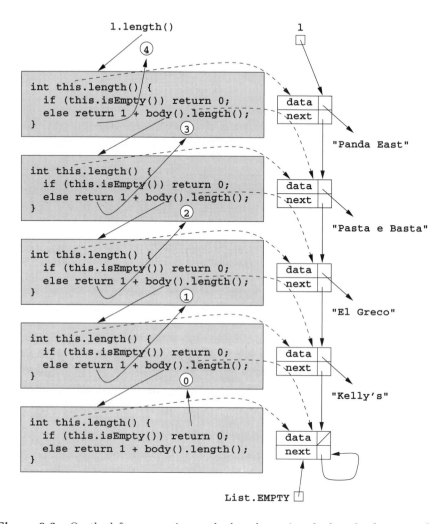

Figure 9.3 On the left, a recursive method to determine the length of a List. On the right, a recursively structured List of favorite lunch spots. Dashed arrows show the correspondence of method identifiers and List elements. Solid arrows on the left show method flow into (downward) and out of (upward) recursion.

```
public int length()
// post: return the number of elements logically in this list
{
    if (isEmpty()) {
        return 0; // empty list has no elements
    } else {
        return 1 + rest().length(); // list is head then rest
    }
}
```

This solution to the problem is beautiful. No local variables or loops are necessary and it directly encodes our thinking about the problem (as opposed to loops that often introduce unnecessary counters, etc.).

Principle 21 *Implement recursive structures using recursive methods.*

Having visited the end of the List in the process of counting elements, we now consider a method that returns the last value stored in the List (see Figure 9.4). If the List is empty, this method should return the null reference. Our thinking is much like that of the length method, except that the value returned is passed back through the recursion unmodified.

```
public Object tail()
// post: return the last value in list
{
    if (isEmpty()) return null;
    else if (rest().isEmpty()) return head();
    else return rest().tail();
}
```

Notice that the structure of both of these methods matches the recursive structure of the List that is traversed (see Figure 9.3): the base case corresponds to the base case of the List structure (the empty List), while the reduction in the problem size involves considering one fewer of the List elements.

For the purposes of comparison, we present an iterative version of length that counts the number of elements using a while loop:

```
public int length()
// post: return the number of elements logically in this list
{
    int result = 0;        // length, ultimately
    List l = this;         // l points to a sublist
    while (!l.isEmpty())
    {
        l = l.rest();      // skip over head, counting it
        result++;
    }
    return result;
}
```

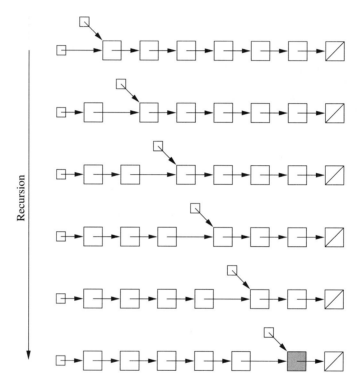

Figure 9.4   The process of finding the end of a `List`. Successively shorter `List`s are considered as recursion deepens. The result is the `head` of a final one-element `List`. The `List.EMPTY` object is indicated by slash.

Notice that there is no easy way of getting rid of the local variables in this last method.

Exercise 9.2 *Write an iterative version of* `tail`.

Because we have hidden the actual implementation using data and procedural abstraction, we are free to make changes to these methods (as the authors seem inclined to do!). The users of the `List` class are protected from the changes and needn't recompile their programs.

Predicates, of course, are a common type of method associated with classes such as `List`. Suppose, for example, we are interested in determining whether or not a particular object is found in the `List`. We can make use of the `equals` method—a method that is defined for all objects in Java—to determine whether or not any element matches the particular value. If we are to really make use of this feature, we should override the `equals` method that we inherit and substitute a suitable method for testing the objects we create.

Principle 22 *Define the* `equals` *method for objects stored in container classes.*

If we make this basic assumption about the items we store in a `List`, we can make use of the `equals` method when checking to see if a `List` contains a particular value. The result is a predicate that works for arbitrarily complex values.

```
public boolean contains(Object x)
// pre: x is not null
// post: returns true if list contains an element with x's value
{
    if (isEmpty()) return false;
    else if (head().equals(x)) return true;
    else return rest().contains(x);
}
```

The base case is, again, the empty `List`. There are no objects in an empty `List`, so the answer must be `false` in this case. Otherwise, the `List` has at least one element (the `head`) and we can compare the desired element to the `head` of the `List`. If these objects are the same under `equals`, then we may return `true`. Otherwise, we have reduced the problem of finding a value in the big `List` to finding a value in the (shorter) `rest` of the big `List`: we need only return the result of the smaller problem. Remember that this is *tail recursion* and that tail recursion can be replaced by a loop. Once again, here is how we might recast a recursive problem using a loop:

```
public boolean contains(Object x)
// pre: x is not null
// post: returns true if list contains x-value as an element
{
    List item = this;
```

```
    while (!item.isEmpty())
    {
        if (item.head().equals(x)) return true;
        item = item.rest();
    }
    return false;
}
```

As with our iterative version of the `length` routine, this method feels a little less natural because we have to keep a reference to the element of the `List` that we're considering (`item`), and that must be initialized to `this`. Furthermore, the loop must "increment" the `item` variable, moving it down the `List` by following the `rest` reference. Some simplification is possible, but it is not clear that we will come up with a solution that is as graceful as the recursive solution.

In some applications, it would be useful to be able to use the `List` structure as though it were similar to a `Vector`. Suppose, for example, we decided to support an `elementAt` method. This method accepts an index and returns the element found at that position in the `List`. We refer to the `head` of the `List` as element zero. The approach is the same as for all of the recursive methods we have seen so far. We begin by considering the base case—when the `List` is empty. Asking for an element at any index in such a `List` would be a strange request. We deal with this by returning the value `null`, an indicator that no reference was found. (A similar approach was taken with the `tail` method.)

Are there other simple base cases? Sure. If the index is zero, we need only return the `head` of the `List`. Otherwise, if the index is greater than zero, the desired value is not the `head`, but a value found in the rest of the `List` at an index that is one less than originally specified. This is encoded as follows:

```
public Object elementAt(int index)
// pre: index is < length of the list
// post: returns the index'th element of the list, where head is zero
{
    if (isEmpty()) return null;
    else if (index == 0) return head();
    else return rest().elementAt(index-1);
}
```

If the `List` is long, indexing the value is not as efficient as it would be if it were stored in a `Vector`. On the other hand, operations like removing an element from the beginning of the structure are less efficient for `Vectors`. (A more detailed analysis of problems like this is the subject of a course on *data structures*.)

We will now consider methods that appear to modify the `List` in a variety of ways. Our first is `append`, which takes a value and appends it to the end of a `List` as the new tail. Clearly, if the `List` is empty, we need only construct a new `List` with just the appended value. Otherwise, we construct a new `List` that has the `head` of the `List` (which must exist and must therefore be skipped over to append to the tail) followed by the `rest` of the `List` appended with the value (see Figure 9.5):

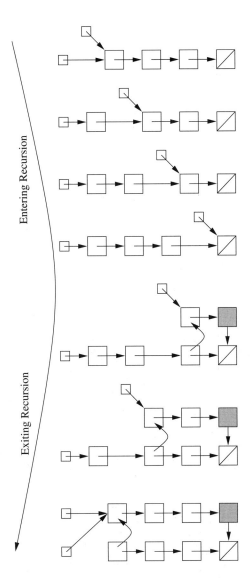

Figure 9.5 Appending a value onto a List: while entering recursion, the end of the List is found; while exiting, a new, longer List is constructed. The gray node is the newly added value. Curved arrows indicate copying of data. The List reference is usually assigned the result of the final List constructor.

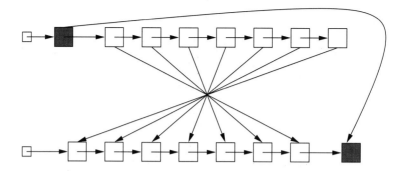

Figure 9.6 The problem of reversing a `List` is related to the problem of reversing the `rest` `List`. Before (above) and after (below) views of the `List` demonstrate that the `head` is appended to the tail of the reversed `rest`.

```
public List append(Object item)
// pre: list is not null
// post: nondestructively appends item onto end of list
{
    if (isEmpty()) return new List(item);
    return new List(head(),rest().append(item));
}
```

The simplicity of methods like `append` is startling.

Because we have an `append` method, reversing a `List` is quite simple. The process of reversing a long `List` can be thought of as taking the `head` off the `List`, reversing the `rest`, and appending what used to be the `head` (see Figure 9.6):

```
public List reverse()
// post: nondestructive reversal of List
{
    if (isEmpty()) return this;
    return rest().reverse().append(head());
}
```

Since, with `elementAt`, we can get the value of a `List` element at a particular location, we now consider how we might construct a new `List` with that element removed. The process is similar to the `elementAt` method, except that returning from the recursion allows us to construct a modified `List` with the node missing (see Figure 9.7):

```
public List removeElementAt(int index)
// pre: index is < length of the list
// post: removes the index'th element of the list, where head is zero
```

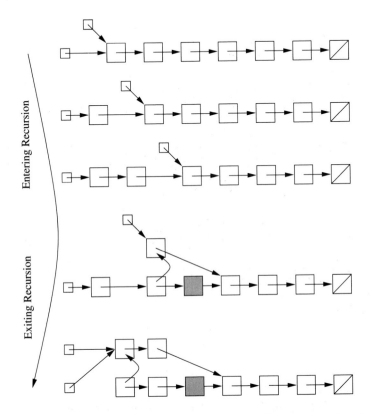

Figure 9.7 The construction of a new `List` during `removeElementAt`, when the index is 2. The gray node is logically removed. Curved arrows indicate copying of data.

```
{
    if (isEmpty()) return this;
    if (index == 0) return rest();
    else return new List(head(),rest().removeElementAt(index-1));
}
```

Finally, we present two utility methods—equals and toString. The equals method returns true if the two Lists are equal length, and each of their elements is pairwise equal. The user, of course, must be aware that the comparisons are between similar types of objects:

```
public boolean equals(Object other)
// pre: other is another List
// post: returns true if other is list with structure similar to this
{
    List that = (List)other;

    if (isEmpty() || that.isEmpty()) return this == that;
    if (!head().equals(that.head())) return false;
    return rest().equals(that.rest());
}
```

The toString constructs a String representation of the List of values. This recursive method depends on the toString method working for each of the elements of the List:

```
public String toString()
// post: print a string representation of this list
{
    if (isEmpty())
    {
        return "";
    } else {
        return head()+" "+rest();
    }
}
```

Exercise 9.3 *What is involved in writing the* clone *method? The result of* clone *should be a logical duplicate of the* List *passed in.*

9.4   Container Classes

Classes like the List class are called *container classes* because they are able to store anything that is of type Object. Every class, however, is ultimately an extension of the Object class, and so the List class is capable of storing any nonprimitive Java type. Thus, the constructor methods allow us to provide any type of object for the head of the List. Although it appears that the actual type of the object is lost when the actual parameter is associated with the formal parameter of the constructor, information about the type of the object is stored with the object itself. Even though we might pass a `String` to the `List` constructor, the reference is stored as a reference to the `Object`. The `Object` is a more general type than the `String` and cannot be assumed to have all the methods associated with the `String`. As a result, it is not possible to call, for example, the `charAt` method on the `head` of a `List`—the method has no reason to believe that a `charAt` method would work. Indeed, most `Objects` don't have `charAt` methods.

If, however, we have some good reason to believe that we know the type more specifically than Java does, we can use a *cast* as a hint to prompt Java to verify that the object is, in fact, that type. So, for example, if we consider the statements:

```
String greeting = "Howdy earthlings";   // line 1
Object token = greeting;                // line 2
    ...                                 // missing code
String phrase1 = token;                 // line 3a
String phrase2 = (String)token;         // line 3b
```

after the assignment of line 2, Java can make no assumption about `token` other than it is an `Object`. In fact, line 3a will not compile because Java is pessimistic. Perhaps there was an assignment of a non-`String` to `token` at the ellipsis, in which case the assignment at line 3a would not be legal. The alternative, line 3b, uses a cast to force Java to ask `token` what type it actually references. If it is a `String`, the assignment progresses. If, however, it is not, the program stops with an error, possibly causing chaos. Programmers, therefore, should only use casts where they are absolutely certain of the type. If they are not certain, the use of casts is ill advised, and the logic of their code should be reconsidered.

Because the values stored in the `List` are of type `Object`, it is usually necessary to recast extracted values to an appropriate type. We saw this technique when we manipulated the results of value-producing methods of the `Vector` class. This decision is usually based on knowledge we have of the way the structure is used. For example, if we know the `List` is constructed only by placing `Strings` in the `List` elements, we can be assured that anything we extract is a `String` value. Here's a familiar example of such a program: it's a version of our poetry program that prints the input back out, in random order on the output:

```
import element.*;
import java.util.Random;

public class ListPoetry
{
    public static void main(String args[])
    {
        ConsoleWindow c = new ConsoleWindow();
        Random g = new Random();
        final int max = 100;
```

ListPoetry

```
            List poem = List.EMPTY;
            String line;
            int i;

            while (!c.input.eof())
            {
                // read in each line, extending the list
                poem = new List(c.input.readLine(),poem);
            }
            while (poem.length() > 0)
            {
                // pick a line
                i = Math.abs(g.nextInt()) % poem.length();
                // print it
                c.out.println(poem.elementAt(i));
                // and remove it
                poem = poem.removeElementAt(i);
            }
        }
    }
```

We note that any updating of the logical structure of poem involves reassign-
ment: when the List is constructed, poem becomes the reference to the new
head element; when elements are removed, the poem becomes a potentially new
reference to a copy of the remaining elements of the List.

As was true with the Vector class, an appealing feature of declaring Lists
as container classes is that *anything* may be stored in the cells, including other
Lists. This forms a structure that is not necessarily linear. If the references
stored within the structure are unique, this general structure is called a *tree*.
Trees are the basis for many algorithms that are more efficient than linear Lists.
Again, this is the subject of many discussions in books on data structures and
algorithms.

Exercise 9.4 *Is it possible to construct a List of values that contains a loop?*
(Such a List would cause an infinite loop when the length method was applied.)

9.5   Chapter Review

In this chapter we have considered a completely dynamic structure that is recursively structured, called a List. The features of the List include

- Pictures are worth a thousand words: when manipulating linked structures, draw pictures to verify the structure of the List objects.

- Lists grow at a uniform rate. In particular, the cost of adding an element
  to the beginning of a List is less expensive than the cost of moving the
  elements of an array or Vector.

- Lists share a single element that serves as an end-of-list mark. This allows all the dynamic `List` methods to be invoked on empty `Lists`.

- Most, if not all, of the `List` methods can be written using recursion in a way that matches the recursive structure of the `List`.

- Like `Strings`, `Lists` cannot be directly modified. Instead, new copies of the `List` are constructed with the modifications incorporated.

- Lists are container classes: they are written to accept `Objects`, but this comes at the cost of having to cast results of methods that return values found within the `List`.

Problems

9.1   Currently, the length of a `List` must be explicitly computed, which can be costly for very long `Lists`. Consider the following modification of the `List` type: each `List` element keeps track of the length of the `List` rooted at this element. For example, the empty list would set this field to zero. Is it possible to set this field once in the life of a `List` element, or must the instance variable be allowed to vary? Explain your reasoning, and describe the pros and cons of such an implementation.

9.2★   Write a method (or methods) that, given a `List`, returns two `Lists`: one containing the even-indexed values and another containing the odd-indexed values.

9.3   Write a method, `index`, that returns the location of the first element of a `List` that matches (using `equals`) an indicated value.

9.4★   Assume that a `List` contains nothing but `Strings`, and that these `Strings` appear in nondecreasing order within the `List`. Write a method that inserts a new `String` into the correct position within the ordered `List`. (Such a method could be the basis for an implementation of *insertion sort*.)

9.5   Develop a new class called `Stack` that only allows the insertion or removal of values from a `List` at the list `head`. (This design process is mainly one of removing methods.) Stacks simulate the behavior of a stack of trays in the dining hall: the last items added to the `Stack` are the first ones to be removed.

9.6   Develop a new class called `Queue` that only allows the insertion at the tail and removal from the `head` of the `List`. (Again, this process is mainly one of removing methods.) Queues simulate the behavior of people lining up at the dining hall: the last items added to the `Queue` are the last ones to be removed.

Chapter 10

Threads

"'Nor, when I bethink me, will I yield now.
Ho, my merry men! Come quickly!'
Then from out the forest leaped Little John
and six stout yeomen clad in Lincoln green."
—Howard Pyle

INSTRUCTIONS MUST BE INTERPRETED BY A PROCESSOR for a computer to perform a computation. We have written a number of Java *programs* that seem to require the complete attention of the Java-oriented machine. In fact, the behavior of a computer is the result of cooperation among many *threads* of execution—sequences of instructions that claim periodic control over a processor for only a short period of time. For example, each window associated with a Java program maintains one or more threads that are responsible for keeping the contents of the window as up-to-date as possible. Most of the time Java hides the details of managing threads, but, on occasion, it is useful for programmers to know how to create and maintain their own threads. The programming of threads is the subject of this chapter.

Before we begin, we point out that we use the term *processor* rather than computer because a single computer might have more than one processor. The use of threads can help us to establish *concurrency*[1] in our programs. The use of concurrency in programming provides us more flexibility in the way we solve programs on one or more processors.

10.1 Thread Concepts

A *thread* is the encapsulation of a piece of code to be executed. Once the thread is created, a piece of code associated with the thread is scheduled to be executed on a processor. The purpose of the thread is to coordinate the execution of the code with other threads.

A newly constructed thread is added to a schedule of threads that is considered by the processor. Over its life, it goes through several important stages (see Figure 10.1). We say that a thread is *running* if the thread's code is currently

---

[1] Strictly speaking, two threads are *run in parallel* if they run at the same time on separate processors. We will say separate threads are *concurrent* if they *appear* to be running in parallel, though they, in fact, may share a single processor. The distinction is largely unimportant to our discussion.

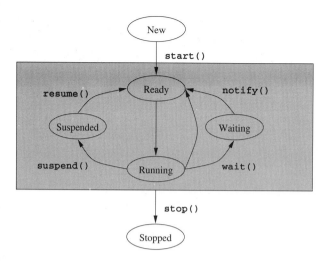

Figure 10.1   The life cycle of `Threads`. A `Thread` is created and enters a cycle of being scheduled and running. At times it may be explicitly suspended or may wait based on an unavailable resource. Finally, the thread can be stopped at any time.

being interpreted by some processor. If, however, the code is not currently being executed, it might be *waiting*. This might happen, for example, if some other thread has control of the processor. The hope would be that the currently running thread would surrender the use of the processor and that the waiting process would get a chance to run itself. When a thread is explicitly told to surrender the processor until further notice, we say the thread is *suspended*; a suspended process must be explicitly *resumed* before it may run again. In extreme cases, a thread may be *stopped* or *killed*, in which case the resources used by the thread—including the processor—are given up permanently for use by remaining threads.

The scheduling of the execution of processes is an important consideration— how processes are scheduled helps to understand how they may interact. If, for example, a single thread runs on the processor continuously, it is impossible for other threads to run or to communicate with it. For portability reasons, there are few constraints on how these processes are actually scheduled. There are, however, hints that the user can provide on the *priority* of a process. High priority processes generally need to be executed soon, while low priority processes are scheduled when little else needs to be done. Armed with these hints, the scheduler can be depended upon to schedule the processor resources fairly.[2]

---

[2] By *fair*, we will mean that no ready thread is held off for an "unreasonable" amount of time. In particular, it is *not* necessarily the case that *fairly* scheduled threads get an *equal* amount of time on the processor.

Thus, as we see in Figure 10.1, the thread goes through a life cycle that is governed by its relationship with the processor's schedule.

10.2 Computing with Java's Threads

In Java, threads are created by extending Java's `Thread` class. The `Thread` class itself does nothing particularly interesting, but it provides a `run` method (which is usually overridden) and a number of other methods that are useful when trying to control the `Thread`'s behavior.

Typically, the `Thread` class is extended with the `run` method overridden to specify the computation that is to be performed. Ideally, it will be executed concurrently with other computations in the Java system. The `Thread` is only useful as long as `run` is being executed: once the `run` method finishes, the `Thread` stops and cannot be restarted. As with any class, the extensions to the `Thread` class may have additional instance variables and methods to facilitate the computation. Any items declared `static` are accessible by any instances of the class. (As we will see a little later, `static` instance variables provide a mechanism for different `Threads` to communicate.)

A newly constructed `Thread` does not run until the `start` method is invoked. This allows the `Thread`'s settings to be adjusted before it is run. Once the `Thread` is running, its instructions are interpreted by a processor. Periodically, however, a `Thread` surrenders its hold on the processor, allowing other `Threads` to execute. A `Thread` stops running in any of the following cases:

- Java decides to schedule another `Thread` for execution, for example, if the current `Thread` has dominated the processor for a long time or if a more urgent `Thread` needs to be executed.

- The `Thread` requires a resource that is not currently available. In such a case, the `Thread` *waits* until it is *notified*.

- The `Thread` is explicitly *suspended*. Suspended `Threads` must be explicitly *resumed*.

- The `Thread` is *stopped*. Stopped `Threads` may not be restarted.

Because many `Threads` must share the same computing resources (processors, data, etc.), it is the programmer's responsibility to make sure that each `Thread` does not unduly dominate its computing resources. In some environments (but not all), `Thread` execution is interleaved in a round-robin fashion, with each `Thread` running for a specific length of time before being rescheduled. In other environments, the programmer is responsible for forcing the `Thread` to yield the processor.

The simplest mechanism is to set the *priority* of a `Thread`. The priority of a `Thread` is set with the `setPriority` method of the `Thread` class. There are three basic levels, with fine gradations in between. `Thread.NORM_PRIORITY` is the default priority of a process, `Thread.MIN_PRIORITY` is the lowest priority and would execute only when no other `Threads` might make use of the CPU, and `Thread.MAX_PRIORITY` is the highest priority that, essentially, schedules the `Thread` continuously. These are integer values and may be adjusted somewhat by adding or subtracting small values. On a round-robin scheduling system, each process that runs at a particular priority runs at about the same rate. The `Thread.MIN_PRIORITY` and `Thread.MAX_PRIORITY` are rarely used. Fine adjustments to `Thread.NORM_PRIORITY` can be used, if necessary, to generate the desired effect.

10.2.1   Example: A Mandelbrot Viewer

In our first example, we consider the use of `Threads` to support multiple drawing windows. Each is supported by an independent `Thread` that computes the *Mandelbrot set* in a portion of the complex plane. (Those less interested in the mathematical details of this computation can skim the next few background paragraphs.)

The Mandelbrot set is generated by looking at the *behavior* of the function

$$z(n, c) = \begin{cases} 0 & \text{if } n = 0 \\ z(n-1, c)^2 + c & \text{if } n \geq 1 \end{cases}$$

Notice that $z(1, c) = c$. Clearly, if c is zero, the value of z never changes. On the other hand, if c is 2, $z(n, c)$ diverges with increasing n. Proving that z diverges for a particular value c is difficult, but if $|z(n, c)| \geq 2$, it must. We use this fact to classify the speed at which z diverges for a particular c: we simply keep track of the smallest n for which the magnitude of $z(n, c)$ becomes larger than 2. For values where the z converges, there is no such n. When z diverges, however, n is finite and provides a rough estimate of the *rate* at which z diverges. For our purposes, here, we will assume that a rate of $n >= 256$ is so slow that the function is likely to be convergent. The value of n can be computed by the following Java method:

```
static int mandelbrot(double re, double im)
// post: computes the rate of divergence of z, Mandelbrot's function
{
    double re0 = re, im0 = im;
    double r2,i2;
    int count;
    for (count = 0; count < 255; count++) {
        r2 = re * re; i2 = im * im; // square (im,re)
        if (r2 + i2 > 4.0) break;   // halt if magnitude > 2
        im = 2 * im * re + im0;     // add (im,re) to square
        re = r2 - i2 + re0;
    }
    return 255-count; // count: 255=> converges, 0=> diverges fast
}
```

Pictures such as the one in Figure 10.2 can be drawn by considering the image to be a view of the complex plane, assigning each pixel a complex value.

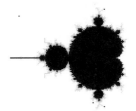

Figure 10.2   A view of the interesting points of the Mandelbrot set.

The color of each pixel is a shade of gray whose intensity is inversely proportional to the speed at which z diverges. Here we present a method that computes an entire image:

MandelThread

```
public void drawMandelbrot(double x0, double y0, double w, double h,
                           int col, int row, int iw, int ih)
// pre: (x0,y0) is lower-left corner of complex plane
//      w,h > 0 determine width of image in complex plane
//      (row,col) is upper-left corner of drawing window
//      iw, ih determine the width and height of the image in window
{
    int r, c;
    for (r = 0; r < ih; r++)
    {
        d.hold();            // stop updating screen
        for (c = 0; c < iw; c++)
        {
            double x;
            double y;
            // determine the speed and color of this pixel
            x = x0+c*(w/iw);
            y = y0+r*(h/ih);
            int speed = Fractal.mandelbrot(x,y);
            d.setForeground(new Color(speed,speed,speed));
            // draw it!
            d.draw(new Pt(col+c,row+r));
        }
        d.release();        // update entire row
    }
}
```

In this method, the rectangular portion of the screen between (col, row) and $(col + iw, row + ih)$ is associated with the complex plane between the points $x_0 + y_0 i$ and $(x_0 + w) + (y_0 + h)i$. The double loop simply computes the speed of divergence and converts it to a new gray Color that is painted on the screen. We use hold and release methods to paint each line of pixels at one time, speeding up the entire computation.

The interesting aspect of the MandelThread class is its run method. Initially, run creates a new DrawingWindow and paints a particular view of the Mandelbrot set on the screen. Once the image is painted, run loops, using new rectangles to generate refined views of the image in independent threads.

```
public void run()
// pre: x0, y0, w, h describe an image region in complex plane
// post: draw mandelbrot image and generate refined images
{
    d = new DrawingWindow(WIDTH,HEIGHT);
    double cx0,cy0,cw,ch;
    // copy the starting coordinates from static variables
    cx0 = x0;
    cy0 = y0;
    cw = w;
    ch = h;
    c.out.println("Picture is ("+cx0+","+cy0+") "+cw+"x"+ch);
    d.clear(d.bounds());
    drawMandelbrot(cx0,cy0,cw,ch,0,0,WIDTH,HEIGHT);
    while (true)
    {
        c.out.println("Scan new rectangle");
        Rect r = scan();  // simple: returns scanned rect
        // compute new complex plane coordinates
        x0 = cx0 + cw/(double)WIDTH*(double)r.left();
        y0 = cy0 + ch/(double)HEIGHT*(double)r.top();
        w = cw * (double)r.width()/(double)WIDTH;
        h = ch * (double)r.height()/(double)HEIGHT;
        // create and start new mandelbrot thread
        MandelThread t = new MandelThread();
        t.setPriority(NORM_PRIORITY-1);
        t.start();
    }
}
```

The computational process begins with a main method. This is responsible for reading the initial bounding complex coordinates of the image and starting the initial thread (at a slightly lower than normal priority). Our version reads in the coordinates from the console. A more graphically oriented program might read the coordinates using the mouse and an initial image.

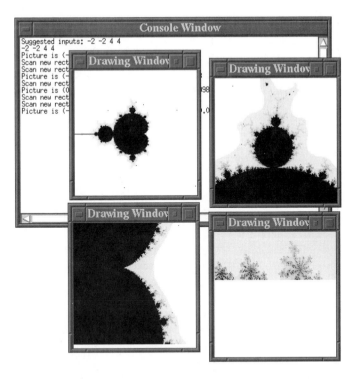

Figure 10.3 A dump of the `mandelThread` program in the midst of computing two simultaneous images (bottom left and right).

```
public static void main(String args[])
{
    MandelThread t = new MandelThread();
    c = new ConsoleWindow();
    c.out.println("Suggested inputs: -2 -2 4 4");
    x0 = c.input.readDouble();
    y0 = c.input.readDouble();
    w = c.input.readDouble();
    h = c.input.readDouble();
    t.setPriority(Thread.NORM_PRIORITY-1);
    t.start();
}
```

Once this process begins, each new image increases the potential concurrency of the application. For example, in Figure 10.3, two images (in the bottom left and bottom right) are computing concurrently.

10.3   Synchronization

As we have seen in our Mandelbrot example, the initial values for each window's computation are gleaned from a `static` instance variable of the class. Because these variables are declared `static`, they are shared among each of the computing `Thread`s. These values are set when the `Thread` that starts up a new window sets them. Because they are shared, it is possible (though not probable) that more than one window might write to these variables at the same time, and at least one of the `Thread`s is likely to find that the value stored in a variable is not what was expected.

There are a number of subtle difficulties that can occur when more than one `Thread` attempts access of a shared resource at the same time, so Java provides a method for ensuring exclusive access to resources, called *synchronization*. Each class and each instance of a class (each object) in Java is provided a *lock*. A lock is a resource that may be *held* by at most one `Thread`. Initially, locks are not held by any `Thread`. Later, a `Thread` might attempt to acquire a lock; if the lock is not currently held, the lock is acquired. If, however, the lock is held by some other `Thread`, the requesting `Thread` is suspended, or made to *wait*. Eventually, when the lock is released, one of the `Thread`s waiting on the lock is *notified* by rescheduling the `Thread` to run while holding the lock. In day-to-day life, we perform locking ourselves. For example, when multiple cars arrive at a four-way intersection with stop signs, it is important that at most one car occupy a particular lane at a time within the intersection. The local law determines how locks are acquired and in what order waiting cars are notified that they now have the lock.

Locks on `static` (classwide) variables are acquired by executing a static method that is declared `synchronized` and, not surprisingly, the lock is released when the method is exited. Methods that are not declared `synchronized` may be executed at any time, no matter what the state of the lock on the class. Thus, when one `Thread` is executing a `synchronized static` method, no other `Thread` is allowed to execute that method, *or any other* `synchronized static` *method* of the object.

Similarly, a lock in a particular *instance* of a class—an object—can be acquired by calling a `synchronized` instance method. During a call to a `synchronized` instance method, other `Thread`s must wait to access any `synchronized` method of *that same object*. Different objects may be the target of similar methods applied by different `Thread`s. If all methods that access a particular instance variable are declared `synchronized`, then the instance variable may only be accessed by a single `Thread` at a time.

10.3.1   Example: A Deli Counter

UnsynchThread

Suppose in the following method that `count` is used to get the value of a `private` counting device and returns that value after it has been incremented. It might be useful, for example, for keeping order in the Berkshire Market, a busy deli with a constant need for a solid synchronization mechanism:

```
private static int ticker = 0;

static public int count()
// post: return a unique counter value
{
    int result = ticker;
    yield();
    ticker++;
    yield();
    return result;
}
```

We should expect that this method might occasionally be interrupted by the scheduling of other threads. In fact, we have inserted `yield`[3] methods here to explicitly force the rescheduling of the current thread in at least the two places indicated. If multiple threads call this method, it is likely that several of the threads will see the very same counter value. In our deli analogy, it's as though someone stepped up and started to grab a ticket and then turned to the person behind them and said, "I'm slow; you grab my ticket too!"

We can test this theory by having five threads take several numbers, stopping when they find a value that is 10 or greater:

```
public void run()
// post: print counter values until one larger than 10 is printed
{
    int ticket;
    do
    {
        ticket = count();
        System.out.println(ticket);
    } while (ticket < 10);
}

public static void main(String args[])
// post: run five threads that fight over the counter
{
    int i;
    for (i = 0; i < 5; i++)
    {
        new UnsynchThread().start();
    }
}
```

The output (modified for brevity), which we hope to be a sequence of unique values, is instead the following:

```
0 0 0 0 0 5 5 5 5 5 10 10 10 10 10
```

---

[3] Every thread has a `yield` method, though most need not explicitly give up control. Our use here is to generate a potentially dangerous interleaving of **Thread** executions.

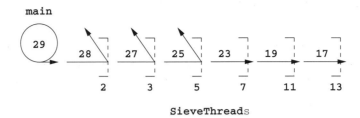

Figure 10.4 The sieve of Eratosthenes, implemented as a lengthening series of threads that implement sieves for increasingly large primes. Numbers are passed from one `SieveThread` to the next, possibly being rejected if they are found to be composite. Numbers emitted from the right form new sieves.

We can see what happens: all five threads are scheduled round-robin and grab the counter value when it is zero. Later, they all increment it once, bringing it to five. The process continues.

We would instead like each process to have, in some order, unfettered access to the `ticker` variable. This is accomplished by declaring `count synchronized`:

```
synchronized static public int count()
```

SynchThread

The result, even with the `yield` methods included, is what would be desired:

```
0 1 2 3 4 5 6 7 8 9 10 11 12 13 14
```

Exercise 10.1 *What happens when the word* `static` *is removed from* `count`? *What happens if static is also removed from* `ticker`?

10.3.2   Example: A Prime Number Sieve

Earlier (in Section 7.1) we worked through an example of the sieve of Eratosthenes. There, we made several passes through an array that crossed out multiples of various values. In this example (see Figure 10.4), we will implement the sieve using a single thread for each prime number found. As increasingly large potential primes are considered, they are passed from one thread (called a `SieveThread`) to another. Composite numbers are eliminated along the way by their smallest prime factor. Any number that makes it through each of the existing sieves is, of course, prime and is the basis for a new sieve that will lengthen the gauntlet.

To accomplish this, we will design a `Thread` class that keeps track of a rudimentary communication channel implemented using an integer and a boolean. The boolean flag indicates to the `SieveThread` whether or not the integer is a usable value. If the flag is true, then the channel (the integer) is a number to be considered for this `SieveThread`. If the flag is false, the channel is empty, waiting for another number to be passed along.

We also will need to make use of two new methods associated with every object: `wait` and `notify`. When a thread holds a lock, the lock may be temporarily surrendered to another thread by calling `wait`. The `Thread` will be suspended as a process *waiting* on the lock and will resume when another `Thread` that later holds the lock calls `notify`. The assumption is that by waiting, some other `Thread` will improve the state of the shared variables, making it possible for this thread to go forward. In our example, the `SieveThread` will `wait` for the next smallest `SieveThread` to pass along an integer and `notify` it that the integer is in the channel.

A feature of this example is that every `SieveThread` will have its own communication channel. The channel is, then, an instance variable of the class and is shared using synchronized instance methods. A little thought will reveal that many integers may be marching through the `SieveThread`s concurrently, so there should be many places to store them.

Not worrying about the `run` method details, we outline that part of the thread that is responsible for communication. It consists of an `int` and `boolean`, along with two synchronized methods, `send`—which a smaller `SieveThread` uses to deliver an `int`—and `receive`—which the `SieveThread` uses to read the value. As is true with many `Thread`-based pieces of code, it's complex, so expect to read it a couple of times!

SieveThread

```java
private boolean inputValid;
private int input;

public SieveThread()
{
    inputValid = false;  // the input buffer isn't being used...yet
}

synchronized public int receive()
// post: read a value from smaller SieveThread
{
    while (!inputValid)
    {
        try
        {
            wait();
        } catch (Exception e) { System.exit(0); }
    }
    inputValid = false;      // at return, input will be gobbled
    notify();                // wake up possible waiting sender
    return input;            // return soon-to-be invalid input
}

synchronized public void send(int n)
// post: write n to larger SieveThread
```

```
    {
        while (inputValid)
        {
            try
            {
                wait();
            } catch (Exception e) { System.exit(0); }
        }
        input = n;              // we have the lock, set buffer
        inputValid = true;      // indicate that the buffer is useful
        notify();               // wake up receiver (if waiting)
    }
```

Of course, when the SieveThread starts up, the input cannot be valid, so the constructor sets the inputValid flag to false. Looking at the send method first, we see that the method is synchronized. Since it is not static, it will first acquire the lock of this particular SieveThread. Once locked, it is impossible for any other Thread to call either send or receive. If the inputValid flag is false, the data we wish to send will not overwrite any data that is there. If, however, the flag is true, we must wait for the SieveThread to call its own read method, clearing the inputValid flag. (The try statement is an unfortunate necessity: it calls the wait method, and if there are any errors—here, referred to as an Exception called e—then the program is halted. In the normal course of waiting in this program, there will be no errors. Still, Java is picky enough to make us catch any errors with the try statement.) Once the inputValid flag is false, the waiting for an empty communication channel is finished, and the data are moved into the buffer. If (as we will see below) someone is waiting for valid data, then inform them of new data by calling notify.

Note that the wait and notify methods take no parameters. The wait and notify methods are performed in the context of the lock that was acquired by the current method. If multiple SieveThreads are waiting, they are waiting on different locks. A notify will only wake those Threads waiting on the same lock.

The action of the receive method is similar. Notice that we make use of the input even after the notify happens. This is because the notify occurs as soon as this process surrenders the lock, and not earlier. We just as easily could have saved the result of the read before the notify had taken place. Understanding these details is difficult, and subtle misunderstandings lead to many "intermittent errors" and "glitches" that make up today's multithreaded software.

Given these primitives, we can now construct the rest of the SieveThread class. The first value a SieveThread receives is prime and will be the base value whose multiples are removed from the stream if encountered. Of course, if a value makes it through *this* SieveThread, then it should be passed along to an even greater SieveThread. The nextSieve object is a reference to the thread of the next larger SieveThread; it is created once and is the target of all the future send calls from here. Here is the full text of the run method:

```
private static final int max = 10000;  // largest prime reported
private int fact;                      // factor sieve uses
private SieveThread nextSieve;         // reference to next sieve

public void run()
{
    fact = receive();
    System.out.println(fact);
    int n;

    // start up next sieve in line
    nextSieve = new SieveThread();
    nextSieve.setPriority(Thread.NORM_PRIORITY-1);
    nextSieve.start();

    for (n = receive(); n < max; n = receive())
    {
        // read values and pass along ones that we don't divide
        if (0 != n % fact) {
            nextSieve.send(n);
        }
    }
}
```

Notice, by the way, that the run method is not synchronized. If it were, it would lock out access to the communication buffer by other Threads.

The only purpose of the main program is to create a single SieveThread and to send it a stream of potential primes, starting with two:

```
public static void main(String args[])
{
    // start up a sieve
    SieveThread source = new SieveThread();
    source.setPriority(Thread.NORM_PRIORITY-1);
    source.start();
    int i;
    for (i = 2; i < max; i++)
    {
        // send it a stream of integers
        source.send(i);
    }
}
```

Because each SieveThread prints its own value, a list of potential primes less than 10000 is presented on the output. As the program runs, a total of 1229 different Threads is created. Not surprisingly, the program slows a bit as the numbers appear, but it is also the case that each prime printed is the result of an increasing amount of computation.

While sieve algorithms such as this are not very effective prime computation techniques, they are amenable to parallelism: when more than one processor can be used to support a single Java computation, threads can be placed on separate processors, speeding up the computation. This can be done without rewriting the original code, where nonthreaded implementations cannot easily make use of more than one processor.

10.3.3 Example: Counting Semaphores

Often, it is useful to limit access to a *collection* of resources. For example, print jobs might be printed on any of a pool of similar printers, but only one job must be printing on a printer at a time. Or a pool of bank tellers might provide access to a queue of bankers in order. Computationally, too, it may be useful to limit the number of `Threads` within a pool that are currently active. One tool can be used in all of these situations: a counting semaphore.

A *semaphore*[4] is a synchronization mechanism that controls access to a shared resource. It provides two operations: `acquire`[5] and `release`. In an implementation of semaphores, `acquire` blocks the current thread until the resource guarded by the semaphore is available, while `release` makes the resource available for others to acquire.

A *counting semaphore* is a semaphore that allows access to n equivalent shared resources (see Figure 10.5). When the semaphore is constructed, a specific value of n is provided. At that point, n consecutive `acquire` operations are immediately successful before one is blocked.

Our treatment of the `send` and `receive` methods in the `SieveThread` example provides us the initial details we will need to implement counting semaphores. Here, though, we will implement the semaphore as a class of its own with synchronized access to instance variables. Within the class, we keep track of the number of outstanding resources that are available.

```
private int count;  // number of resources currently available

public Semaphore(int number)
// pre: number > 0
// post: construct a binary semaphore; controls a single resource
{
    count = number;
}

public Semaphore()
// post: construct a binary semaphore; controls a single resource
{
    this(1);
}
```

---

[4] A semaphore is a signal used on railways at both ends of a shared set of rails. At any time, at most one approaching train is given the signal to use the track.
[5] Originally, these operations were given the cryptic names P (Dutch for *passeren* or "pass by") and V (Dutch for *vrijgeven*, or "release"). With due respect to Dutch, we use more descriptive names in our treatment here.

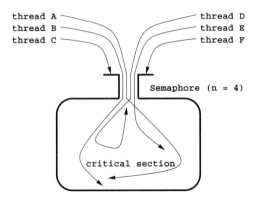

Figure 10.5 Counting semaphores control access to critical sections of a program. Here, four threads are allowed access while two others wait. As threads leave the section, waiters are notified that they may proceed.

Initially, of course, the constructor sets this to the maximum number of resources, but at other times, this number may become negative as the number of threads requesting a resource exceeds the number available.

Now, to acquire a resource, we must check to see if any resources are available. If there are, we decrement the inventory and return, allowing the `Thread` to continue. If there are no available resources, we wait until we are notified by a thread holding a resource that one is now available.

```
synchronized public void acquire()
// post: awaits allocation of a resource
{
    while (count <= 0)
    {
        try {
            wait();
        } catch (Exception e) { System.exit(0); };
    }
    count--;
}
```

To release a resource, we simply increment the number of resources and notify any waiting processes that the inventory has changed:

```
synchronized public void release()
// post: frees resource
{
    count++;
    notify();
}
```

Since both `acquire` and `release` are declared `synchronized`, at most one `Thread` will be allowed to update the state of the inventory (although many `Threads` may be waiting to enter one of the methods, or may be explicitly waiting on a positive change in the inventory of the resources).

We can now easily control the number of threads that are executing a section of code at any time through the use of a counting semaphore. At the top of the *critical section*, each `Thread` acquires the section, and at the bottom, the `Thread` releases the resource:

Critical

```
static Semaphore threadController;

public void run()
{
    threadController.acquire();
    ...
    if (...) new Critical().start();
    ...
    if (...) new Critical().start();
    ...
    threadController.release();
}

public static void main(String args[])
{
    threadController = new Semaphore(10);
    new Critical().start();
}
```

Notice again that the method `run` is not itself declared `synchronized`. Instead, the semaphore is synchronized, and threads will not be allowed to advance without a semaphore `acquire`. In fact, because the entire thread is controlled by the semaphore, we can be sure that even though large numbers of threads are created, the processor is not distracted by any more than 10 at time.

Of course, a counting semaphore that controls a single resource (a *binary semaphore*) is, effectively, a simple lock that could be implemented using Java's standard synchronization techniques. Still, the simplicity of the use of binary `Semaphores` makes them an appealing alternative, and many systems use semaphores to control the allocation of resources.

Exercise 10.2 *Reimplement the prime number sieve by removing synchronization on the* `SieveThread` *class, replacing it with* `Semaphores`.

Once implemented, of course, `Semaphores` can be used in any application. The ability to diversity the synchronization mechanisms of a language that supports multithreaded applications is a very positive feature. Concurrent applications are difficult to design, and often an alternative means of synchronizing resources can simplify the ultimate solution.

10.4   Chapter Review

In this chapter, we have seen how we can use threads to schedule concurrent computations.

- New threads are usually developed as a subclass of Java's `Thread` class.

- The `Thread` class provides many methods that are useful in controlling thread behavior. `start`, `stop`, `yield`, `wait`, and `notify` all control the current state of a thread.

- The priority of a thread determines the likelihood that a thread will be scheduled soon. It may be adjusted (with care) using the `setPriority` method of the `Thread` class.

- Class variables are shared among all instances of a class, while instance variables are usually shared through the use of methods.

- Successful sharing of variables demands appropriate use of synchronization primitives or semaphores. Java provides a rich set of supporting utilities for sharing of resources.

- Multithreaded applications allow the programmer a greater variety of approaches to solving problems, some of which might make use of parallel execution of threads on different processors.

Chapter 11

Machines

"Computer science is no more about computers than
astronomy is about telescopes."
—E. W. Dijkstra

WE HAVE SPENT SO MUCH TIME CONSIDERING SOFTWARE that it is easy to forget that a computer is involved. In this chapter we consider various machines that are of interest to computer scientists. Recall that when Java "compiles" code, it is simply translating your human readable Java into another language that is easier for computers to understand. Still, Java runs on so many different types of computers, it is hard to know *what* should be part of an ideal universal language for machines. In this chapter, we investigate three machines that are important to computer scientists and, as we will see, none of these is implemented in hardware!

11.1 Java's Virtual Machine

When we write programs in Java, we hope to be able to write programs that run on a great many *platforms*. Loosely speaking, a platform is a configuration of hardware and an operating system. We need only open a magazine to understand that there are a great variety of approaches to computing.

So the makers of Java sidestepped the issue of appropriate hardware and opted to meet the various platforms half way (see Figure 11.1): Java compiles to the *Java Virtual Machine* (or *JVM*)—a machine that exists only as a specification—and the various vendors would build programs that simulated the behavior of the virtual machine on top of their platforms. This virtual machine has certain basic characteristics, including a graphical console, a mouse with at least one button, large chunks of memory, and a system for storing files. The unique aspect of the JVM is that the language designers determined the features of the machine.

It is certainly beyond the scope of this book to describe the features of the JVM in any detail, but you can easily peek at the machine's interface with your environment using a *disassembler*. A disassembler is responsible for interpreting a compiled program in a manner that makes the program readable by (persistent) humans. In some environments, a Java utility called `javap` provides this function, while in others a debugger can show you disassembled code.

As an example of what the JVM language looks like, we disassemble the code for the very first program of this text, a program called `Greeting`, which we reproduce here:

Greeting

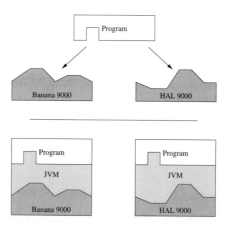

Figure 11.1   Above: portable programs must mesh well with a variety of computing environments. Below, the Java Virtual Machine masks the differences between machines and provides a similar virtual target machine in each environment.

```
public class Greeting
{
    public static void main(String[] args)
    {
        // welcome the user
        System.out.println("Welcome to Java.");
    }
}
```

This is how the JVM sees the code:

```
Compiled from Greeting.java
public synchronized class Greeting extends java.lang.Object
{
    public static void main(java.lang.String[]);
    public Greeting();
}

Method void main(java.lang.String[])
   0 getstatic #7 <Field java.io.PrintStream out>
   3 ldc #1 <String "Welcome to Java.">
   5 invokevirtual #8 <Method void println(java.lang.String)>
   8 return

Method Greeting()
   0 aload_0
   1 invokespecial #6 <Method java.lang.Object()>
   4 return
```

As you can see, even though the program we wrote specifies one method, there are now two. The second method is the default constructor, should we decide to construct a `Greeting` object. Clearly, that was not our intent, and so we will ignore that code. The two lines just below the disassembled header of the `main` procedure fetch the output stream (`System.out`) and the string we wish to print (`"Welcome to Java."`). These values are placed in a listlike structure called a *stack*. Then the `invokevirtual` command calls the `println` method. This method absorbs the two values last placed on the stack and prints the `String` to `System.out`. The final instruction, `return`, is the standard method for returning from a valueless procedure.

The sequence of numbers beside the disassembled instructions are offsets, measured in addressable memory units, or *bytes*. We can see, then, that the `getstatic` method takes three bytes (from 0 up to 3), while the `ldc` (load constant) instruction takes only two. Fortunately, these are not considerations of the Java programmer! Instead, they disappear with the abstraction of the Java language. On the other hand, the virtual machine, which understands the code we disassembled, does not concern itself with many of the details of the underlying machine. Are we running on a Banana 9000 or a HAL 9000? *Those* details disappear with the abstraction that supports the JVM.

So the Java Virtual Machine provides a suitable platform on which Java programs may run no matter *where* they were compiled. Arguably, this is the first successful experiment with a language that is truly portable. An unfortunate side effect, however, is that Java programs run slowly compared to programs written in other languages that are compiled for specific platforms. Programs can make use of features that are particularly suited for particular platforms. Java, however, cannot make use of those features unless they are implemented very efficiently in the JVM. Most agree the price of simulating the JVM will be increasingly well worth the portability of code compiled with Java.

Perhaps the most important feature of the JVM is its *security*. As machines that sit on our desktop become more exposed to a greater variety of forces—forces like the Web, experimenting programmers, and increasingly powerful software—the stability of the computer is increasingly important, *and* increasingly tested. The JVM and Java itself provide a significant number of safeguards against attacks by the inhospitable world outside the machine, as well as the unfortunate logic of programs within the machine. For example, Java provides simple checks on boundaries of array, `String`, and `Vector` indexing. The authors have spent many an hour accidentally writing code that accesses parts of an array that are well beyond the space allocated. Java's ability to stop a program that accesses an array beyond its bounds keeps the programmer from reaching into parts of memory that are not under the programmer's control. When languages don't provide these checks the integrity of the machine is at risk. Other security features make it difficult for Java programs written elsewhere to write or modify files on your machine. To download and run programs that modify the local file system is to endanger your machine.

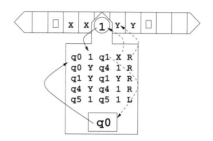

Figure 11.2 The Turing machine, a universal theoretical model of a computer. This machine is in state q_0. At each step, the state and the tape cell under the reader determine the instruction (bold arrows). The instruction determines the new cell value, new state, and next cell to be processed (dashed arrows).

Exercise 11.1 *In some languages, it is possible to explicitly* destroy *objects, even if they are the target of multiple references. Why does Java not allow this?*

In the end, we see that the Java Virtual Machine facilitates portable and secure programming, features that are important to programmers of computers that participate in the increasingly complicated world of computing.

11.2   The Turing Machine

Just what a computer *can* compute is an important subject to theoretical computer scientists. While our expectations of what a suitable computer is have changed dramatically over recent decades, there has been no change in the underlying model of a computing device. Indeed, the machine attributed to Alan Turing was originally formulated as a possible (theoretical) mechanism for answering any mathematical question. Formulated in 1936, the machine predates the modern view of computing but remains the best common understanding of what it means to be a computer.

The basic Turing machine (see Figure 11.2) consists of an infinite *tape*, a finite portion of which is actually used. The tape is composed of individual cells and, within each cell, any of an *alphabet* of symbols may be written. The contents of the tape essentially represent the contents of the memory of a modern processor. To manipulate the contents of the tape, the Turing machine is equipped with rudimentary reading, and a writing mechanism (called a *tape head*) is allowed to access a single cell at a time. Internally, the Turing machine is in one of a finite number of *states* that are controlled by a fixed, finite number of instructions called a *program*. Typically, one symbol of the tape's alphabet is a special mark called the "end-of-tape" mark (here, □); it is placed on either end of the initial string of symbols that make up the input. The tape head is placed on the left end of the input, and the program runs until the machine halts by entering a state for which there is no suitable instruction, usually leaving the tape head at the extreme left.

Typically, each instruction is composed of five parts:

- A current state (usually written q_i). For this instruction to execute, this state must match the current state of the machine.

- A tape symbol to be read. For this instruction to execute, this symbol must reside in the cell under the tape head.

- A next state. This is the next state of the machine.

- A tape symbol to be written. If executed, this instruction causes this symbol to be written to tape.

- A direction. Either "left" or "right," indicating which neighboring cell is to be moved under the tape head.

An example of a Turing machine program to multiply a unary (tally-mark) representation of an integer by two can be found in Figure 11.3. The machine begins with a number between two end-of-tape marks. The tape head then finds the left-most 1, rewrites it to the symbol X, and moves right. At the right end of the tape, the symbol Y is inserted, lengthening the tape by one cell. The machine then moves left, looking for the last remaining 1. When no tallies are left to be duplicated, the Y (and later, X) marks are rewritten as tally marks. The machine halts because there is no instruction to handle the machine in state q_5 at the left end of the tape.

Turing machines are just as expressive as what we consider to be a conventional machine: programs written for conventional computers can be simulated on a Turing machine, and *vice versa*. This simple fact allows us to use the Turing machine as a concise description of what it means to be a computer. For example, to say that something can or cannot be computed is to say that it can or cannot be computed on a Turing machine. Thus, while Turing machines are often the target architecture used within technical proofs, the results are usually appreciated as statements about any reasonably powerful computer. In particular, the equivalence of Turing machines and physical machines allows us to make statements about whether or not an actual machine can compute certain things. For example, it is known that no Turing-equivalent machine can determine whether or not a machine will stop on a particular input.

Exercise 11.2 *Write a Turing machine program that compares two unary numbers (separated by a special symbol). If the numbers are equal, it writes an '='
in the left-most cell; otherwise it writes an '!' at that location.*

Some of the most interesting computer science involves determining the tractability of certain ways of solving problems. The Turing machine allows us to make general statements about computers without having any particular machine in mind.

State	Read	State	Write	Dir	State	Read	State	Write	Dir
q_0	□	q_0	□	R	q_3	1	q_3	1	L
q_0	1	q_1	X	R	q_3	X	q_0	X	R
q_0	Y	q_4	1	R	q_3	Y	q_3	Y	L
q_1	1	q_1	1	R	q_4	Y	q_4	1	R
q_1	Y	q_1	Y	R	q_4	□	q_5	□	L
q_1	□	q_2	Y	R	q_5	1	q_5	1	L
q_2	any	q_3	□	L	q_5	X	q_5	1	L

	Before	After	
State	Goal	Tape	State
q_0	Find left-most 1	□$\underline{1}$11□	q_0
q_0	Change to X, move to right end	□X11$\underline{\ }$□	q_1
q_1	Extend by writing Y before end mark	□X11$\underline{Y}$□	q_3
q_3	Find next left-most 1, change to X	□$XX\underline{1}Y$□	q_1
q_1	Extend string	□$XX1Y\underline{Y}$□	q_3
q_3	Find next left-most 1, change to X	□$XXX\underline{Y}Y$□	q_1
q_1	Extend string	□$XXXYY\underline{Y}$□	q_3
q_3	Find left-most Y, change Y's to 1's	□$XXX\underline{1}11$□	q_5
q_5	Moving left, change X's to 1's	$\underline{□}$111111□	—

Figure 11.3 Above, a Turing machine program to double a unary number. Below, the status of the tape at various points in the doubling of the number 3 (underscore indicates head position).

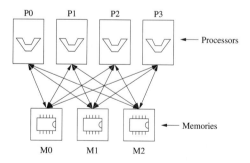

Figure 11.4 The parallel random access machine, a universal theoretical model of a parallel computer.

11.3   The P-RAM

Another model for a computer is the random access machine, or *RAM*. A RAM is similar to a Turing machine but has memory that may be randomly accessed by the computer. The instructions that control the processor must be able to read and write to memory and are written in simple language that is sufficiently powerful to make it equivalent to a Turing machine. The machine is "random access" because there is no penalty for accessing one particular memory location over another. Each memory cell takes "unit time" to access.

A *Parallel RAM* or *P-RAM* is a computer composed of several processors attached to several memories (see Figure 11.4). The memories are "shared" because any processor may access any *shared* memory location within a single unit of time. Programs for P-RAM computers are usually written so that, at each step, every processor executes a single instruction. If more than one processor attempts to read the same memory location at the same time, each processor gets a copy of the memory. It is illegal to mix reads and writes to a single location at the same time.

Computer scientists use models similar to the P-RAM to develop algorithms that allow multiprocess and multithreaded programs to solve problems with parallelism more quickly than they might be solved on a single sequential processor. Some problems, of course, feature a behavior that makes them inherently sequential; the use of threads for implementing these types of programs is only for ease of programming, and not for increasing performance. Other potentially parallel programs make use of threads to expose concurrency that is not easily identified in languages without threads.

Exercise 11.3 *Suppose* 52 *people are to sort* 52 *cards of a deck into ascending order. Can this be done more quickly than if one person sorted the deck of cards?*

Computer scientists have developed languages like Java to provide features, like threads, that are not a standard part of traditional languages, in hopes that programmers can make better use of the machines—both virtual and physical.

11.4   Chapter Review

We have seen three different types of machines, none of which is intended for implementation in hardware. These machines play an important role for computer scientists in their studies of what computers can and cannot do. In particular,

- The Java Virtual Machine allows programmers to develop programs for many hardware configurations at once. In fact, some of these platforms may not be available for testing by the programmer; instead, the virtual machine provides a standard environment that provides the security that is essential for modern, portable programming.

- The Turing machine provides a standard platform for proofs developed by theoretical computer scientists. While the Turing machine is both simple to program and impossible to build, it is a powerful tool for making general statements about all devices considered to be computers.

- The P-RAM is a theoretical model for parallel computation that scientists can use to model the behavior of multithreaded and multiprocessing algorithms. Languages like Java promise to provide improved performance on machines that allow parallel execution of threads (including the P-RAM). Traditional languages without threads or explicit parallelism may limit the approaches to solving complex problems in the most efficient manner possible.

While programming is an important tool for computer scientists to solve problems, it is also important to understand what languages and computers can (and cannot) do so that programming can be as effective as possible.

Appendix A
Selected Answers

"What is that which has one voice and yet
goes on four legs in the morning,
two legs at noon,
and upon three legs in the evening?"
—The Sphinx

"Man, who in childhood creeps on hands and knees,
in manhood walks erect,
and in old age walks with the aid of a staff."
—Oedipus

Chapter 0

0.1 Really, visit the web site!

0.3 Here, in the back!

0.5 At Library of Congress call number `QA76.73.J38`.

0.7 Among other things, it may make programs less portable. We have already seen this problem with the various interpretations of HTML documents.

Chapter 1

1.1 (a) An `int`, (b) a `double`, (c) a `long`, (d) an `int`, (e) a `boolean`, (f) a `char`, (g) a `boolean`.

1.3 Because for both primitive and reference types, the first statement is a tautology and the second is a fallacy.

1.5 `3600*hours` represents the same quantity of time in seconds.

1.7 `seconds = millis/1000; millis %= 1000;` etc.

1.10 The earth travels a mere 0.00117 inch in one nanosecond.

1.11 A micromile is about 0.63 inch.

1.13 See `FactorialAns.java`. It may be found in the on-line answer section.

1.15 The duration of the piece is approximately 1 minute, 35 seconds. Over 912 notes, the bow travels approximately 152 feet. The bow travels, then, at only about 1.1 miles per hour. The average speed of a bumblebee, in contrast, has been measured to be at least 6.4 miles per hour. It undoubtedly flies faster outside the lab.

1.16   To develop a boolean answer to the question: Are there duplicates in the list? you must keep each selected birthday in one of 23 different integer variables. You must then compare each birthday with every other—a total of $\frac{23*22}{2} = 253$ comparisons!

Chapter 2

2.2   Hint: These points appear on a circle, every 72 degrees.

2.4   All are legal. (a) prints 3, (b) prints 12, (c) prints 12, (d) prints 12, (e) prints 3.

2.6   Hint: Begin by filling the two circles and erasing everything *above* the lip line.

2.9   This is easiest if you draw the two lines, and then clear and draw rectangles over them.

2.12   Hint: See Appendix D.

2.13   See `FillSqAns.java`. It took us 4.31 seconds without the `hold` and `release`. With the hold and release it took 0.1 seconds!

2.15   Fill an arc and clear its "top."

Chapter 3

3.2   Because a switch statement can only handle specific cases. The rules apply to all values of an integer.

3.6   See `AdvancesAns.java`.

3.8   The loop computes the approximate number of digits necessary to print a positive number.

3.11   Any `if` statement may be substituted with a `for` loop. The problem, for example, is solved with the addition of a boolean variable, go:

```
for (go = true; go && d.mousePressed(); go = false)
    c.out.println("Let go!");
```

3.16   See `PrimeAns.java`.

Chapter 4

4.1   See `MaxAns.java`.

4.6   See `PushButtonAns.java`.

4.10   See `BinRepAns.java`.

4.14   See `TimeMouseAns.java`.

4.16   See `SmoothRollerAns.java`.

Chapter 5

5.1   The empty string.

5.2   Yes. The `toString` method can actually be called on a `String` constant!

5.5   If n is less than 1, the string is left unchanged.

5.9   See `UntabifyAns.java`.

5.11   Hint: Make use of the fact that you can convert any type to a `String`.

5.12   Any bits that are set in a character will invert the corresponding bits in the checksum. If that character is missing or different, the recomputed checksum will be different.

Chapter 6

6.1   See `RecursiveAddAns.java`.

6.4   It is interesting to note the relationship the solution has with the code that generates the sequence:

```
public static int syrLength(int n)
// post: returns length of Syracuse sequence beginning with n
{
    if (n <= 1) return 1;
    else if (n%2 == 0) return syrLength(n/2);
    else               return syrLength(3*n+1);
}
```

6.5   See `BinaryStringAns.java`.

6.7   All `for` loops can be cast as recursive procedures.

```
static void forLoop(int i, int n)
{
    if (i < n)
    {
        s();
        forLoop(f(i),n);
    }
}
// later, call forLoop with initial value of i
    forLoop(initial, n);
```

6.11   See `GCDAns.java`.

6.16   See `ParsleyAns.java`.

Chapter 7

7.1   Yes.

7.3   Using a loop, move each of the following elements toward the front of the array by one element. It must be done from the lower index first. Decrement the count.

7.5   The procedure would select the last button in the array that contains the mouse. By reversing the loop or by exiting the loop prematurely the earliest button can be selected.

7.7   A `Vector` can contain any object. Simply allocate a `Vector` of `Vector` objects. The notation is quite bulky and is similar to the complex array declaration described within the text.

7.12 Hint: This problem can be solved using recursion on smaller and smaller arrays.

7.15 See `BirthdayAns.java`.

7.17 See `ShuffleAns.java`.

Chapter 8

8.1 Code reuse occurs through inheritance. It is important because programmers don't want to waste their time writing the same code over and over.

8.3 See `CounterAns.java`.

8.6 It should be declared `private`. It's not useful to create an empty name if it cannot be changed.

8.7 See `TriCloneAns.java`.

8.9 The upper bound is not necessary. If we use a `Vector`, the limitation is removed, but at the cost of a little slowdown. The change does not affect users of the `WordList` class because the instance variables are private.

8.10 The `Point` class has easily accessible data but does not support basic operations on points. It is also difficult to modify implementations.

8.12 The reuse of code means that bugs are likely to be localized in one piece of code. Fixing the bugs for several classes might be accomplished by fixing an appropriate base class.

Chapter 9

9.2 See `ListSplitAns.java`.

9.4 See `OrderedInsertAns.java`.

Appendix B

Basics

*"Break any of these rules
sooner than say anything outright barbarous."*
—George Orwell

B.1 Principles of Java Programming

1. A useful principle is not fact, but a guide. (Page xiii)

2. Use comments to make your programs readable. (Page 4)

3. Experiment. (Page 7)

4. Spell out and capitalize words in identifiers. (Page 11)

5. Initialize variables before they are used. (Page 16)

6. Use parentheses to make explicit the order of evaluation. (Page 26)

7. Later drawing usually obscures earlier work. (Page 43)

8. Program with a reader in mind. (Page 46)

9. Inverting a drawing an even number of times makes it disappear. (Page 60)

10. Use the `while` loop to do something *zero or more times*. (Page 76)

11. Use the `do-while` loop to do something *at least once*. (Page 76)

12. The `for` loop is best used when counting or iterating a specific number of times. (Page 81)

13. The structure of the program should model the structure of the problem. (Page 99)

14. Pre- and postconditions provide an easy method for formalizing your documentation. (Page 102)

15. Functions don't generate output. (Page 110)

16. Return a result on the last line of a function. (Page 111)

17. Seek symmetry in design. (Page 135)

18. Recursive methods perform tests to identify one or more simple base cases. In other cases progress is made toward the solution using recursion to solve a simpler problem. (Page 151)

19. Declare instance variables of classes `private`. (Page 206)

20. The base case of a recursive class should, itself, be an instance of the class. (Page 240)

21. Implement recursive structures using recursive methods. (Page 245)

22. Define the `equals` method for objects stored in container classes. (Page 247)

B.2   Primitive Data Types in Java

Java supports a number of data types that are primitive. These types are not themselves, objects, although for most there are object *wrapper* classes that facilitate manipulation of primitive types as objects.

Name	Type	Range	Default Value
`boolean`	boolean	`true` or `false`	`false`
`char`	character data	any character	`\0 (NUL)`
`int`	integer	$-2^{31} \ldots 2^{31} - 1$	0
`long`	long integer	$-2^{63} \ldots 2^{63} - 1$	0
`float`	real	$-3.4028E38 \ldots 3.4028E38$	0.0
`double`	double precision real	$-1.7977E308 \ldots 1.7977E308$	0.0

B.3   Capitalizing Identifiers in Java

Here's a set of guidelines for capitalization in Java. Undoubtedly, there are counterexamples to almost every one of them, but a simple set of rules should go a long way.

Packages.   Names of packages are always entirely lowercase letters, even if acronyms:

```
element
java.lang
java.awt
java.vecmath
```

General.   Multiple-word mixed-case identifiers capitalize letters of embedded words:

```
DrawingWindow
moveTo
```

Classes. Names of permanent classes should start with a capital letter:

```
System
Math
DrawingWindow
```

Names of programs are, arguably, less permanent and could be started with lowercase letters:

```
public class yingYang {...}
```

(It should be pointed out that, in this book, we're in the habit of capitalizing program identifiers.)

Methods. Names of all methods begin with lowercase letters:

```
sin
currentTimeMillis
main
min
drawLordJeff
```

Instance variables. Names of instance variables begin with lowercase letters:

```
static DrawingWindow d;
Element headOfList;  // head of a linked list
```

Names of `final` objects (constants) are all caps, with words separated by underscores ('_'):

```
public static final double PI = 3.14159265358979323846;
private static final int INVERT_MODE = 1;
```

Locals. Local variables and constants always begin with lowercase letters:

```
int x,y;
final static int maxTimes = 10;
Double piBy2 = Math.PI/2;
```

This allows us to recognize that `java.lang.Math.sin` is a method within the object `Math`, which resides in package `java.lang`.

B.4   The ASCII Code

American Standard Code for Information Interchange subset of UNICODE								
char		Name	char		Name	char		Name
0	nul	null, end string	43	+	plus	86	V	upper v
1	soh	start heading	44	,	comma	87	W	upper w
2	stx	start text	45	-	minus	88	X	upper x
3	etx	end text	46	.	period	89	Y	upper y
4	eot	end transmission	47	/	slash	90	Z	upper z
5	enq	enquiry	48	0	zero	91	[	l. bracket
6	ack	acknowledge	49	1	one	92	\	backslash
7	bel	bell	50	2	two	93	]	r. bracket
8	\b	backspace	51	3	three	94	^	caret
9	\t	horizontal tab	52	4	four	95	_	underscore
10	\n	newline	53	5	five	96	`	backquote
11	vt	vertical tab	54	6	six	97	a	lower A
12	\f	form feed	55	7	seven	98	b	lower B
13	\r	carriage return	56	8	eight	99	c	lower C
14	so	turn cursor on	57	9	nine	100	d	lower D
15	si	turn cursor off	58	:	colon	101	e	lower E
16	dle	data link escape	59	;	semicolon	102	f	lower F
17	dc1	device control 1	60	<	less	103	g	lower G
18	dc2	device control 2	61	=	equals	104	h	lower H
19	dc3	device control 3	62	>	greater	105	i	lower I
20	dc4	device control 4	63	?	question	106	j	lower J
21	nak	negative ack.	64	@	at sign	107	k	lower K
22	syn	synchronous idle	65	A	upper a	108	l	lower L
23	etb	end trans. block	66	B	upper b	109	m	lower M
24	can	cancel	67	C	upper c	110	n	lower N
25	em	end medium	68	D	upper d	111	o	lower O
26	sub	substitute	69	E	upper e	112	p	lower P
27	esc	escape	70	F	upper f	113	q	lower Q
28	fs	file separator	71	G	upper g	114	r	lower R
29	gs	group separator	72	H	upper h	115	s	lower S
30	rs	record separator	73	I	upper i	116	t	lower T
31	us	unit separator	74	J	upper j	117	u	lower U
32		space	75	K	upper k	118	v	lower V
33	!	exclamation/bang	76	L	upper l	119	w	lower W
34	"	quotation	77	M	upper m	120	x	lower X
35	#	pound/hash/splat	78	N	upper n	121	y	lower Y
36	$	dollar sign	79	O	upper o	122	z	lower Z
37	%	percent	80	P	upper p	123	{	l. brace
38	&	ampersand	81	Q	upper q	124			pipe
39	'	quote	82	R	upper r	125	}	r. brace
40	(	left paren	83	S	upper s	126	~	tilde
41	)	right paren	84	T	upper t	127	del	delete
42	*	asterisk	85	U	upper u			

Appendix C

Contest Problems

*"Anyone who has never made a mistake
has never tried anything new."*
—Albert Einstein

PROGRAMMERS GET A GREAT DEAL of experience programming by solving
problems. Some problems are difficult because the appropriate representation
within a machine is unexpected or complex. Such problems are interesting because they're not immediately obvious and, as one's understanding of computer
science matures, one's view on how to solve these problems effectively will undoubtedly change.

We present here a number of problems that are typical of those found in
a programming contest. Each may be solved using the Java you have learned
within this text, but we are also certain that returning to these problems after
some time will yield different solutions—especially as you learn more about the
art and science of programming.

Typically, programming contests place limits on the time allowed to solve
problems. Cumulative points are garnered for writing a solution that compiles, a
solution that solves the problem for some of the inputs, and a solution that solves
the problem for all inputs. When considering possible inputs, it is particularly
important to consider the absolute simplest cases.

Here are some typical rules one might allow:

1. Rulings of the judges are final and are not to be contested.

2. You have two hours to solve all of these problems. Any problems submitted
   before the end of the two hours will be graded. Because grading is difficult,
   contestants should not wait for results of grading before continuing with
   the contest.

3. Five points will be awarded any problem that is submitted and *runs correctly on all tests*. Partial credit (based on a running program) is possible.
   Only one submission of a correct problem will be considered.

4. Any problem graded and found to be incorrect will be returned, with a
   penalty of one point. All incorrect submissions will be graded and penal-
   ized. Reasons for incorrect submissions:

   - Program would not compile (reason not indicated).
   - Program fails on one or more inputs (inputs not indicated).

- Program had to be terminated after an unreasonable length of time (inputs not indicated).

- Program had a run-time error (inputs and reason not indicated).

5. In the event of a tie for first, tie-breaking mechanisms might consider

  - Speed of the program, or computational prowess within a fixed interval of time, or

  - Elegance of solution.

The tie-breaking mechanism actually used is determined by the judges before the contest but announced only just before final reconsideration of the programs in question. Programmers therefore should program for speed and elegance as a rule.

6. Teams submitting programs not conforming to the spirit of the contest will be disqualified from participating.

Problem 0. Write a program that accepts a string and prints out each of the permutations of the letters of the string. If the letters of the string are unique, then each of the permutations is printed exactly once. For example, given the string

```
word
```

the following output might be generated:

```
dorw
dowr
drow
drwo
dwor
dwro
. . .
```

Problem 1. Assume you are a vending machine in a U.S. post office and you return change in the form of penny stamps, 20-cent postcards, and 33-cent stamps. For purposes of reducing the number of times the machine needs to be restocked, it is important to hand over, in change, the smallest number of postal items. For example, if five cents in change is necessary, five penny stamps are returned. If 42 cents in change is necessary, two postcards and two penny stamps are returned. Write a program that determines a minimum number of postal items that may be returned for any particular monetary value.

Problem 2. The Mersenne primes are of the form $2^n - 1$. For example, at the time of this writing, the current largest known prime is $2^{23021377} - 1$. Write a program to print the decimal value of $2^n - 1$ for an entered number n. (For how large a value of n can this value be computed in less than a minute?)

Problem 3. The following popular sliding piece puzzle is called the fifteen puzzle. The goal is to slide the pieces within the 4×4 grid to arrange the pieces in increasing order. For the purposes of this problem, the missing tile will be represented by the number 0; at any time, it may be swapped with any immediately adjacent numeric tiles above, below, to the left, or to the right. After reading in the numbers of the tiles (the space tile is represented as a 0) that appear in each row of a configuration, print out either YES or NO, indicating whether the puzzle can be solved or not. For example, the puzzle

```
 1  2  3  4
 5  6  0  7
 9 10 12  8
13 14 11 15
```

would generate the solution

```
YES
```

while the puzzle

```
 1  2  3  4
 5  6  7  8
 9 10 11 12
13 15 14
```

would generate the solution

```
NO
```

Problem 4. (Due to Knuth.) Suppose you are given 100 gold coins labeled with numbers 1 through n. Coin n has weight (and worth) that is $\sqrt{n}$. Given one minute of computation, how close can you come to dividing the 100 coins into two piles of 50 coins each of nearly equal weight. The output should be a difference in the weights, followed by a list of the 50 labels of coins on one side of the scale.

Problem 5. Write a program that, given an arbitrary integer n, prints the one or two closest prime numbers to n.

Problem 6. Given a list of words as input, write out any longest word that, when typed, is typed using either entirely the left or the right hand. Consider only words composed of alphabetic letters found on a "QWERTY" (a six-letter word typed only by the left hand) keyboard.

Problem 7. Assume that the earth is a perfect sphere with radius 4000. Write a program that accepts two points on the earth and prints the shortest distance between them. The coordinates are signed floating point numbers representing degrees north latitude and east longitude.

Problem 8. Write a program that reads an integer $n > 1$ and the latitude and longitude coordinates (see format, above) of n points of interest (logically labeled 0 through $n-1$) on a planet of radius 1000. After at most a minute of computation, it prints the length of a round-trip tour that is as short as can be found, along with a permutation of integers 0 through $n-1$ that represents the order of points visited.

Appendix D

Documentation of Selected Classes

*"Keeping a language as simple and as regular as possible
has always been a guideline in my work.
The description of Pascal took some 50 pages,
that of Modula 40, and Oberon's a mere 16 pages.
This I still consider to have been genuine progress."*
—Niklaus Wirth

THIS BOOK MAKES USE OF SELECTED CLASSES from the Java Development Kit. Further details on classes can be found at http://java.sun.com. Here, we outline selected methods of classes discussed within this book. Each method is described using a precondition and a postcondition. The postcondition describes what will happen if you run the method; the precondition describes what must be true for the postcondition to be guaranteed. All methods described here are public.

D.1 The Color Class

The java.awt.Color class provides access to predefined and customized colors. To be used, it must be imported with the statement

```
import java.awt.Color;
```

Many monitors support three color "guns" that generate red, blue, and green colors on the display. Thus, colors are specified as a mixture of these three colors at different intensities. The Color constants are usually sufficient for everyday use. To generate shades of a color, scale all intensities by an equal amount. To generate shades of gray, specify three equal intensities (white is the most intense, black is the least). Color.black is the default foreground color, and Color.white is the default background color.

```
static final Color Color.black;    // Color(0.0,0.0,0.0)
static final Color Color.darkGray; // Color(0.25,0.25,0.25)
static final Color Color.gray;     // Color(0.5,0.5,0.5)
static final Color Color.lightGray;// Color(0.75,0.75,0.75)
static final Color Color.white;    // Color(1.0,1.0,1.0)
static final Color Color.red;      // Color(1.0,0.0,0.0)
static final Color Color.pink;     // Color(1.0,0.68,0.68)
```

```
static final Color Color.orange;    // Color(1.0,0.78,0.78)
static final Color Color.yellow;    // Color(1.0,1.0,0.0)
static final Color Color.green;     // Color(0.0,1.0,0.0)
static final Color Color.cyan;      // Color(0.0,1.0,1.0)
static final Color Color.blue;      // Color(0.0,0.0,1.0)
static final Color Color.magenta;   // Color(1.0,0.0,1.0)

Color(float red, float green, float blue)
// pre: 0.0f <= red, green, blue <= 1.0f
// post: creates a new color object with indicated red, green, blue
//       intensities; higher values are more intense

Color(int red, int green, int blue)
// pre: 0 <= red, green, blue <= 255
// post: creates a new color object with indicated red, green, blue
//       intensities; higher values are more intense

Color brighter()
// post: returns a brighter version of this color, if possible

Color darker()
// post: returns a darker version of this color, if possible

boolean equals(Other other)
// pre: other is a valid Color
// post: returns true if this and other are equivalent colors

int getRed()
int getGreen()
int getBlue()
// post: returns intensity of specific color between 0 and 255;
//       higher values are more intense
```

D.2   The Math Object

The `java.lang.Math` library is imported automatically in all Java programs. The methods of the `Math` class are declared static because they are to be applied to primitive types (usually `doubles`). It is always necessary to prefix the method name with the class name, `Math`. Users should be aware that all angles are specified in *radians*. To convert degrees to radians, multiply by `Math.PI/180.0`. To convert back to degrees, multiply by `180.0/Math.PI`. To compute logarithms in bases other than e, recall a base b log of n can be computed as `Math.log(n)/Math.log(b)`.

```
// interesting constants:
static final double Math.E = 2.7182818284590452354;
static final double Math.PI = 3.14159265358979323846;
```

```
static double Math.random()
// post: returns random value uniformly distributed between 0 and 1

static int Math.max(int a, int b)
static long Math.max(long a, long b)
static float Math.max(float a, float b)
static double Math.max(double a, double b)
// post: returns the larger of a and b

static int Math.min(int a, int b)
static long Math.min(long a, long b)
static float Math.min(float a, float b)
static double Math.min(double a, double b)
// post: returns the smaller of a and b

static int Math.abs(int value)
static long Math.abs(long value)
static float Math.abs(float value)
static double Math.abs(double value)
// post: returns the magnitude of value

static double Math.ceil(double value)
// post: returns smallest integer not less than value

static double Math.floor(double value)
// post: returns largest integer that does not exceed value

static int Math.round(float value)
static long Math.round(double value)
// post: computes integer value closest to value; floor(value+0.5)

static double Math.exp(double p)
// post: returns e to the power p

static double Math.log(double value)
// pre: value > 0
// post: returns power to which e must be raised to get value

static double Math.sqrt(double value)
// pre: value >= 0
// post: returns the square root of value

static double Math.pow(double base, double p)
// pre: base > 0, or base == 0 and p > 0, or base < 0 and p integral
// post: raises base to power p

static double Math.sin(double theta)
// post: returns sine of theta (expressed in radians)
```

```
static double Math.cos(double theta)
// post: returns cosine of theta (expressed in radians)

static double Math.tan(double theta)
// post: returns tangent of theta (expressed in radians)

static double Math.asin(double value)
// pre: Math.abs(value) <= 1
// post: returns an angle (between -pi/2 and pi/2) whose sin is value

static double Math.acos(double value)
// pre: Math.abs(value) <= 1
// post: returns an angle (between 0 and pi) whose cos is value

static double Math.atan(double value)
// post: returns an angle (between -pi/2 and pi/2) whose tan is value

static double Math.atan2(double y, double x)
// post: returns the angle (between -pi and pi) ray (0,0)-(x,y)
//       makes with the positive x axis; NOTE ORDER OF PARAMETERS
```

D.3 The Random Class

Random numbers can be generated with the use of java.util.Random. They are made available to Java programs with the import statement:

```
import java.util.Random;
```

The construction of a Random provides the user a random number generator, from which a sequence of random values may be generated. Since the default random number generator uses the current time as a seed, multiple generators should not be constructed close together without dedicated seeds. Section 8.3.3 discusses the problems of generating effective random numbers.

```
Random()
// post: construct a random number generator;
//       seed based on current time

Random(long seed)
// post: construct a random number generator;
//       seed is provided by the user

void setSeed(long seed)
// post: resets the seed of the generator to seed

int nextInt()
// post: returns a random int from a uniform distribution
```

```
///      value may be negative

long nextLong()
// post: returns a random long from a uniform distribution
//       value may be negative

int nextFloat()
// post: returns a random float from a uniform distribution
//       value falls between 0.0f and 1.0f

double nextDouble()
// post: returns a random double from a uniform distribution;
//       value falls between 0.0 and 1.0

double nextGaussian()
// post: returns a random double from a normal distribution whose
//       mean is 0.0 and whose standard deviation is 1.0
```

D.4   The String Class

The `java.lang.String` class is automatically imported to all Java programs. Strings are *immutable*: they may not be directly modified. Instead, modifications to Strings are accumulated in a new `String` constant. As a result, `String` references are reassigned whenever the value might change. Strings also make significant use of the '+' operator, which concatenates a pair of `String` values. When objects are used where Strings are needed, the `toString` method of the object is silently called to produce a `String` representation of the object. Thus, programmers of new classes are encouraged to consider overriding the `toString` method inherited from the `Object` class. The use of the `String` class is discussed in great detail in Chapter 5. The `String` class has a very large interface; we describe a useful subset of the methods here:

```
String()
// post: constructs an empty string

String(String other)
// pre: other is not null
// post: constructs a copy of string other

int length()
// post: returns the number of characters stored within the string

char charAt(int index)
// pre: 0 <= index < length()
// post: returns the character at the index'th location;
//       indexing begins at 0
```

```
boolean equals(Object other)
// pre: other is a valid String object
// post: returns true if the strings are equal

boolean equalsIgnoreCase(Object other)
// pre: other is valid String object
// post: returns true if the strings are equal, where
//       upper- and lowercase characters are considered the same

int compareTo(Object other)
// pre: other is a valid String object
// post: returns an integer less than, equal to, or greater than zero
//       if this is less than, equal to, or greater than other

boolean startsWith(String other)
// pre: other is not null
// post: returns true iff this begins with the prefix other

boolean endsWith(String other)
// pre: other is not null
// post: returns true iff this ends with the suffix other

int indexOf(int ch)
// post: returns the index of the first occurrence of character ch,
//       or -1 if not found

int indexOf(String other)
// pre: other is not null
// post: returns the starting location of first occurrence of other
//       in this, or -1 if not found

int lastIndexOf(int ch)
// post: returns the index of the last occurrence of character ch,
//       or -1 if not found

int lastIndexOf(String other)
// pre: other is not null
// post: returns the starting location of last occurrence of other
//       in this, or -1 if not found

String substring(int index)
// pre: 0 <= index < length()
// post: returns the substring of this starting at index and
//       extending to the end of this string

String substring(int start, int follow)
// pre: 0 <= start <= follow <= length()
// post: returns substring of characters starting at start
//       and ending at follow-1
```

```
String concat(String other)
// pre: other is not null
// post: returns string constructed of this followed by other;
//        equivalent to this + other

String toLowerCase()
// post: returns a lowercase version of this string

String toUpperCase()
// post: returns an uppercase version of this string

String trim()
// post: returns this string without leading and trailing spaces

static String valueOf(Object value)
// pre: other is not null
// post: returns string representation of reference value

static String valueOf(int value)
static String valueOf(long value)
static String valueOf(float value)
static String valueOf(double value)
static String valueOf(boolean value)
// post: returns string representation of any primitive value
```

D.5   The System Object

The `java.lang.System` object is automatically imported in all Java programs. Typically, `System.in` and `System.out` are streams used for reading and writing. At the time of this writing, it was difficult to make reasonable use of the `System.in` stream for elementary programmers. Instead, the `ConsoleWindow` class is suggested (see Appendix E.1 and Chapter 2 for more details). Two methods of `System` are, however, quite useful:

```
static long System.currentTimeMillis()
// post: returns the number of thousands of seconds since 1969

static void System.exit(int code)
// post: stops the Java Virtual Machine with exit status code
//        (often 0); never returns
```

D.6   The Thread Class

The `java.lang.Thread` class forms the basis for implementing threads in Java. The class is automatically imported in all Java programs. A typical use of the `Thread` class is to use it as the basis for an extension, overriding the `run` method. It should be noted that all execution in Java happens within the context of a *current thread*. Methods declared `static` affect the currently running thread. Threads are covered extensively in Chapter 10.

```
static final int Thread.MIN_PRIORITY; // least scheduled
static final int Thread.MAX_PRIORITY; // most scheduled
static final int Thread.NORM_PRIORITY;// normal scheduling


static Thread currentThread()
// post: returns the currently executing thread

static void yield()
// post: pause and reschedule the currently executing thread

static void sleep(long millis) throws InterruptedException
// post: causes the currently executing thread to sleep at least
//       millis thousandths of a second

void run()
// post: the computation to be performed; by default nothing;
//       OVERRIDE THIS METHOD

void start()
// post: starts the thread running the run method

void stop()
// post: stops the thread; it cannot be restarted

void suspend()
// post: suspends this thread indefinitely

void resume()
// post: resumes suspended thread

int getPriority()
// post: returns the current priority of the thread

void setPriority(int prio)
// post: Thread.MIN_PRIORITY <= prio <= Thread.MAX_PRIORITY
// post: sets the thread's priority to prio
```

D.7   The Vector Class

The class `java.util.Vector` implements a variable length array of references to objects. To make use of `Vectors`, you must have the following import:

```
import java.util.Vector;
```

As a `Vector` grows, it is lengthened in an efficient manner. As with arrays, it is possible to generate errors by accessing a `Vector` beyond its current bounds. `Vectors` are only able to store references to objects; primitive values must be stored within arrays. When objects are retrieved from a `Vector`, their type must be explicitly cast. If methods like `contains` are to be used, programmers should remember to override the `equals` method of the objects stored within the `Vector`. The use of arrays and `Vectors` is discussed in Chapter 7.

```
Vector()
// post: construct an empty vector of values

void addElement(Object item)
// post: adds item to end of Vector

Object clone()
// post: returns a copy of this Vector;
//       elements are not cloned

boolean contains(Object item)
// pre: item is not null
// post: returns true if item equals a value in the Vector;
//       equality is determined by the equals method

Object elementAt(int index)
// pre: 0 <= index < size()
// post: returns the index'th element of the vector;
//       the first element has index 0

Object firstElement()
// pre: size >= 0
// post: returns the first element of the vector

Object lastElement()
// pre: size >= 0
// post: returns the last element of the vector

int indexOf(Object item)
// pre: item is not null
// post: returns the index of the first occurrence of item,
//       as tested by equals; returns -1 if item does not occur

int indexOf(Object item, int start)
// pre: item is not null; 0 <= start < size()
```

```
// post: returns the index of the first occurrence of item,
//       as tested by equals, search begins at index start

void insertElementAt(Object item, int index)
// pre: 0 <= index <= size()
// post: inserts item in vector; will be located at index'th position

void removeElementAt(int index)
// pre: 0 <= index < size()
// post: removes the item located at index; vector is one shorter

void setElementAt(Object item, int index)
// pre: 0 <= index < size()
// post: replaces object at location index with item

void boolean removeElement(Object item)
// pre: item is not null
// post: removes first occurrence of item from vector;
//       returns true if successful
```

Appendix E

The `element` Package

"The secret to creativity is knowing how to hide your sources."
—Albert Einstein

THIS APPENDIX DESCRIBES THE USER-ACCESSIBLE CLASSES of the `element` package (see Figure E.1). The purpose of the `element` package is to provide a simple, JDK-consistent set of classes for performing input, output, and graphics in Java applications. Each class is presented as a class "interface"—the publicly accessible features of each method and instance variable. To make use of these classes, of course, it is necessary to have an

```
import element.*;
```

statement in source files that make use of `element` package classes.

Each method is provided with a postcondition and an optional precondition. The precondition states conditions that are expected to be true before the method is called. If there is no precondition, the method may be called without concern. The postcondition makes statements about what will be true after the method is completed, provided that the precondition was true. These more formal comments help to verify that methods are being called correctly.

Some features of many of these classes are discussed in Chapter 2, while examples of the use of these classes, of course, are demonstrated throughout the text. Users interested in the latest electronic documentation or programmers interested in the internals of these classes are encouraged to look to the on-line resources (see `http://www.mhhe.com/javaelements`).

E.1 The `ConsoleWindow` Class

```
public class ConsoleWindow
{
    public PrintWriter out;    // the output stream
    public InputStream in;     // the input stream
    public ReadStream input;   // the input ReadStream

    public ConsoleWindow()
    // post: constructs a 24x80 console window

    public ConsoleWindow(int rows, int cols, String name)
    // post: constructs a rows by cols window titled name
```

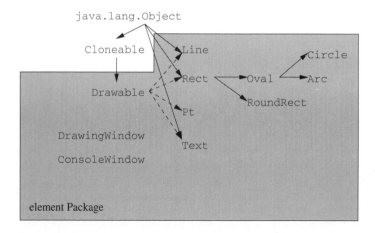

Figure E.1 The hierarchy of graphical classes and interfaces. Solid lines indicate extensions; dashed lines indicate implementation. Only those classes and interfaces in the gray area are classes of the `element` package.

```
        public String toString()
        // post: constructs a string describing the window
    }
```

Textual communication between the user and program can be accomplished through the standard system console (`System.in`, `System.out`, etc.). The `ConsoleWindow`, however, constructs a dedicated, portable, and easily configured window for more formal textual communication. Because of the relatively non-user friendly nature of textual communication in Java, the `ConsoleWindow` class provides access to an input `ReadStream` (see below) that filters the basic `InputStream` accessed through `in`. The parameterless constructor displays a window with 24 rows and 80 columns; alternative dimensions may be specified in the two-parameter constructor. Usually, one window is constructed, but several are also possible. In large programs, the console window is usually declared as a `static private` variable and initialized in the `main` method.

E.2   The `ReadStream` Class

```
    public class ReadStream extends FilterInputStream
    {
        public ReadStream()
        // post: constructs a pascal-like stream based on System.in

        public ReadStream(InputStream strm)
```

```
// pre: strm is a valid input stream
// post: constructs a pascal-like stream based on strm

public boolean eof()
// pre: are we at the end-of-file?

public char peek()
// post: returns next character in stream, without consuming it

public boolean eoln()
// post: returns true if next stream char is an eoln char

public void readln()
// post: reads input stream until end-of-line (\r or \n or \n\r)

public void skipWhite()
// post: input pointer is at EOF, or nonwhitespace char

public String readString()
// post: reads next word as string

public boolean readBoolean()
// post: returns next boolean value read from input

public char readChar()
// post: returns next character, or 0 for eof

public void pushbackChar(char c)
// post: pushes back character, possibly clearing EOF;
//       if c == 0, does nothing

public double readDouble()
// post: reads in double value

public float readFloat()
// post: reads floating point value and returns value

public short readShort()
// post: reads a short integer from stream

public int readInt()
// post: reads an integer from stream

public long readLong()
// post: reads a long integer from stream

public String readLine()
// post: reads remainder of line; returns as string
}
```

The ReadStream class (most often, the input stream from a ConsoleWindow) filters an InputStream (usually the in stream from the same ConsoleWindow) for general use. Unlike the InputStream, the ReadStream is used to read primitive types from the input. For example, ints are read with the readInt method, booleans are read with the readBoolean method, and chars are read with readChar. Contiguous, nonwhitespace characters ("words") are read with readString. Spaces, tabs, and newlines are skipped before reading, except in the case of readChar, where careful reading of whitespace may be useful.

The ReadStream has, in addition, a notion of end-of-line and end-of-file marks, typed as a *carriage return* and *control-D*, respectively. The readLine method returns a string of all white and nonwhite characters remaining on the line before the end-of-line mark (the mark is consumed, but not returned). When the result of readLine is not important, readln can be used. The methods eoln and eof test for the occurrence of each of these marks in the next character of input. (Programmers may peek at the next character of input and return a character pushBackChar to be read again.) Whitespace is not skipped before the eoln and eof tests, so the user usually explicitly calls skipWhite to ensure, for example, that an eof is exposed before testing. Since the end-of-line mark is considered whitespace, skipWhite consumes these characters, and the programmer may miss end-of-line marks if tests are preceded by skipWhite. Examples of ReadStream-based input and output appear in Chapter 2.

E.3   The DrawingWindow Class

```
public synchronized class DrawingWindow
{
    public DrawingWindow()
    // post: constructs a 200x200 standalone drawing window

    public DrawingWindow(int width, int height)
    // post: constructs a drawing window of desired dimensions

    public DrawingWindow(int width, int height, String title)
    // pre: 0 <= width, height; title is a valid string
    // post: constructs a named window with desired dimensions

    public void hold()
    // post: delays updating the screen until matching release

    public void release()
    // post: releases a hold on the drawing window

    public Rect bounds()
    // post: returns rectangle describing bounds of window

    public Pt getMouse()
    // post: returns the current mouse position as a Pt
```

```
public boolean mousePressed()
// post: returns true if mouse is pressed

public Pt awaitMousePress()
// post: blocks until mouse is pressed;
//        returns point of press

public Pt awaitMouseRelease()
// post: blocks until mouse is released;
//        returns point of release

public Pt awaitMouseClick()
// post: blocks until mouse is released;
//        returns point of press

public char awaitKey()
// post: blocks until a keystroke
//        returns character associated with key

public void moveTo(int x, int y)
// post: sets the current position to (x,y)

public void moveTo(Pt p)
// post: sets the current position to point p

public void move(int dx, int dy)
// pre: current position has been set previously
// post: changes the current position by (dx,dy)

public void lineTo(int x, int y)
// post: draws a line from current position to (x,y);
//        (x,y) becomes the new current position

public void lineTo(Pt p)
// pre: the current position has previously been set
// post: draws a line from current position to (x,y)

public void line(int dx, int dy)
// pre: the current position has been set
// post: draws a line relative from current position by (dx,dy)

public void setForeground(java.awt.Color c)
// pre: c is a valid Color
// post: the pen is filled with that color for drawing

public void setBackground(Color c)
// pre: c is a valid Color
// post: the eraser is filled with that color for erasing
```

```
            public void paintMode()
            // post: sets the drawing mode to paint

            public void invertMode()
            // post: sets the drawing mode to invert

            public void fill(Drawable d)
            // pre: d is a valid drawable object
            // post: fills in the drawable object, d

            public void clear(Drawable d)
            // pre: d is a valid drawable object
            // post: the drawable object is erased

            public void draw(Drawable d)
            // pre: d is a general drawable object
            // post: object d drawn (or inverted) on the drawing window
        }
```

The `DrawingWindow` provides a simple dedicated, portable, and JDK-similar canvas on which the programmer may draw. In addition, the mouse location may be determined relative to the `DrawingWindow`. The great number of methods belies the simplicity of the class.

Several methods query the mouse: `getMouse` returns the current mouse location within the window. The `mousePressed` method returns `true` if any of the mouse buttons are pressed and may be used for polling the mouse. To avoid polling, `awaitMousePress` (or `awaitMouseRelease`) suspends the program until the mouse is pressed (or released). `awaitMouseClick` returns when the mouse is next pressed and then released. Each of these routines returns the position of the mouse at the time of the specified event. It is important to note that on some systems, a mouse leaving the window may no longer be logically part of the drawing window and that windows have different manners of being selected as the *current window*.

The `awaitKey` suspends and returns the next character typed while the drawing window was active. The character is not displayed.

Basic drawing is accomplished through absolute drawing commands (`move-To` and `lineTo`) or relative commands (`move` and `draw`). Each of these updates a *current position*: the absolute commands set the position explicitly, and the relative commands move as an offset from the current position. Only the `line` and `lineTo` methods potentially leave marks on the screen.

More complex drawing is accomplished by the `draw`, `fill`, and `clear` methods. The arguments to these methods must be `Drawable` and include the `element` package's `Pt`, `Line`, `Rect`, `Oval`, and others (see below). Generally, `draw` draws the outline of the object in the foreground color; `fill` draws the solid object, including the outline; and `clear` erases by drawing in the background color.

The `bounds` method returns a `Rect` that may be used to locate objects within the drawing window (for example, `bounds().center()` returns the window's center point around which a circle might be centered). The `clear` method clears the screen and is equivalent to `d.clear(d.bounds())`.

The methods `hold` and `release` are used in pairs to suspend and resume the updating of the screen, respectively. While suspended, drawing occurs offscreen. The offscreen canvas is used to update the screen when the appropriate `release` occurs. When complex painting operations are to be performed, these methods can be used to perform a single, comprehensive update.

Color drawings can be accomplished by setting the foreground (`setFore-ground`) and background (`setBackground`) colors. The foreground color is used by the `draw` and `fill` methods, while the background color is used by the `clear` method. Colors are defined in the JDK package, `java.awt.Color` and include `Color.red`, `Color.green`, `Color.blue`, `Color.black`, `Color.white`, and others (see Appendix D).

The methods `paintMode` and `invertMode` tell the `DrawingWindow` to apply paint directly, or invert black and white pixels. See Chapter 2 for details.

E.4   The Drawable Interface

```
public interface Drawable extends Cloneable
{
    public int height();
    // post: returns the height of the drawable object

    public int width();
    // post: returns the width of the drawable object

    public int left();
    // post: returns the left-most coordinate of the bounding
    //       box containing the drawable object

    public int right();
    // post: returns the right-most coordinate of the bounding
    //       box containing the drawable object

    public int bottom();
    // post: returns the bottom-most coordinate of the bounding
    //       box containing the drawable object

    public int top();
    // post: returns the top-most coordinate of the bounding
    //       box containing the drawable object

    public void center(Pt p);
    // post: sets the center of the bounding box of drawable to p;
    //       the dimensions remain the same
```

```
      public Pt center();
      // post: returns the center of the bounding box of
      //       the drawable object

      public void drawOn(DrawingWindow d);
      // post: draws outline of this object on window d;
      //       same as d.draw(this)

      public void fillOn(DrawingWindow d);
      // post: draws the interior of this object on window d;
      //       same as d.fill(this)

      public void clearOn(DrawingWindow d);
      // post: erases this object from window d;
      //       same as d.clear(this)
}
```

This interface describes the methods that are shared among all objects that may be drawn on a drawing window. A number of primitive objects—including Pt, Line, Rect, and others—implement this interface and, therefore, may be passed to DrawingWindow methods. The height and width return the logical dimensions of the object. Usually these correspond to the dimensions of the smallest bounding Rect that contains the object, but not always (for example, the Arc object may span only a portion of the Rect that bounds the Arc's ellipse). To determine the location of the object, methods like top may be called. The center function computes the logical center of the object—the mean of the horizontal and vertical bounds—and not necessarily the center-of-mass. The single-parameter center procedure moves the object by relocating its center point to p. Methods drawOn, fillOn, and clearOn are equivalent to d.draw(this), d.fill(this), and d.clear(this) and are provided to allow graphics operations from the point of view of the Drawable object.

Users may construct their own Drawable objects (for example, houses, cows, etc.); this is discussed in detail in Section 8.5.2.

E.5   The Pt Class

```
  public class Pt implements Drawable
  {
      public Pt()
      // post: constructs a point object

      public Pt(Pt p)
      // post: constructs a point, like p

      public Pt(int x, int y)
      // post: constructs the point (x,y)
```

```
public int x()
// post: returns the horizontal coordinate of the point

public int y()
// post: returns the vertical coordinate of the point

public void x(int x)
// post: sets the horizontal coordinate to x

public void y(int newy)
// post: sets the new vertical coordinate

public void move(int dx, int dy)
// post: moves point by (dx,dy)

public void moveTo(int x, int y)
// post: sets point to (x,y)

public void moveTo(Pt p)
// pre: p is not null Pt
// post: sets this to new p

public void fillOn(DrawingWindow d)
// pre: d is not null
// post: draws this point on d

public void clearOn(DrawingWindow d)
// pre: d is not null
// post: erases this point from d

public void drawOn(DrawingWindow d)
// pre: d is not null
// post: draws this point on d

public boolean equals(Object p)
// pre: p is not null
// post: returns true if this and p are equal
}
```

The Pt class defines a point in the screen coordinate system and, as a result, is defined by a horizontal and vertical coordinate pair. As with all element objects, a Pt may be copied by constructing one Pt from another. These values may be retrieved with the parameterless x and y methods or changed with the single-parameter versions. Several trivial methods (left and right, etc.) are provided to support the Drawable interface. A point drawn or filled is guaranteed to occupy a single pixel. Since the x and y coordinates are integers, the equals test returns true when corresponding coordinates are equal.

The JDK defines a logically similar but unrelated class, Point.

E.6   The Line Class

```
public class Line implements Drawable
{
    public Line()
    // post: constructs a trivial line segment at origin

    public Line(Line l)
    // pre: l is a valid line segment
    // post: this is a copy of l

    public Line(Rect r)
    // post: constructs a line from a rectangle

    public Line(int x0, int y0, int x1, int y1)
    // pre:  w >= 0, h >= 0
    // post: constructs rectangle with top left at (x,y),
    //       width w, height h

    public Line(Pt p, Pt q)
    // pre: p and q are valid points
    // post: constructs a line segment from the two endpoints

    public int left()
    // post: returns the left-most coordinate of the segment

    public int right()
    // post: returns the right-most coordinate of the segment

    public int top()
    // post: returns the top-most coordinate of the segment

    public int bottom()
    // post: returns the bottom-most coordinate of the segment

    public void left(int x)
    // post: adjusts line so that it falls to the right of x

    public void right(int x)
    // post: adjusts line so that it falls to the left of x

    public void top(int y)
    // post: adjusts line so that it falls below y

    public void bottom(int y)
    // post: adjusts line so that it falls above y

    public int width()
    // post: returns the horizontal distance between endpoints
```

```
public int height()
// post: returns the vertical distance between endpoints

public Pt center()
// post: returns the midpoint of the line segment

public void center(Pt p)
// pre: p is the desired midpoint of line
// post: the line is moved to make p the midpoint

public Pt here()
// post: returns one endpoint of the line

public Pt there()
// post: returns another endpoint of the line

public boolean contains(Pt p)
// pre: p is not null
// post: returns true if p lies on line segment

public void fillOn(DrawingWindow d)
// pre: d is a valid drawing window
// post: line is drawn on window d in the current mode

public void clearOn(DrawingWindow d)
// pre: d is a valid drawing window
// post: line is erased from window d in the current mode

public void drawOn(DrawingWindow d)
// pre: d is a valid drawing window
// post: line is drawn on window d in the current mode

public boolean equals(Object other)
// pre: other is a valid line segment
// post: returns true if two rects are equal valued
}
```

The Line class allows the user to specify a segment of a line between two
points. A line may be constructed from two Pt objects, four integers (considered
as two pairs of coordinates), another Line, or as the (rarely used) negative-
slope diagonal of a Rect. The left, right, top, and bottom methods return
the bounds of the smallest containing rectangle. Changing any of these values
with the corresponding one-parameter function *moves* the Line, preserving its
geometry. Two lines are equal if their endpoints are (in some order) equal: in
other words, if they are *geometrically* equal. Careful thought demonstrates that
the bounding coordinates do not give enough information to reconstruct the
Line entirely, so the methods here and there return the endpoints in some
order. Lines that are painted with drawOn and fillOn appear the same.

E.7 The Rect Class

```
public class Rect implements Drawable
{
    public Rect()
    // post: constructs a trivial rectangle at origin

    public Rect(Pt p1, Pt p2)
    // post: constructs a rectangle between p1 and p2

    public Rect(Drawable o)
    // post: constructs a rectangle, based on another drawable object

    public Rect(int cx, int cy, int r)
    // pre: radius >= 0
    // post: constructs a radius r square centered about (cx,cy)

    public Rect(Pt p, int r)
    // pre: radius >= 0
    // post: constructs a radius r square centered about (cx,cy)

    public Rect(int x, int y, int w, int h)
    // pre:  w >= 0, h >= 0
    // post: constructs a rectangle with upper left (x,y),
    //       width w, height h

    public boolean contains(Pt p)
    // pre: p is a valid point
    // post: true iff p is within the rectangle

    public int left()
    // post: returns left coordinate of the rectangle

    public int top()
    // post: returns top coordinate of the rectangle

    public int right()
    // post: returns right coordinate of the rectangle

    public int bottom()
    // post: returns the bottom coordinate of the rectangle

    public int width()
    // post: returns the width of the rectangle

    public int height()
    // post: returns the height of the rectangle

    public void width(int w)
    // post: sets width of rectangle, center and height unchanged
```

```
public void height(int h)
// post: sets height of the Rect; center and width unchanged

public void left(int x)
// post: sets left to x; dimensions remain unchanged

public void top(int y)
// post: sets top to y; dimensions remain unchanged

public void bottom(int y)
// post: sets bottom to y; dimensions remain unchanged

public void right(int x)
// post: sets the left coordinate; dimensions unchanged

public Pt center()
// post: returns center point of rectangle

public void center(Pt p)
// post: sets center of rect to p; dimensions remain unchanged

public void move(int dx, int dy)
// post: moves rectangle to left by dx and down by dy

public void moveTo(int left, int top)
// post: moves left top of rectangle to (left,top);
//       dimensions are unchanged

public void moveTo(Pt p)
// post: moves left top of rectangle to p

public void extend(int dx, int dy)
// post: moves sides of rectangle outward by dx and dy

public void fillOn(DrawingWindow d)
// pre: d is a valid drawing window
// post: the rectangle is filled on the drawing window d

public void clearOn(DrawingWindow d)
// pre: d is a valid drawing window
// post: the rectangle is erased from the drawing window

public void drawOn(DrawingWindow d)
// pre: d is a valid drawing window
// post: the rectangle is drawn on the drawing window

public boolean equals(Object other)
// post: returns true iff two rectangles are equal
}
```

The Rect class (not to be confused with the similar JDK object, Rectangle), describes a rectangular region on the screen whose edges are vertical or horizontal. Rect objects may be copied from other Rect objects or constructed from a top-left point and a width and height, or as the unique rectangle that bounds two points. The parameterless left, right, top, and bottom return the bounding coordinates, while width and height determine the dimensions. The parameterless center method returns the center point. Similar methods taking parameters relocate the Rect, preserving dimensions. The extend method takes two integers—dx and dy—and modifies the horizontal and vertical coordinates to increase the width and height by 2dx and 2dy, preserving the center. Negative values will shrink the Rect toward its center.

One Rect equals another if they are the same geometrically. A Rect contains a Pt if filling the Rect would paint the Pt. The clearOn method essentially fills the Rect with the background color, erasing all the contained pixels.

E.8   The Circle Class

```
public class Circle extends Oval
{
    public Circle()
    // post: constructs a trivial circle at origin

    public Circle(Drawable d)
    // post: constructs a circle from a drawable object

    public Circle(int x, int y, int r)
    // pre:  r >= 0
    // post: constructs circle with center at (x,y), radius r

    public Circle(Pt p, int r)
    // pre:  r >= 0
    // post: constructs circle with center p, radius r

    public boolean contains(Pt p)
    // post: returns true iff p is within circle

    public int radius()
    // post: returns radius of circle

    public void radius(int r)
    // pre:  r >= 0<br>
    // post: sets radius of the circle

    public void fillOn(DrawingWindow d)
    // pre:  d is a valid drawing window
    // post: the circle is filled on the drawing window d
```

```
    public void clearOn(DrawingWindow d)
    // pre: d is a valid drawing window
    // post: the circle is erased from the drawing window

    public void drawOn(DrawingWindow d)
    // pre: d is a valid drawing window
    // post: the circle is drawn on the drawing window

    public boolean equals(Object other)
    // post: returns true if two rects are equal
}
```

The `Circle` object describes circular regions in screen coordinates. `Circle` objects may be copied from other `Circle` objects or constructed from a center point and a radius, or a horizontal and vertical coordinate and a radius. The `center` and `radius` may be queried or modified with the parameterless and one-parameter methods, respectively.

The `Circle` may also be used wherever a `Rect` may be used. As a result, the parameterless `left`, `right`, `top`, and `bottom` methods (inherited from the `Rect` object) return the bounding coordinates, while `width` and `height` determine the dimensions (they will always be equal). Similar methods taking parameters relocate the `Circle`, preserving dimensions. The `extend` method takes two integers—`dx` and `dy`—which must be equal, and modifies the radius by 2`dx`, preserving the center. Negative values will shrink the `Circle` toward its center.

One `Circle` equals another if they are the same geometrically. A `Circle` contains a `Pt` if filling the `Circle` would paint the `Pt`. The `clearOn` method essentially `fills` the `Circle` with the background color, erasing all the contained pixels.

E.9   The `Oval` Class

```
    public class Oval extends Rect
    {
        public Oval()
        // post: constructs a trivial oval at origin

        public Oval(Oval r)
        // pre: r is a valid Oval

        public Oval(Pt p, Pt q)
        // pre: p and q are valid points
        // post: constructs an oval bounded by two points

        public Oval(Rect r)
        // post: constructs an oval bounded by a rectangle r
```

```
        public Oval(int x, int y, int w, int h)
        // pre:  w >= 0, h >= 0
        // post: constructs oval with top left at (x,y),
        //       width w, height h

        public boolean contains(Pt p)
        // pre: p is a valid point
        // post: true iff p is within the oval

        public void fillOn(DrawingWindow d)
        // pre: d is a valid drawing window
        // post: the oval is filled on the drawing window d

        public void clearOn(DrawingWindow d)
        // pre: d is a valid drawing window
        // post: the oval is erased from the drawing window

        public void drawOn(DrawingWindow d)
        // pre: d is a valid drawing window
        // post: the oval is drawn on the drawing window

        public boolean equals(Object other)
        // post: returns true iff two ovals are equal
    }
```

The Oval object describes elliptic regions in screen coordinates. The major and minor axes of the ellipse are oriented horizontally and vertically. Oval objects may be copied from other Oval or Rect-like objects or constructed from a top-left point and a width and height, or from two points that determine the smallest bounding rectangle.

The Oval may also be used wherever a Rect may be used. As a result, the parameterless left, right, top, and bottom return the bounding coordinates, while width and height determine (in some order) the major and minor diameters. The parameterless center method returns the center point. Similar methods taking parameters relocate the Oval, preserving its dimensions. The extend method takes two integers—dx and dy—and modifies the horizontal and vertical radii by dx and dy, preserving the center. Negative values will shrink the Oval toward its center.

One Oval equals another if they are the same geometrically. An Oval contains a Pt if filling the Oval would paint the Pt. The clearOn method essentially fills the Circle with the background color, erasing all the contained pixels.

E.10   The Arc Class

```
public class Arc extends Oval
{
    public Arc()
    // post: constructs a circle at origin

    public Arc(Pt p, Pt q)
    // pre: p and q are valid points
    // post: constructs oval bounded by p and q

    public Arc(Rect r, int strt, int angl)
    // post: constructs an arc bounded by r,
    //       swept for angl degrees, starting at strt

    public Arc(int x, int y, int w, int h, int strt, int angl)
    // pre:  w >= 0, h >= 0
    // post: constructs arc with top left at (x,y), width w,
    //       height h, and sweep angl from starting angle strt

    public Arc(int x, int y, int w, int h)
    // pre:  w >= 0, h >= 0
    // post: constructs an oval with top left at (x,y),
    //       width w, height h

    public Arc(Arc r)
    // pre: r is a valid arc
    // post: this is a copy of r

    protected static int canonical(int angle)
    // post: reduces an angle to a value between 0 and 359

    public boolean contains(Pt p)
    // post: returns true iff p is within confines of the arc

    public int start()
    // post: returns the starting angle of the arc

    public int angle()
    // post: returns the span of the arc, in degrees

    public void start(int strt)
    // pre: strt is an angle
    // post: arc is rotated to start at angle strt

    public void angle(int angl)
    // pre: angl is a sweep, in degrees
    // post: the angle is changed to sweep out angle degrees
```

```
        public void fillOn(DrawingWindow d)
        // pre: d is a valid drawing window
        // post: the arc is filled on the drawing window d

        public void clearOn(DrawingWindow d)
        // pre: d is a valid drawing window
        // post: the arc is erased from the drawing window

        public void drawOn(DrawingWindow d)
        // pre: d is a valid drawing window
        // post: the arc is drawn on the drawing window

        public boolean equals(Object other)
        // post: returns true iff two arcs are equal
    }
```

The Arc object describes portions of elliptic regions of the screen. The major and minor axes of the ellipse are oriented horizontally and vertically. The portion of the containing Oval that is part of the Arc is determined by a *starting angle* and a *sweep*. Both are measured in (positive or negative) degrees, with zero degrees pointing to the right and increasing counterclockwise. Arc objects may be copied from other Arc or Rect-like objects or constructed from a top-left point and a width, height, start, and sweep, or from two points that determine the smallest bounding rectangle and a start and sweep. Dropping the start and sweep generates an ellipse.

The Arc may also be used wherever a Rect may be used. As a result, the parameterless left, right, top, and bottom return the bounding coordinates *of the defining* Oval, while width and height determine (in some order) the major and minor diameters of the bounding Oval. The parameterless center method returns the center point while start and angle return the starting and sweep angles, respectively. Similar methods taking parameters relocate and reorient the Arc. The extend method takes two integers—dx and dy—and modifies the horizontal and vertical radii by dx and dy, preserving the center. Negative values will shrink the Arc toward its center.

One Arc equals another if they are the same geometrically. The contains predicate tests to see if filling the Arc would paint the Pt. The drawOn method draws a portion of an elliptic frame (but not the radial line segments), while fillOn generates a pie-shaped wedge. The clearOn method essentially fills the Arc with the background color, erasing all the contained pixels.

E.11   The RoundRect Class

```
public class RoundRect extends Rect
{
    public RoundRect()
    // post: constructs a trivial rectangle at origin

    public RoundRect(Pt p, Pt q)
    // pre: p and q are valid points
    // post: constructs a RoundRect bounded by p and q

    public RoundRect(Rect r, int cw, int ch)
    // post: constructs a rounded rectangle

    public RoundRect(int x, int y, int w, int h, int cw, int ch)
    // pre:  w >= 0, h >= 0
    // post: constructs rectangle with top left at (x,y),
    //       width w, height h

    public RoundRect(int x, int y, int w, int h)
    // pre:  w >= 0, h >= 0
    // post: constructs rectangle with top left at (x,y),
    //       width w, height h

    public RoundRect(RoundRect r)
    // pre: r is not null
    // post: constructs a rounded rectangle like r

    public int cornerWidth()
    // post: returns the width of the corner oval

    public int cornerHeight()
    // post: returns the height of the corner oval

    public void cornerWidth(int cw)
    // pre: cw >= 0
    // post: sets the width of the corner oval

    public void cornerHeight(int ch)
    // pre: ch > 0
    // post: sets the height of the corner oval

    public boolean contains(Pt p)
    // pre: p is not null
    // post: returns true iff p is within the rounded rect

    public void fillOn(DrawingWindow d)
    // pre: d is not null
    // post: draws this filled rounded rectangle on d
```

```
        public void clearOn(DrawingWindow d)
        // pre: d is not null
        // post: erases this rounded rectangle on d

        public void drawOn(DrawingWindow d)
        // pre: d is not null
        // post: draws this rounded rectangle on d

        public boolean equals(Object other)
        // pre: other is not null RoundRect
        // post: returns true if two RoundRects are equal
    }
```

The RoundRect class describes a rectangular region on the screen whose edges are vertical or horizontal and whose corners are constructed from the four quadrants of an Oval. (A RoundRect with corner arcs of zero radius appears as a Rect while a RoundRect with corner arcs of width and height greater than or equal to the width and height of the RoundRect appears as an Oval.) RoundRect objects may be copied from other Rect-like objects or constructed from a top-left point and a width and height and a corner arc horizontal and vertical radius, or as the unique unrounded rectangle that bounds two points. The parameterless left, right, top, and bottom return the bounding coordinates, while width and height determine the dimensions. The parameterless center method returns the center point, while the cornerWidth and cornerHeight methods return the radii of the corner arcs. Similar methods taking parameters relocate or "re-round" the RoundRect. The extend method takes two integers—dx and dy—and modifies the horizontal and vertical coordinates to increase the width and height by 2dx and 2dy, preserving the center. Negative values will shrink the RoundRect toward its center.

One RoundRect equals another if they are the same geometrically. A RoundRect contains a Pt if filling the RoundRect would paint the Pt. The RoundRect drawOn method draws the frame of the RoundRect, while the fillOn method paints the interior with the foreground color as well. The clearOn method essentially fills the Rect with the background color, erasing all the contained pixels.

E.12 The Text Class

```
public class Text implements Drawable
{

    public Text(char c)
    // post: construct a text using c, with lower left at origin

    public Text(long i)
    // post: construct a text using i, with lower left at origin

    public Text(Object s)
    // post: s is a not null object
    // post: construct a Text representation of s at origin

    public Text(Object s, int left, int bottom)
    // post: s is a not null object
    // post: construct a text using s.toString;
    //       with lower left at (left,bottom)

    public Text(Object s, Pt p)
    // pre: s is not null, p is not null
    // post: construct rep of s with lower left at p

    public Text(Text that)
    // pre: that is not null
    // post: this is a copy of that

    public int left()
    // post: returns the left coordinate of the text

    public int right()
    // post: returns the right coordinate of the text

    public int top()
    // post: returns the top coordinate of the text

    public int bottom()
    // post: returns the bottom coordinate of the text

    public void left(int x)
    // post: sets the left coordinate of the text,
    //       relocating text

    public void right(int x)
    // post: sets the right coordinate of the text,
    //       relocating text

    public void top(int y)
    // post: sets the top coordinate of the text, relocating text
```

```
public void bottom(int y)
// post: sets the bottom coordinate of the text,
//       relocating text

public int width()
// post: returns the width of the text

public int height()
// post: returns the height of the text

public Pt center()
// post: returns the center of the text

public void center(Pt p)
// pre: p is not null
// post: relocates the center of the text at p

public boolean contains(Pt p)
// pre: returns true if the text's bounding rect contains p

public void fillOn(DrawingWindow d)
// post: draws the text on the drawing window

public void clearOn(DrawingWindow d)
// post: erases the text from the drawing window

public void drawOn(DrawingWindow d)
// post: draws the text on the drawing window

public boolean equals(Object other)
// pre: other is not null Text
// post: returns true if two Texts are equal
}
```

The Text object is a Drawable object that supports the display of strings in the DrawingWindow. A Text object may be constructed from another Text, a String, or most primitive types (including char and long, etc.), or as any Java Object. For general Objects, the toString method is used to construct the representation. Text objects are constructed with their lower-left coordinate at the origin, unless an alternative location is provided.

As a Drawable object, the bounds of a Text may be determined by left, right, top, bottom, and center. The text may be relocated, as well, using the similarly named single-parameter methods.

One Text object equals another if they are composed of equal Strings located at equal points. The methods drawOn and fillOn both draw the text, while clearOn erases the text from the drawing window.

Index